Natural Resources, Extraction and Indigenous Rights in Latin America

"Marcela Torres Wong has written a tour de force on the extractive conflicts in Latin America and the rights of indigenous peoples, specifically in the countries of Mexico, Peru, and Bolivia. Her methodological diversity and her on the ground filed techniques serve not only to demystify our previous understandings of indigenous peoples rights and their struggles to survive in a global political economy, but she also shines light on and captures the geo-political realities of Green Criminology and sustainability in the 21st century."

—Gregg Barak, Professor of Criminology and Criminal Justice at Eastern Michigan University, USA

In 1989, the International Labor Organization stated that all indigenous peoples living in the postcolonial world were entitled to the right to prior consultation on activities that could potentially impact their territories and traditional livelihoods. However, in many cases, the economic importance of industries such as mining and oil condition the way that governments implement the right to prior consultation.

This book explores extractive conflicts between indigenous populations, the government and oil and mining companies in Latin America, namely Mexico, Peru and Bolivia. Building on two years of research and drawing on the state-corporate and environmental crime literatures, this book examines the legal, extralegal, illegal and political strategies used by the state and extractive companies to avoid undesired results produced by the legalization of the right to prior consultation. It examines the ways in which prior consultation is utilized by powerful indigenous actors to negotiate economic resources with the state and extractive companies while also showing the ways in which weaker indigenous groups are incapable of engaging in prior consultations in a meaningful way and are therefore left at the mercy of negative ecological impacts. It demonstrates how social mobilization—not prior consultation—is the most effective strategy in preventing extraction from moving forward within ecologically fragile indigenous territories.

Marcela Torres Wong is a Peruvian lawyer and anthropologist at the Pontificia Universidad Catolica del Peru. She has a PhD in Political Science from The American University in Washington, DC. Since 2017, she has worked as a full-time professor and researcher in the Latin American Faculty of Social Science (FLACSO) in Mexico City. Her research interests include indigenous movements, extractive industries and socio-environmental conflicts in Latin America. She has received grants from the Inter-American Foundation (IAF), the Tinker Foundation and the Centre National de la Recherche Scientifique (CNRS).

Crimes of the Powerful

Gregg Barak, Eastern Michigan University, USA
Penny Green, Queen Mary University of London, UK
Tony Ward, Northumbria University, UK

Crimes of the Powerful encompasses the harmful, injurious, and victimizing behaviors perpetrated by privately or publicly operated businesses, corporations, and organizations as well as the state mediated administrative, legalistic, and political responses to these crimes.

The series draws attention to the commonalities of the theories, practices, and controls of the crimes of the powerful. It focuses on the overlapping spheres and inter-related worlds of a wide array of existing and recently developing areas of social, historical, and behavioral inquiry into the wrongdoings of multinational organizations, nation-states, stateless regimes, illegal networks, financialization, globalization, and securitization.

These examinations of the crimes of the powerful straddle a variety of related disciplines and areas of academic interest, including studies in criminology and criminal justice; law and human rights; conflict, peace, and security; economic change, environmental decay, and global sustainability.

Revisiting Crimes of the Powerful
Marxism, Crime and Deviance
Edited by Steven Bittle, Laureen Snider, Steve Tombs and David Whyte

Torture as State Crime
A Criminological Analysis of the Transnational Institutional Torturer
Melanie Collard

Natural Resources, Extraction and Indigenous Rights in Latin America
Exploring the Boundaries of Environmental and State-Corporate Crime in Bolivia, Peru and Mexico
Marcela Torres Wong

For more information about this series, please visit: https://www.routledge.com/Crimes-of-the-Powerful/book-series/COTP

Natural Resources, Extraction and Indigenous Rights in Latin America

Exploring the Boundaries of Environmental and State-Corporate Crime in Bolivia, Peru and Mexico

Marcela Torres Wong

Routledge
Taylor & Francis Group
LONDON AND NEW YORK

First published 2019
by Routledge
2 Park Square, Milton Park, Abingdon, Oxon OX14 4RN

and by Routledge
711 Third Avenue, New York, NY 10017

Routledge is an imprint of the Taylor & Francis Group, an informa business

British Library Cataloguing-in-Publication Data
A catalogue record for this book is available from the British Library

Library of Congress Cataloging-in-Publication Data
A catalog record has been requested for this book

ISBN: 978-0-8153-8152-5 (hbk)
ISBN: 978-1-351-21024-9 (ebk)

Typeset in Bembo
by codeMantra

MIX
Paper from responsible sources
FSC® C013056

Printed and bound in Great Britain by
TJ International Ltd, Padstow, Cornwall

To the Indigenous Peoples of Latin America and their fight for Justice

Contents

List of figures and tables

List of figures

List of tables

Acknowledgments

First and foremost, I would like to thank all the interview respondents who dedicated their time and provided their expertise to enrich this book. I would like, in particular, to thank my dear friends Guster Bártenes (Peru), Deysi Choque (Bolivia) and Rosalinda Dionisio (Mexico), remarkable indigenous leaders and environmental activists who have generously shared their knowledge and experiences with me during this journey. Their deep understanding of indigenous struggles opened up the avenues of research that encouraged me to study extractive conflicts. I would also like to thank Todd Eisenstadt, Gisela Zaremberg, Maya and GreggBarak for their thoughtful comments on the chapters that make up this book and Monserrat Rangel for her valuable editorial assistance. Finally, all my gratitude to my parents, Maria and Javier, for their unconditional support.

Introduction

Indigenous peoples and the extractive industry

On June 5, 2009, then-President Alan García's government dispatched police and military forces against thousands of indigenous activists who were blocking lands from access by state oil company, Petro Peru. The resulting "Baguazo Massacre" left 34 dead and hundreds more injured, among them both protestors and armed forces. At the time, García intended to advance hydrocarbon extraction within the Peruvian Amazon. Yet he faced unexpected indigenous opposition. Protestors amassed from 65 ethnic groups to oppose García's executive decrees seeking to privatize indigenous territories. As a result of these new decrees, only simple-majority approval from community members would be required to sell off indigenous lands, which under extant laws could not be privatized. With this new legal frame, the Peruvian government attempted to promote exploration of oil and gas reserves in the Amazonian forest.

Using a legal discourse to channel their interests, the indigenous protestors claimed that Convention 169 approved by the International Labor Organization (ILO Convention 169) in 1989 granted them the right to prior consultation. Indigenous communities were to be consulted, formally and properly, on any measure that could directly or indirectly affect their territories and traditional way of living (Articles 6, 7 and 8 of ILO Convention 169). When no prior consultation occurred, protestors took over a petroleum distribution station and pipeline juncture, roads and town squares, demanding cancellation of the decrees. After a several-month standoff, García's government ordered the Peruvian military to intervene, leading to the deadly outcome.

From the government perspective, García was not doing anything illegal, but indigenous protestors disregarded constitutional norms establishing that the elected government is entitled to administer subsoil resources, such as minerals and hydrocarbons, in the national interest. Instead, they claimed that ILO Convention 169 gave them the right to control the use of their territories. Indigenous organizations argued that they rejected the extractivist economic model put forward by the García government as this threatened their natural environment. Amazonian indigenous communities were committed to the protection of Mother Earth as well as to ensuring the survival of future indigenous generations.

Peru ratified ILO Convention 169 in the context of human rights protection; therefore, this international treaty has had constitutional status since 1994 (Chirif 2015a). Still, President García disobeyed the rules contained in the international norm. The Peruvian government chose repression over consultation, and violence took place. International and national human rights organizations criticized repressive measures and put pressure on the government, prompting García to suspend the controversial decrees.

The platform presented by protestors in the heat of conflict implied that once governments implemented the right to prior consultation through consultation procedures, indigenous groups would say "no" to extraction. Upon the assumption that communal lands represent the most valuable resource the indigenous own, many environmental activists saw these procedures as mechanisms to prevent the expansion of extractivism into fragile ecosystems. During the 2000s, many environmentalist and human rights organizations undertook intense campaigns directed at governments' failure to acknowledge the rights granted by ILO Convention 169.

International pressure caused by increasing conflicts involving indigenous territories created the conditions for state implementation of ILO Convention 169. From the mid-2000s onward, some governments began to carry out prior consultation procedures. The evidence presented throughout this book, however, demonstrates that within a decade of the rise of prior consultation procedures, indigenous communities in numerous countries have not chosen to reject extraction. On the contrary, all consulted groups have agreed to projects, with some using prior consultation procedures to negotiate for significant economic resources from extractivists. Findings also indicate that it is only in the absence of these procedures that indigenous communities can prohibit extractive industries within their lands. Surprisingly, the implementation of the right to prior consultation would be detrimental—not helpful—in deterring the expansion of extractivism into indigenous territories. *How can we explain these results in light of increasing conflict surrounding indigenous lands and the extractive industry?*

Over the last two decades, indigenous movements in various parts of the world have emerged to defend their ancestral territories and tradition from potentially destructive mega projects. Green criminologists have offered extensive documentation of the negative effects that natural resource exploitation by the private industry has on the environment of nearby communities (Stretesky and Lynch 2011; Long et al. 2012; Pearse et al. 2013; Ruggiero and South 2013; White 2013). In this endeavor, scholars emphasize how state actors permit or facilitate environmental crimes by enabling corporate access to natural resources (Zilney et al. 2006; Ruggiero and South 2013; White

2013). A growing body of pro-indigenous legislation at the international level is now in force, and many countries have recognized indigenous rights, at least partially. Yet the results of extant legislation are dissatisfying for many indigenous rights supporters. Through the lens of green criminology—and using struggles over mining and hydrocarbon projects in Latin America as a useful window into a global problem—this book offers one explanation as to how the political and economic management of natural resources by governments and multinational companies influences the implementation of indigenous rights while reshaping indigenous movements' goals.

The intersection of indigenous rights and environmental crime

The Baguazo Massacre is not an isolated event. Similar conflicts over the control of indigenous lands, especially those potentially containing valuable minerals and hydrocarbons, continue to proliferate around the world. In 2017, Global Witness revealed that 197 people were killed worldwide for defending their lands, forests and rivers against destructive industries, and 40 percent of them were members of indigenous groups (Global Witness 2016). According to the same source, mining and oil operations are the two activities at the heart of conflict and were linked to 33 killings in 2016. Lack of prosecutions, however, would complicate the identification of the individuals responsible for the killings (The Guardian 2017).

With social conflicts on the rise, mining and hydrocarbon companies keep pushing governments worldwide to ease legal restrictions and expand resource frontiers into new regions (Ebus and Kuijpers 2015). Whether in the Virunga Park in the Democratic Republic of the Congo or the Aguaragüe in Bolivia, governments manipulate national laws and institutions to authorize extraction in sites where such operations would otherwise be prohibited. Despite the numerous adverse social and environmental impacts of these projects, state actors are enticed by the revenues that the mining and hydrocarbon industries might channel to state coffers and favored constituencies (in the form of license fees, taxes and royalties). State agencies, then, frame controversial extractive operations as motors for economic development and therefore extensively support these projects (Seoane and Algranati 2005; Deheza and Ribet 2012). Furthermore, using the argument that governments in underdeveloped countries have limited budgets, oil and mining companies, along with a growing number of consultants who are hired by these companies (Cleary 2011, 2012), carry out environmental and social impact reports used to determine whether such projects should move forward. Extractive companies are thus judge and jury of their own impact assessments. Together, these conditions have a central role in explaining why, even when regulation exists to oversee the impacts of industrialized extraction, extant laws are not used for halting extractive projects for environmental reasons.

ILO Convention 169 and the protection of indigenous peoples' territories

Exploration and extraction of minerals, oil and gas are frequently attempted in remote indigenous villages far away from the places where strategic business decisions are made (Carrington et al. 2015:243). The most common cause of social unrest is then attributed to the fact that governments and extractive companies generally agree on the terms of exploration and exploitation operations without including the voice of the indigenous communities whose environments could be damaged by such activities (Tauli-Corpuz 2017). Passed in 1989, ILO Convention 169 states that all indigenous populations in the postcolonial world have the right to live in their ancestral territories according to their customary norms and political institutions. With this convention, an obligation was created for governments to conduct proper prior consultation procedures with their indigenous population regarding any activity potentially affecting their lands (Lapidoth 1997:16–17; Kymlicka 2001:23–24).

Using ILO Convention 169 as a symbol of their struggle, indigenous movements claim that indigenous organizations, not the government, should be the ones to decide the future of their territories (Plant 2002:209). By mirroring the legal language used in international law to address the demands of millions of people from dozens of countries, indigenous groups demand the right to live according to their own social and political structures (Stavenhagen 2002:24; Hernández-Díaz 2007:35). Despite progress in legislation, concerns about the impact of extractive industries on indigenous water sources, lands and culture continue to be predominant among indigenous organizations and their supporters. In light of these concerns, senior mining researcher Roger Moody estimates that 50–80 percent of mineral expansion worldwide is planned on indigenous lands (Wolf 2016).

In this context, the alliance between indigenous peoples and the environmental movement has become stronger over the last few decades. During the energy crises in the 1970s, environmentalists began to challenge both left- and right-wing parties' obsession with economic growth (Temkin 2017:143). Given the increasing concerns over the finite nature of natural resources, indigenous living based on activities such as agriculture, fishing and hunting appeared to many environmentalists as ecologically sustainable in contrast to industrialized resource extraction. Overlapping goals translated into organizational resources from international actors for indigenous organizations generally located in the Global South. However, as will be explored shortly, the sustained expansion of extractive projects has disrupted the natural connections between these two movements.

The expansion of extractivism in Latin America

Over the last two decades, mining and hydrocarbon operations have caused violent upheavals among indigenous communities. As of today, nearly

64 percent of the world's extractive conflicts take place in the Latin American region (Özkaynak et al., 2015). Furthermore, Latin American countries are pioneers in implementing the indigenous right to prior consultation (Cerqueira 2015). As of today, 14 of the 22 countries that ratified ILO Convention 169 are Latin American. Given these considerations, the Latin American context affords unique opportunities to evaluate the interaction between the legal implementation of indigenous rights and national politics aimed at expanding extractivism.

In most Latin American countries, the expansion of mining and hydrocarbon extraction has been the direct consequence of neoliberal reforms implemented in the 1990s (Slack 2009; Arce 2014). Neoliberal policies sought to limit the scope of the state in order to grant greater autonomy to private investors and achieve a dramatic increase in export revenues. Such policies included the privatization of strategic mining and hydrocarbon industries. Latin American economic growth since the turn of the century has relied primarily upon the exports of commodities, fueled in part by skyrocketing Chinese demand.

Today, nearly 27 percent of global investment in mining and 52 percent of the worldwide investment in gold and copper are concentrated in Latin America (Arce 2014). While the mining industry has been present in the region since precolonial times, it has transformed and modernized over the last decades. Foreign investment in mining projects was followed by the introduction of the open-pit method and the use of cyanide in the extractive process to separate the mineral from the surrounding rocks (Broad and Cavanagh 2017). These new techniques spread rapidly across Latin American countries, allowing mining companies to extract minerals found in diminutive sizes that had been impossible to extract with the use of old mining methods (Bebbington and Bury 2013).

Currently, the mining industry is capital-intensive and does not require a large labor force. In addition, the use of sophisticated technology allows the removal of sizable expanses of lands to extract as much mineral as possible, negatively affecting the agricultural economies that are often found nearby mining projects (Bury 2004; Bebbington et al. 2008; Himley 2010; Perreault 2014; Eisenstadt and West 2017). Moreover, the need for great amounts of water for extractive operations and the discharge of wastewater into natural waterways often impact the quantity and quality of water sources needed by adjacent populations (Bridge 2004). All these reasons have led many scientists to conclude that in certain countries and areas, mining should be prohibited (Broad and Cavanagh 2017).

The lack of job opportunities for locals and environmental degradation has led to strong opposition by surrounding communities. This industry is responsible for more than 200 socio-environmental conflicts taking place in the Latin American region. Mexico and Peru head the list, with both the biggest gold reserves and the largest number of conflicts (Observatory of Mining Conflicts in Latin America n.d.). Amid increasing violence within the mining industry, control over mineral-rich lands has become central to the political agendas of powerful mining lobbies and indigenous advocacy groups alike.

The hydrocarbons industry is also central to Latin American economies. The region holds 20 percent of proven global oil reserves and 4 percent of global natural gas reserves (BP Statistical Review of World Energy 2017). Whereas the majority of large-scale mining projects are controlled by multinational corporations, most hydrocarbon production is carried out by state-owned companies (Bebbington and Bury 2013:54). State control of this sector has spurred a sort of "resource nationalism" in countries such as Bolivia and Mexico, preventing anti-oil mobilization (De la Fuente 2013; Perreault 2013). In comparison with the mining industry, social conflicts over this industry have been less numerous, and hydrocarbon projects are usually perceived as less disruptive to the environment (De la Fuente 2013; Perreault 2013; The Dialogue 2015).

Still, severe environmental contamination is produced by this industry (Eisenstadt and West 2017). Hydrocarbon extraction is generally advanced in isolated areas where there is little oversight of the extractive process (Bebbington and Scurrah 2013:173). Numerous ethnic groups living in places such as the ecologically fragile Amazon basin have suffered the contamination of their rivers and fauna due to oil spills, pipeline ruptures and the deficient closure of oil wells (Fraser 2014; Eisenstadt and West 2017). As most of these communities lack the means to satisfy their basic needs, oil companies in these localities exercise state-like functions, representing one of the few sources of services for indigenous populations (Crabtree and Crabtree-Condor 2012); this hinders opposition to this industry. Nationally owned oil company Mexican Petroleum, or PEMEX, in Mexico exemplifies this situation. Due to long-standing clientelist relationships with nearby communities, PEMEX can advance extraction projects rather smoothly in spite of visible contamination to lands, mangrove swamps, rivers and seawater (Vargas 2015).

Nevertheless, traditional areas and methods for hydrocarbon exploitation have begun to change in Latin America. Falling oil prices since 2014 have diminished funds available for governments in Venezuela, Mexico, Argentina, Brazil, Bolivia, Colombia and Ecuador (BBC Mundo 2005). Currently, these countries struggle to maintain incomes generated from the exports of oil and gas while simultaneously attempting to fulfill their domestic energy demands. Exploration activities are encouraged in areas that formerly prohibited extractive industries. National parks and ecological reserves in the Amazon—shared by Brazil, Peru, Bolivia, Ecuador, Colombia, Venezuela and Surinam—and the El Chaco desert—shared by Bolivia, Paraguay and Argentina—are increasingly used to search for new energy sources. In addition, unconventional oil and gas production, such as fracking, is becoming increasingly attractive for governments in the region. This is, in part, due to the influence of the US Energy Information

Administration, whose reports estimate that great amounts of oil and gas exist within Latin American countries and could be extracted using new techniques (Pérez-Castellón 2016:159).

However, in 2001, the US Environmental Protection Agency estimated that fracking in the United States used 70–140 billion gallons of water per year. This is equivalent to the total amount of water used each year by up to five million people (Doyle and Whitmore 2014). These figures are alarming, especially if we take into consideration the fact that two-thirds of the world's population currently live in areas that experience water scarcity for at least one month a year (Mekonnen and Hoekstra 2016). By 2025, 1.8 billion people are expected to be living in countries or regions with absolute water scarcity, and two-thirds of the world's population could be under water stress conditions (United Nations Department of Economic and Social Affairs n.d.). Despite the substantial contribution to carbon dioxide (CO_2) emissions and environmental harms to water sources associated with mineral, oil and gas extractions, forecasts for the coming 20 years suggest that investments in the extractive industry sector will continue to grow (Doyle and Whitmore 2014).

The right to prior consultation in Latin America

During the neoliberal heyday of the 1990s in Latin America, mining and hydrocarbon concessions were granted almost automatically to multinational companies that requested permission from the government to operate. The right to prior consultation of indigenous communities remained unimplemented, even though almost all Latin American countries had already committed to ILO Convention 169. In the 2000s, leftist governments came to power in the aftermath of widespread anti-neoliberal contention. New governments in the Andes promised to address the unequal distribution of resources and ecological degradation that were associated with the extractivist model. At the beginning of their administrations, progressive presidents in Bolivia and Ecuador undertook innovative political reforms to enhance indigenous participation in national politics as well as to protect environmentally fragile regions. Both countries included the institutionalization of prior consultation procedures as key components of new constitutional orders. In 2007, President Correa launched the Yasuní project intended to keep the Ecuadorian Amazon free of hydrocarbon exploitation (Mena 2013). In 2008, the Ecuadorian Constitution granted legal rights to Mother Nature and declared environmental protection a national priority. Similarly, Bolivia passed a 2010 law, "*Ley de derechos de la Madre Tierra*," addressing the importance of protecting "the rights of Mother Earth" and establishing the government's commitment to doing just that.

Nonetheless, favorable prices of minerals during the commodity boom that began around 2003 and continued for roughly a decade, coupled with the peak in the price of oil in 2008, pushed new presidents to maintain extractivism, although with a greater degree of state intervention (Gray Molina 2010; Hinojosa 2012). Even with progressive legislation in place, both governments abandoned their environmental promises and continued pursuing extractive policies as aggressively as the neoliberal regimes that preceded them. Yet, through economic redistribution, these governments attempted to overcome the "natural resources curse" that inevitably condemns resource-rich countries to structural inequality and underdevelopment (Weber-Fahr 2002; Humphreys et al. 2007; Gudynas 2009; Hinojosa 2012). "Neo-extractivism," as this model was labeled, allowed leftist governments to maintain the support of their constituents and win reelection while still pursuing extractive projects. However, these governments lost popularity among environmentalists and indigenous rights advocates who initially saw in these new administrations an opportunity to migrate toward ecologically sustainable economic models.

Given the shortcomings in governments' adoption of prior consultation, several international provisions have followed to increase the protection of indigenous territories. There is increased oversight of financial institutions to ensure that they are not complicit in the violation of indigenous peoples' rights. This is reflected by the incorporation of requirements to obtain indigenous peoples' free, prior and informed consent (FPIC) with regard to extractive projects into the policies of many of the major financial institutions (FAO 2014). However, as of today, the role of the extractive industry sector in sustaining the region's economic growth hinders the protection of the integrity of indigenous territories.

The biased implementation of the right to prior consultations is one manifestation of the political influence of the extractivist stakeholders on domestic policies. In this vein, subsequent chapters will demonstrate that during the first years that prior consultation legislation was in effect, Latin American governments used *de facto* discretionary power to avoid consultations with indigenous groups that were likely to have radical stances against extraction, generally found in the mining sector. In turn, such procedures were mostly conducted in the hydrocarbon sector, where indigenous groups were prone to accept extraction (see Chapter 3).

Still, selective government enforcement of the right to prior consultation is only one element that helps to explain why all consultations in Bolivia, Peru and Mexico have resulted in indigenous approval. Systematic indigenous approval of extractive projects was unexpected by some of the fiercest advocates of the right to prior consultation. Many indigenous rights and environmentalist organizations argue that these procedures—when applied—do not meet international standards; instead, state agencies manipulate indigenous leaders to obtain their consent. While this might be true, Chapter 2 shows that indigenous peoples are not homogeneous, and their attitudes toward the extractive industry vary depending on these groups' historic relationships with state actors as well as oil and mining companies.

Latin American indigenous populations number around 45 million, representing almost 9 percent of the entire population of the region (CEPAL 2014). Despite their considerable size and the valuable natural resources contained beneath their lands, this population exhibits the highest levels of economic and political marginalization across the subcontinent (CEPAL 2010). Cases such as the Baguazo in Peru frequently depict indigenous groups as comprised of radical activists, struggling against mega projects to preserve their long-standing and harmonious relations with Mother Nature. Romanticizing indigenous struggles, no doubt, served as a powerful tool to nourish the discourse of environmentalists and other advocacy groups worldwide (Albert 2004) that finally led to the legalization of the right to prior consultation. However, in most cases, indigenous communities do not inhabit untouched environments isolated from modern society. Interaction with the West and the increasing advancement of outsiders into their lands have had devastating effects on native economies and political organizations for centuries. Historical dispossession of their environmental resources and discrimination toward their traditional livelihoods have placed many indigenous communities in critical living conditions. As indigenous peoples continue to be pushed away from their ancestral territories, and natural resources become scarce, it is hard for indigenous leaders to maintain cultural and political control of their territories (Chirif 2015b). In several rural areas where environmental conditions are rough and activities such as agriculture and cattle raising are difficult to develop, extractive industries are the most viable opportunity by which young indigenous members can make a living (Arce 2014:21). The following chapters show how these conditions, combined with state agencies' bias toward extractive projects, explain why indigenous groups choose bargaining over radical environmental stances once they are offered the right to prior consultation.

Notwithstanding, this book presents evidence demonstrating that indigenous groups committed to defending the environment do exist. While the extractive industry represents a viable opportunity for many impoverished indigenous groups to access economic resources, anti-extractivist stances prevail among some indigenous communities and can spark violent battles against the extractive industry (Guha and Martinez-Alier 1997; Guha 2000; Arellano-Yanguas 2011; Arce 2014). The use of new extractive techniques, such as the open-pit mining method, directional drilling, super-deep ocean drilling and fracking technologies, has triggered the emergence of opposition movements in various parts of the world (Bebbington and Bury 2013). As a result, some indigenous populations do not view economic agreements as sufficient compensation for the environmental damage associated with modern extraction technologies (Pegg 2006; Urkidi and Walter 2011). In this vein, Chapter 4 presents cases where indigenous communities refuse to engage in prior consultation procedures with their governments and choose social mobilization to prevent extraction.

The cases of Bolivia, Peru and Mexico

Bolivia, Peru and Mexico were selected as country cases because they have a number of factors in common that make them comparable, such as the presence of large indigenous populations, economically significant hydrocarbon and mining industries, and a history of resource-based conflicts involving indigenous groups. Similar prior consultation outcomes were found in spite of differences in national political settings. Variables such as government ideology, the influence of indigenous movements on national politics and the scope granted by the government to the right to prior consultation—three factors that social scientists associate with the advancement of indigenous rights in Latin America (Yashar 2005; Van Cott 2008; Lucero 2009 and Albó 2012)—do not appear to have a significant impact on the outcomes of prior consultation procedures in these three cases.

Over the course of two-year research, governmental and Non-governmental organizations (NGOs) databases, and reports documenting the results of prior consultation procedures in each country were examined. Research also included fieldwork within 11 indigenous municipalities containing minerals and hydrocarbon reserves in the three countries. The process-tracing method was utilized to obtain information and establish the causal chain in extractive conflicts. Sixty semi-structured interviews were conducted with indigenous activists, indigenous rights lawyers, environmentalists, state officials, NGO employees and social scientists studying the conflicts examined in this book. These data were complemented by newspapers, visits to indigenous territories and participant observation to gauge the current circumstances, as represented by public events, protests and related activities. Data reveal that all prior consultations conducted in the countries under study up until the end of 2017 resulted in indigenous approval of extractive projects. As detailed in Chapter 3, governments used diverse legal and political strategies to avoid consulting on controversial mining projects and successfully navigated through consultations within the hydrocarbon sector.

Subsequent chapters divide indigenous municipalities into two types: those who participated in prior consultation procedures and those who did not. In the first type of municipality, only indigenous groups with sufficient political power to "threaten" the government were able to derive meaningful economic benefits in exchange for allowing extraction. Unexperienced indigenous groups with incipient forms of political organizations accepted projects without obtaining economic compensation. In municipalities where prior consultation did not take place, politically powerful indigenous groups, through social and legal mobilization, were able to prohibit extraction. As in the first type of municipality, the weakest groups complied with the government projects without obtaining compensation. Tables I.1–I.4 show the indigenous municipalities selected for examination in Bolivia, Peru and Mexico.

Table I.1 Political Power with Enforcement of Prior Consultation

Country	*Region*	*Municipality*	*Extractive Company*
Peru	Loreto	Andoas	Pacific Stratus Energy
Bolivia	Santa Cruz	Takovo Mora	Yacimientos Petrolíferos Fiscales Bolivianos (YPFB)
Mexico	Sonora	Yaquis	Petróleos Mexicanos (PEMEX)

Source: Author's elaboration.

Table I.2 No Political Power with Enforcement of Prior Consultation

Country	*Region*	*Municipality*	*Extractive Company*
Peru	Ucayali, Loreto	Kukama Kukamiria-Capanahua	Pluspetrol
Bolivia	La Paz	TIOC Moseten	YPFB Petroandina

Source: Author's elaboration.

Table I.3 Political Power with No Prior Consultation

Country	*Region*	*Municipality*	*Extractive Companies*
Peru	Cajamarca	San Esteban de Chetilla	Shield. Estrella Gold and Wild Acre Metals
Bolivia	Oruro	Challapata	EmusaOrvana (Bolivian-Canadian) Castillian Resources (Canada)
Mexico	Oaxaca	Capulálpam de Méndez	Company Continuum Resources (Canada) Sundance Minerals (Canada)

Source: Author's elaboration.

Table I.4 No Political Power with No Prior Consultation

Country	*Region*	*Municipality*	*Extractive Companies*
Peru	Apurimac	Cotabambas/Grau	Xtrata Copper (Anglo-Swiss)
Bolivia	La Paz	Corocoro, Pacajes	Comibol and Kores (Bolivia and South Korea)
Mexico	San Luis Potosí	Cerro San Pedro	New Gold, Inc. (Canada)

Source: Author's elaboration.

Environmentalism or redistribution?

The economic utility that prior consultation affords to some indigenous groups is often perceived rather negatively by some environmentalist's organizations, who see prior consultation procedures as mechanisms to buy off indigenous approval. For these organizations, prior consultation is a window dressing institution designed to maintain the "status quo" as opposed to a mechanism of political participation that can transform the administration of natural resources (Xantomila 2017). However, a sector of indigenous rights supporters still see prior consultation as a legitimate and, more importantly, accessible mechanism that the indigenous can utilize to have direct access to otherwise restricted economic resources (see Chapter 2).

This book does not attempt to put an end to this debate. Instead, the central aim is explaining why prior consultation is not a mechanism for protecting indigenous lands from the impacts of extraction. The economic importance of the mining and hydrocarbon industries conditions the way Latin American governments implement the right to prior consultation. Likewise, the dependence on extractivism of many impoverished indigenous groups prompts them to see prior consultation procedures as a bargaining chip instead of a legal channel to prevent industrialized resource extraction within their lands. In this endeavor, the book emphasizes governments' use of Latin America's weak institutions to avoid undesired effects that might derive from consulting indigenous communities about environmentally threatening projects. Selective enforcement of prior consultations and negotiations with politically powerful indigenous groups enable governments to advance billionaire extractive projects at the expense of indigenous rights to their lands and natural resource. Likewise, the book evidences how the historical and continued political and economic marginalization of indigenous peoples places these groups at a crossroads in the face of the extractive industry.

Choosing negotiation over rejection seems like the most viable opportunity indigenous groups have for escaping prevailing poverty. Yet systematic approval of extractive operations—now achieved through the implementation of prior consultation procedures—puts indigenous environments and the survival of ancestral cultures at serious risk.

Overall, the book reflects on the connections between unexpected prior consultation outcomes and a legal order where nation-states possess an undeniable privilege over the use of the law (Barak 2015). The current uses of prior consultation procedures in Latin America are produced by this privilege and could contribute to push environmental crime away from the spotlight. In a context in which new mechanisms for diminishing environmental harm are increasingly needed, this study highlights the urgency of safeguarding the rights of indigenous peoples, especially their rights to their lands, territories and resources. By examining three Latin American countries, the book demonstrates that the legalization of prior consultation has not been the most adequate way to achieve this goal. Furthermore, findings shed light on potential outcomes in countries with similar economic and political arrangements, where prior consultation is demanded but is not yet a reality. Finally, new venues for indigenous rights advocates and environmental activists are pointed out in the hopes of contributing to their task of protecting indigenous natural environments.

Organization of the book

This book consists of five core chapters. Chapter 1: *What do indigenous peoples want?* distinguishes between indigenous groups seeking to prohibit extraction on their lands—referred to as anti-extractivists—and those groups seeking to profit from the extractive industry—referred to as pro-extractivist indigenous. Further, the chapter identifies the main sources of indigenous political power *vis-à-vis* the state and mining and hydrocarbon projects. The central argument is that whether intending to prohibit extraction or obtain economic benefits, indigenous communities must have sufficient mobilization capacities for persuading the state to deliver indigenous demands.

Chapter 2: *Ecological defense or bargaining over indigenous lands?* examines why prior consultation is not ideal for indigenous groups fighting extractive companies. The chapter shows that variation in the national influence of indigenous movements, the legal scope given by the government to the right to prior consultation and the government ideology do not result in different prior consultation outcomes in Latin America. On the contrary, prior consultation is equally implemented by Latin American governments, which use these procedures as bargaining chips to negotiate resources from the most powerful indigenous groups while also using their de facto discretionary power to avoid consultations with anti-extractivist indigenous groups. The central argument is that the legalization of the right to prior consultation in

Latin America can help the most powerful pro-extractivist indigenous communities achieve economic agreements, but these procedures are useless for anti-extractivist indigenous movements.

Chapter 3: *Rights do not matter, political power does* presents the empirical cases that illustrate the argument presented in Chapters 1 and 2. The chapter compares cases of resource-rich indigenous municipalities in which prior consultation rights were enforced, with contrasting results for indigenous populations. The first part discusses the cases of Andoas (Peru), Takovo Mora (Bolivia) and the Yaqui people (Mexico). In these cases, indigenous political power manifested through high levels of mobilization capacities made prior consultation a meaningful mechanism for redistribution of economic resources in favor of indigenous populations. The chapter describes the intense processes of negotiation that followed prior consultation in all these cases. Several mechanisms of political pressure, as well as indigenous ability to obtain considerable concessions, are addressed. The second part analyzes the cases of the Kukama Kukamiria (Peru) and the Mosetén (Bolivia). Prior consultation was also enforced in these cases, yet consulted groups were politically demobilized and did not obtain significant economic benefits.

Chapter 4: *There is nothing to consult here!* compares and analyzes resource-rich indigenous municipalities in which tension over the control of natural resources was present, but prior consultation was not conducted, leading to different results for the indigenous. The first part of the chapter examines the cases of Challapata (Bolivia), Chetilla (Peru) and Capulálpam de Méndez (Mexico) in which sustained social mobilization culminated in the prohibition of extraction. The chapter examines indigenous resistance against extractive industries and illustrates how indigenous mobilization, operating in the absence of prior consultation, prompted the state to suspend or cancel extractive projects. The second part of the chapter presents the cases of Cotabambas and Grau (Peru), Corocoro (Bolivia) and Cerro San Pedro (Mexico), in which mobilization over extractive projects was not strong enough to succeed. This chapter demonstrates that a lack of sufficient mobilization capacities prevented indigenous groups from both prohibiting mining projects and negotiating extractive resources.

Chapter 5: *Prior consultation and the expansion of extractivism in Latin America* examines how the implementation of prior consultation rights in three Latin American countries has served to validate the extractive industry sector. This chapter highlights the irony of prior consultation being detrimental—not beneficial—in the protection of indigenous territories from extraction. Here, we see that environmental protection functions have been mistakenly attributed to economically and politically marginalized indigenous groups. In this regard, the chapter highlights the inadequacy of linking indigenous people's rights with ecological causes for policymaking purposes. On the other hand, the chapter emphasizes the opportunities created by prior consultation and the open paths for indigenous movements and environmentalists in the protection of fragile ecosystems.

Finally, the conclusion reexamines extractive conflicts in Latin America in light of state-corporate environmental crime studies. Disputes over the control of natural resources are born out of the structural inequality that defines the Latin American region. Indigenous peoples continue to lag behind the general population with regard to basic services and quality of life. Ironically, these communities usually inhabit areas containing valuable minerals and hydrocarbons, and are the most affected by the impacts of extractive activities. In economies that are heavily dependent on the exports of commodities, such as Latin America's, environmental degradation becomes bearable as exploitation of natural resources remains profitable for main stakeholders. The chapter emphasizes that states are not autonomous; instead, law enforcers are deeply susceptible to economic interests created by extractive industries. Governments unfold diverse legal and political strategies to misuse the right to prior consultation in accordance with their own interests. Structural inequalities between indigenous peoples and main stakeholders in the extractive industry are not attacked. Furthermore, issues concerning environmental harm to indigenous territories are overlooked. Continuing under this prior consultation framework, violent confrontations between indigenous peoples, state actors and multinational companies are likely to increase.

References

Albert, Bruce. 2004. "Territorialidad, etnopolítica y desarrollo: A propósito del movimiento indígena en la Amazonía brasileña." In Alexandre Surrallés and Pedro García Hierro (eds) *Tierra adentro. Territorio indígena y percepción del entorno. Copenhague: IWGIA, 221–258.*

Arce, Moises. 2014. *Resource Extraction and Protest in Peru.* Pittsburg: University of Pittsburg Press.

Arellano-Yanguas, Javier. 2011. *¿Minería sin fronteras? Conflicto y desarrollo en regiones mineras del Perú.* Lima: IEP.

Barak, Gregg. 2015. *On the Invisibility and Neutralization of the Crimes of the Powerful and their Victims, Introduction to the Routledge International Handbook of the Crimes of the Powerful.* June. Available at: www.greggbarak.com/whats_new_10.html (Accessed May 23 2017).

BBC Mundo. 2005. Hidrocarburos en América Latina. BBC Mundo. Available at: http://news.bbc.co.uk/hi/spanish/specials/newsid_4562000/4562409.stm#top (Accessed June 20 2017).

Bebbington, Anthony, and Martin Scurrah. 2013. "Hydrocarbon Conflicts and Indigenous People in the Peruvian Amazon: Mobilization and Negotiation along the Rio Corrientes" In Anthony Bebbington and Jeffrey Bury (Eds.) *Subterranean Struggles. New Dynamics of Mining, Oil and Gas in Latin America.* Austin: University of Texas Press. DOI: 10.7560/748620.

Bebbington, Anthony, Dani de Haan, and A. Walton M. 2008 (Eds.). *Institutional Pathways to Equity: Addressing Inequality Traps*. Washington DC: World Bank.

Bebbington, Anthony, and Jeffrey Bury. 2013. *Subterranean Struggles. New Dynamics of Mining, Oil and Gas in Latin America*. Austin: University of Texas Press. DOI: 10.7560/748620.

BP Statistical Review of World Energy. 2017. BP Statistical Review of World Energy June 2017. Available at: www.bp.com/content/dam/bp/en/corporate/pdf/energy-economics/statistical-review-2017/bp-statistical-review-of-world-energy-2017-full-report.pdf (Accessed June 30 2017).

Bridge, Gavin. 2004. Contested Terrain: Mining and the Environment. *Annual Review of Environmental Resources* 29: 205–259.

Broad, Robin, and John Cavanagh. 2017. Historic Wins for Democracy and Rights in El Salvador. *Ethics & International Affairs*, June 19, 2017. Carnegie Council. Available at: www.ethicsandinternationalaffairs.org/2017/historic-wins-democracy-rights-el-salvador/ (Accessed April 21 2018).

Carrington, Kerry, Russel Hogg, and Alison McIntosh. 2015. The Hidden Injuries of Mining: Frontier Cultural Conflict. In Avi Brisman, Nigel South and Rob White (eds) *Environmental Crime and Social Conflict: Contemporary and Emerging Issues*. Ashgate Publishing Limited.

Cleary, Paul. 2011. *Too Much Luck: The Mining Boom and Australia's Future*. Collingwood, Victoria: Black Inc.

Cleary, Paul. 2012. *Minefield: The Dark Side of the Mining Boom*. Collingwood, Victoria: Black.

CEPAL. 2010. *La hora de la igualdad. Brechas por cerrar, caminos por abrir*. Santiago de Chile: Comisión Económica para América Latina y el Caribe.

CEPAL. 2014. *Los pueblos indígenas en América Latina. Avances en el último decenio y retos pendientes para la garantía de sus derechos. Síntesis*. Santiago de Chile: Comisión Económica para América Latina y el Caribe.

Cerqueira, Daniel. 2015. "Por un fundamento ético-jurídico de la participación diferenciada de los pueblos indígenas en las decisiones estatales." *Themis, Revista de Derecho*, 67. Lima: Pontificia Unversidad Catolica del Perú.

Chirif, Alberto. 2015a. Los 20 años del convenio 169 de la OIT en el Perú. ¿Algo que celebrar?. Sevindi April 23 2015. Available at: https://www.servindi.org/actualidad/128507 (Accessed June 30 2018).

Chirif, Alberto. 2015b. ¿Cuál es la situación de los territorios indígenas en la coyuntura actual? Curso taller *Políticas de desarrollo, territorio y consulta previa*. Organizado por el Fórum Solidaridad Perú, realizado en Tarapoto, 1–3 July. Available at: www.servindi.org/actualidad/134946 (Accessed February 28 2017).

Crabtree, Jonh, and Isabel Crabtree-Condor. 2012. The Politics of Extractive Industries in the Central Andes. In Anthony Bebbington (ed.) *Social Conflicts, Economic Development and Extractive Industries*. London, Hague: Routledge, 2012. 46–64.

De la Fuente, Aroa. 2013. *La explotación de los Hidrocarburos y los Minerales en México: un Análisis Comparativo*. Mexico: Heinrich Boll Stieftung.

Deheza, Elizabeth, and Ugo Ribet. 2012. Latin America's Mining Boom. The Socio-environmental and Security Dynamics in the Case of Colombia. *The RUSI Journal* 157(5): 22–31.

Doyle, Cathal, and Andy Whitmore. 2014. *Indigenous Peoples and the Extractive Sector. Towards a Rights-Respecting Engagement*. Baguio city and London: Tebtebba, Indigenous Peoples Links and Middlesex University.

Ebus, Bram, and Karly Kuijpers. 2015. The State-Corporate Tandem Cycling Towards Collision: State-Corporate Harm and the Resource Frontiers of Brazil and Colombia. In Avi Brisman, Nigel South, Rob White (eds) *Environmental Crime and Social Conflict. Contemporary and Emerging Issues*, Ashgate Publishing Limited, 125–152.

Eisenstadt, Todd, and Karleen West. 2017. Environmentalism in a Climate-Vulnerable State: Rainforests, Oil, and Political Attitudes along Ecuador's Extractive Frontier. *Journal of Comparative Politics* 49(1): 231–251.

FAO. 2014. *Respecting free, prior and informed consent. Practical guidance for governments, companies, NGOs, indigenous peoples and local communities in relation to land acquisition*. Governance of tenure technical guide No. 3. Rome: Food and Agriculture Organization.

Fraser, Barbara. 2014. Oil Spill in the Amazon Sickens Villagers, Kills Fish. A Recent Rupture of Peru's 39-Year-Old Northern Crude Oil Pipeline has Terrified Kukama Villagers along the Marañón River. *Environmental Health News* 23. Available at: www.scientificamerican.com/section/environmental-health-news/?page=5 (Accessed April 30 2016).

Global Witness. 2016. Exposing the Truth. Annual Report. Available at: www.globalwitness.org/en/about-us/exposing-truth/?accessible=true (Accessed April 01 2018).

Gray Molina, George. 2010. "The Challenge of Progressive Change Under Evo Morales." In Kurt Weyland (Ed.) *Leftist Governments in Latin America: Successes and Shortcomings*. New York: Cambridge University Press, 2010, 140–179.

Gudynas, Eduardo. 2009. Diez tesis urgentes sobre el nuevo extractivismo. Contextos y demandas bajo el progresismo sudamericano actual. *"Extractivismo, política y sociedad"*. November 2009. Quito: CAAP (Centro Andino de Acción Popular) and CLAES (Centro Latino Americano de Ecología Social). Guha Ramachandra. 2000. *Environmentalism: A Global History*. Oxford: Oxford University Press.

Guha, Ramachandra, and Juan Martínez Alier. 1997. *Varieties of Environmentalism. Essays North and South*. London: Earthscan.

Hernández-Díaz, Jorge. 2007. *Ciudadanias Diferenciadas en un estado multicultural. Los Usos y Costumbres en Oaxaca*. Mexico City: Siglo XX Editores S.A.

Himley, Matthew. 2010. *Frontiers of Capital: Mining, Mobilization, and Resource Governance in Andean Peru*. Doctoral Dissertation. Syracuse: Syracuse University.

Hinojosa, Leonith (Ed.). 2012. Gas y desarrollo. *Dinámicas territoriales rurales en Tarija, Bolivia*. La Paz, Bolivia: Fundación Tierra–CERDET.

Humphreys, Macartan, Jeffrey Sachs, and Joshep Stiglitz (Eds.). 2007. *Escaping the Resource Curse. Journal of Cleaner Production* 14(3–4): 376–387. New York: Columbia University Press.

ILO. 1989. *Convention Concerning Indigenous and Tribal Peoples in Independent Countries*. (Entry into force: 05 September 1991) Adoption: Geneva, 76th ILC session (27 June). International Labour Organization. Available at: www.ilo.org/dyn/normlex/en/f?p=NORMLEXPUB:12100:0::NO::P12100_ILO_CODE:C169 (Accessed April 01 2018).

Kymlicka, Will. 2001. *Politics in the Vernacular: Nationalism, Multiculturalism, and Citizenship*. Oxford: Oxford University Press.

Lapidoth, Ruth. 1997. *Autonomy, Flexible Solutions to Ethnic Conflicts*. Washington DC: US Institute of Peace.

Long, Michael, Paul Stretesky, and Michael Lynch et al. 2012. Crime in the Coal Industry: Implications for Green Criminology and Treadmill of Production. *Organization & Environment* 25(3): 328–346.

Lucero, Jose Antonio. 2009. "Decades Lost and Won: Indigenous Movements and Multicultural Neoliberalism in the Andes." In John Burdick, Phillips Oxhorn, and Roberts Kenneth (Eds.) *Beyond Neoliberalism in Latin America: Societies and Politics at the Crossroads*. New York: Palgrave Macmillan.

Mekonnen, Mesfin, and Arjen Hoekstra. 2016. Four Billion People Facing Severe Water Scarcity. *Science Advances* 2(2), e1500323. Available at: www.ncbi.nlm.nih.gov/pubmed/26933676 (Accessed April 02 2018).

Mena, Paúl. 2013. ¿Por qué fracasó el proyecto ambiental de Yasuní en Ecuador? Ecuador: BBC Mundo. Available at: www.bbc.com/mundo/noticias/2013/08/130816_ecuador_yasuni_causas_fracaso_lps (Accessed June 19 2016).

Observatory of Mining Conflicts. N.d. Mining Conflicts in Latin America. Available at: www.conflictosmineros.net/ (Accessed December 01 2017).

Özkaynak, Begüm, Beatriz Rodríguez-Labajos, and Cem Iskender Aydin. 2015. *Towards Environmental Justice Success in Mining Resistances: An Empirical Investigation*. EJOLT Report 14 (April).

Pearse, Guy, D. McKnight, and B. Burton. 2013. *Big Coal: Australia's Dirtiest Secret*. Sydney: NewSouth.

Pegg, Scott. 2006. Mining and Poverty Reduction: Transforming Rhetoric into Reality. DOI: 10.1016/j.jclepro.2004.06.006.

Pérez-Castellón, Ariel. 2016. El desembarco del fracking en América Latina. Available at: http://farn.org.ar/wp-content/uploads/2016/07/11Castello%CC%81n.pdf.

Perreault, Tom. 2013. "Nature and Nation: The Territorial Logics of Hydrocarbon Governance in Bolivia." In Anthony Bebbington and Jeffrey Bury (Eds.) *Subterranean Struggles: New Geographies of Extractive Industries in Latin America*. Austin: University of Texas Press, 67–90.

Perreault, Tom (Ed.). 2014. *Mineria, agua y justicia social en los andes: experiencias comparativas de Perú y Bolivia*. La Paz: Justicia Hídrica, Centro de Ecología y Pueblos Andinos; Fundación PIEB.

Plant, Roger. 2002. "Latin America's Multiculturalism: Economic and Agrarian dimensions." In Rachel Sieder (Ed.) *Multiculturalism in Latin America, Indigenous Rights, Diversity and Democracy*. New York: Palgrave McMillan.

Ruggiero, Vincenzo, and Nigel South. 2013. Toxic State–Corporate Crimes, Neo-Liberalism and Green Criminology: The Hazards and Legacies of the Oil, Chemical and Mineral Industries. *International Journal for Crime, Justice and Social Democracy*, 2(2): 12–26.

Seoane, Taddei, and C. Algranati. 2005. *The New Configurations of Popular Movements in Latin America*. Buenos Aires: Consejo Latinoamericano de Ciencias Sociales.

Slack, Keith. 2009. "Digging Out from Neoliberalism: Responses to Environmental (Mis) Governance of the Mining Sector in Latin America" In John Burdick, Phillips Oxhorn, and Roberts Kenneth (Eds.) *Beyond Neoliberalism in Latin America: Societies and Politics at the Crossroads*. New York: Palgrave Macmillan, 117-134.

Stavenhagen, Rodolfo. 2002. Indigenous Peoples and the State in Latin America: An Ongoing Debate. In Rachel Sieder (Ed.) *Multiculturalism in Latin America, Indigenous Rights, Diversity and Democracy*. New York: Palgrave McMillan.

Stretesky, Paul, and Michael Lynch. 2011. 'Coal Strip Mining, Mountaintop Removal, and the Distribution of Environmental Violations across the United States, 2002–2008. *Landscape Research* 36(2): 209–230.

Tauli-Corpuz, Victoria. 2017. Report of the Special Rapporteur of the Human Rights Council on the Rights of Indigenous Peoples. Available at: http://unsr.vtaulicorpuz.org/site/images/docs/annual/2017-annual-ga-a-72-186-en.pdf (Accessed March 1 2018).

Temkin, Benjamin. 2017. Los sindicatos estadounidenses y el movimiento ambientalista: La experiencia de la década de 1970. *Revista de historia internacional.* XII.

The Dialogue. 2015. Local Conflicts and Natural Resources. Available at: www.thedialogue.org/wp-content/uploads/2015/05/Local-Conflicts-and-Natural Resources-FINAL.pdf (Accessed May 29 2016).

The Guardian. 2017. Environmental Defenders Being Killed in Record Numbers Globally, New Research Reveals. Available at: www.theguardian.com/environment/2017/jul/13/environmental-defenders-being-killed-in-record-numbers-globally-new-research-reveals (Accessed February 28 2017).

United Nations Department of Economic and Social Affairs. N.d. International Decade for Action Available at www.un.org/waterforlifedecade/scarcity.shtml (Accessed April 10 2018).

Urkidi, Leire, and Mariana Walter. 2011. Dimensions of Environmental Justice in Anti-Gold Mining Movements in Latin America. *Geoforum* 42: 683–695. Barcelona: Institut de Ciència i Tecnologia Ambientals.

Van Cott, Donna Lee. 2008. *Radical Democracy in the Andes.* New York: Cambridge University Press.

Vargas, Cecilia. 2015. Devasta PEMEX desde hace años comunidades de Tabasco. Available at: www.la-verdad.com.mx/devasta-pemex-desde-hace-anos-comunidades-tabasco-24864.html (Accessed February 28 2018).

Weber-Fahr, M. 2002. Treasure or Trouble? Mining in Developing Countries. *World Bank and IFC Mining and Development Series.*

White, R. 2013. Resource Extraction Leaves Something Behind: Environmental Justice and Mining. *International Journal for Crime, Justice and Social Democracy* 2(1): 50–64. DOI: 10.5204/ijcjsd.v2i1.90.

Wolf, Jedamiah. 2016. A Thanksgiving Story: Extractive Industries Exploit Standing Rock Sioux and Indigenous People. Available at: www.planetexperts.com/thanksgiving-extractive-industries-exploit-indigenous/ (Accessed February 28 2018).

Xantomila, Jessica. 2017. En México no se consulta a los indígenas. La Jornada, November 15. Available at: www.jornada.unam.mx/2017/11/15/sociedad/041n3soc (Accessed February 28 2017).

Yashar, Deborah. 2005. *Contesting Citizenship in Latin America. The Rise of Indigenous Movements and the Postliberal Challenge.* New York: Cambridge University Press.

Zilney, Lisa Anne, Danielle McGurrin, and Sammy Zahran. 2006. Environmental Justice and the Role of Criminology: An Analytical Review of 33 Years of Environmental Justice Research. *Criminal Justice Review* 31: 47–62.

Chapter 1

What do indigenous people want?

Introduction

Indigenous movements in the developing world are typically framed as struggles against the dispossession of their natural resources (Harvey 2003; Bebbington et al. 2008; Bebbington and Bury 2009; Perreault 2014). As argued by Ebus and Kuijpers (2015), by cutting off local communities' access to their lands and water sources, multinational corporations have ensured that violence ensues. Over the last two decades, the alliances between indigenous rights movements and environmentalists have provided greater leverage to indigenous communities over the extractive industry (Doyle and Whitmore 2014). With resources from Non-Governmental Organizations (NGOs), numerous indigenous groups have strengthened their political organizations while becoming one of the most visible public faces of the global environmentalism.

This chapter shows, however, that the convergence of indigenous people's goals and environmentalists' agendas is not necessarily the best window to understanding extractive conflicts. Systematic indigenous approval of mining and hydrocarbon projects resulting from prior consultation procedures unveils the gap between indigenous political discourse and practice. With the aim of beginning to unpack this contradiction, this chapter argues that indigenous peoples' engagement in conflicts is not always driven by the desire to prohibit extraction on their territories. In most cases, indigenous communities use environmental protest as a means to obtain a more even distribution of extractive revenues.

Drawing from fieldwork in Bolivia, Peru and Mexico, the following sections offer analytical tools for distinguishing between pro-extractivist indigenous and anti-extractivist indigenous. Likewise, the chapter examines the underlying conditions that make both types of indigenous groups politically stronger *vis-à-vis* the state and extractive companies. Finally, the chapter dwells upon the urgency of improving indigenous peoples living conditions as a key element for safeguarding their territories from potentially destructive industries.

Latin America's impoverished indigenous peoples

In the international arena, various norms including ILO Convention 169 (1989) and the United Nation Declaration of the Rights of Indigenous Peoples (2007) recognize indigenous people's rights to maintain and strengthen their distinct political, economic and cultural institutions. In light with these norms, states have the obligation to guarantee their indigenous citizens the integrity of their territories and natural environments, as well as the full enjoyment of all human rights and fundamental freedoms recognized in international human rights law (Article 1° United Nation Declaration of the Right of Indigenous Peoples 2007). Yet in spite of extant legislation, everyday indigenous communities all over the world face dispossession of land, impacts of large-scale development projects, forced relocation and a host of other abuses (United Nations Department of Public Information 2010).

There are approximately 370 million indigenous peoples worldwide, making up 5 percent of the global population; however, they also account for about 15 percent of the world's extreme poor (United Nations Department of Public Information 2010). In Latin America, the indigenous population number 45 million living across the 20 countries that comprise the region. There are over 522 different ethnic groups from the Patagonia to northern Mexico, many of which have inhabited their territories since precolonial times (UNICEF 2009). Nevertheless, a high correlation persists between poverty and being member of an indigenous group. The 2013 report elaborated by the United Nation Development Programme on political participation of indigenous peoples in Latin America shows that indigenous peoples own little, often unproductive land and live below the poverty line (UNDP 2013).

Governments' failure to improve indigenous populations' living conditions has been deepened by the increment in the number of extractive projects in areas inhabited by indigenous communities. Resource extraction remains one of the main causes of dispossession from indigenous agricultural lands and water sources not only in Latin America but also in Canada, Australia and Africa (Carrington et al. 2015). Due to historical and ongoing overrun of extractive companies and other colonizers, indigenous territories continue to be reduced causing negative impacts on these groups' ancestral relationship with their lands and natural resources (Chirif 2015). The expansion of extractive activities jeopardizes the survival of indigenous cultures either by forcing these groups to migrate due to environmental degradation or by transforming indigenous men and women into low-skilled wage workers (Brisman et al. 2015:18). In the words of the former special rapporteur on the rights of indigenous peoples, James Anaya, the extractive industry might as well be the most pervasive source of the challenges to the full exercise of indigenous human rights (Doyle and Whitmore 2014:xiv).

Pro-extractivist indigenous vs anti-extractivist indigenous

The negative impacts on indigenous people's health, lands, water and sacred places have become more visible over the last few decades. Furthermore, the economic benefits produced by the extractive industry have not translated into a significant improvement in indigenous people's quality of life (Arellano-Yanguas 2011). On the contrary, these industries represent a major threat to the natural resources upon which many indigenous communities depend to achieve long-term survival (Mrema et al. 2009, cited by Milburn 2015:59).

However, mining and hydrocarbon projects might also represent the most viable way for numerous indigenous communities living in extreme poverty conditions to access economic resources. Some scholars argue that no real ecologists would exist if multinational companies offered the communities legitimate development opportunities (Devlin and Yap 2008:20). Research on Bolivia's hydrocarbon industry would seem to corroborate this argument. Evidence from this country demonstrates that many indigenous communities use prior consultation procedures to negotiate extractive resources with the state (see Chapter 3). This corroborates previous research showing that indigenous groups do not use consultations with the government to reject extraction (Pellegrini and Ribera 2012; Falleti and Riofrancos 2018).

Positions for and against extractive activities correspond to the different conditions existing in indigenous territories that lead them to mobilize. Social movements' theorists conceptualize social struggles as responses to disruptive changes that either pose a new threat to some segment of the population or grant new opportunities to potential challengers (Tilly 1978; Tarrow 1998; McAdam 1999; Goldstone and Tilly 2001). Whether extractive industries pose an ecological threat or represent an economic opportunity depends on the socioeconomic reality the group faces at the time disruptive changes take place. Nevertheless, distinguishing indigenous communities mobilizing to achieve anti-extractivist goals from those seeking to obtain economic resources is not an easy task, as both groups frame their struggles using environmental discourses (Arellano Yanguas 2011; Arce 2014). The sections that follow emphasize the characteristics of local economies, market integration, dependence on natural resources and access to information as the main factors contributing to the formation of indigenous attitudes toward the extractive industry.

Pro-extractivist indigenous groups

The characteristics of indigenous communities vary from region to region. Furthermore, indigenous groups are not internally homogeneous. Research shows that disagreements between indigenous members usually deepen when they have to decide to allow or prohibit extractive industries within communal lands. Therefore, it is very likely that anti-extractivist and pro-extractivist stances coexist in one single locality. Whereas for some members, resource extraction represents a source of ecological destruction, for others, these activities represent a means to escape poverty (Roblero 2011; Hernández 2014). Despite this duality, previous studies demonstrate that pro-extractivist positions generally end up prevailing in most cases (Arellano-Yanguas 2011). This is consistent with the fact that a large part of Latin America's indigenous population lack alternative development options that can surpass the incomes expected from giving up their lands for extractive operations.

As of today, subsistence agriculture, fishing and hunting do not generally provide sufficient resources to cover indigenous basic needs. In these cases, geographic isolation makes things worse for indigenous families. The lack of access to broader markets prevents these communities from trading their products, curtailing economic mobility. Extractive companies in these contexts are perceived as one of the few sources of economic expansion. Employees of such companies require provision of services such as lodging, food and entertainment. Increasing demands for these services create conditions for the emergence of new businesses near the places where employees live (Wise and Shtylla 2007:9). The expectations of greater economic growth prompt disadvantaged indigenous communities to accept extractive projects.

Chapter 3 presents several cases of pro-extractivist indigenous communities complying with resource extraction. Geographic disconnection and insufficient subsistence economies push Amazonian tribes from the Mosetén ethnic group in Bolivia, and from the Kukama Kukamiria and Capanahua ethnic groups in Peru to approve hydrocarbon operations in their lands, in the hopes of accessing to jobs and basic services. The chapter also shows that pro-extractivist indigenous groups are generally found in places where mining and hydrocarbon companies operate for long periods. Over time, the presence of extractive companies generates local economic dependence and discourages the emergence of alternative sources of income (MMSD 2002:276). Guaraní indigenous communities in Bolivia, for instance, have coexisted with the hydrocarbon industry for extended periods and systematically comply with gas extraction. Similarly, the Amazonian ethnic groups of Datem del Marañon, in Peru, accept the continuity of oil extraction, as hydrocarbons are the dominant industry in the area.

In addition, favorable attitudes toward extractive industries might be reinforced by episodes of nationalization of these industries, which have historically fostered far-reaching nationalist feelings among the population. In some countries, nationalist sentiment toward state-owned industries prevented the formation of opposition movements, even at the expense of the environment. In Bolivia for example, mining workers had a leading role in the Revolution of 1952 that then resulted in the nationalization of the mining industry (Grindle 2003). Enduring nationalist feelings discouraged the formation of anti-mining movements in the highlands of Oruro and Potosí despite extended ecological harms caused by the ongoing extraction of minerals (Perreault 2014). A similar scenario is observed in the hydrocarbon industry in Mexico, in which nationalist feelings toward state-owned oil companies, and strong economic ties between the state enterprise PEMEX and surrounding communities prevented the emergence of anti-oil movements (De la Fuente 2013; The Dialogue 2015).

Hence, indigenous communities lacking alternatives to the extractive industry, either because they lack local economies that are sufficient to guarantee adequate standard of living or because they are dependent on incomes from extractive companies, are likely to be pro-extractivist. For them, resource extraction does not represent a major threat to their living, as they have little to lose and potentially much to gain from relinquishing their land. In these cases, the enforcement of prior consultation procedures could serve as an innovative mechanism to negotiate extractive profits. Yet, as evidenced in Chapter 3, adequate provisions to prevent environmental harms to indigenous ecosystems are generally absent in these negotiations.

Anti-extractivist indigenous groups

Previous research shows that true anti-extractivist struggles led by indigenous peoples to protect the environment occur, but constitute a minority of cases of indigenous mobilization (Arellano Yanguas 2011; Arce 2014). Research confirms that barring economic depravity as the root cause for mobilization, there are communities that are skeptical of the environmental sustainability of extractive projects. Moreover, such communities do not believe that extractive industries are capable of improving current living conditions for people living close to extraction sites. Instead, indigenous peoples engaging in anti-extractivist mobilization are convinced that the damages caused by industrialized resource extraction would be greater than the benefits they could reap from it (Zavaleta 2014:6).

Generally, anti-extractivist protestors have viable economic systems in place that are threatened by extractive companies (Arellano-Yanguas 2011; Arce 2014). For instance, Arce finds that anti-mining struggles are likely to emerge and succeed in cases in which well-established, agricultural-based social organizations exist. Mineral extraction directly jeopardizes water sources needed for agricultural, as well as local control of lands (Arce 2014: 22). Following this argument, radical opposition to "big mining" projects (particularly to open pit mining) originates because opponents perceive that these projects threaten existing agricultural economies while lacking the capacity of generating comparable benefits.[1]

This chapter adds to previous studies by arguing that agricultural economies must not only be present for anti-extractivist mobilization to emerge, but they must also represent viable economic systems for indigenous communities (in opposition to subsistence agriculture). This requires that agriculturally based economies exhibit specific characteristics. Mexican anthropologist Aracely Burguete argues that indigenous communities with access to external revenue sources are most likely to be defensive of their lands and natural resources. According to Burguete, communities with "mixed economies" have more to lose from harms to their environment than communities that only have subsistence economies like agriculture, fishing or hunting to cover their basic needs (Aracely Burguete, personal communication, March 11, 2015).

Low migration rates are generally a signal that viable economic systems are in place as people do not have to leave their hometown in search of jobs. Connections to major cities—crucial for indigenous populations to trade their products and obtain cash to buy products lacking in their own communities—bolster indigenous economies. In addition, connectivity allows indigenous populations to have access to circulating narratives about the negative ecological impacts of extractive companies. Chapter 4 illustrates this argument through case studies of powerful anti-mining mobilizations emerging within the indigenous municipalities of Challapata in Bolivia and Chetilla in Peru. Both municipalities, catalogued as extremely poor by official statistics, exhibit well-established "mixed economies" based on both agriculture and informal commerce. Connections to capital cities allow informal indigenous traders to sell their products abroad without having to migrate to other cities searching for jobs. Furthermore, these connections grant them access to information about the environmental impacts associated with the mining industry. These conditions propelled the formation of anti-mining movements in both places, counteracting state attempts to implement mining projects.

On the other hand, the emergence of nontraditional economic sectors among the indigenous also creates new conditions for anti-extractivist mobilization to manifest. Ecological tourism, for instance, is emerging within some indigenous municipalities as an additional source of income. The purpose of ecotourism is the exchange of resources between indigenous populations in need of money and foreigners seeking untouched environments and ecological ways of living (Valcuende del Río et al. 2012). The implementation of extractive projects represents a threat to the viability of this new economy, as it damages the image of indigenous communities as ecologically harmonious. Chapter 4 presents the case of the indigenous municipality of Capulálpam de Méndez in Oaxaca, catalogued as ecotourist municipality by the Mexican government. Strikingly, the government also attempted to implement an open-pit mining project in this municipality and faced opposition by the local population.

Hence, anti-extractivist indigenous mobilization usually takes place within indigenous communities that are capable to cover their basic needs and have access to goods produced outside their territories. Access to cash incomes, low migration rates, connections to capital cities and access to broader markets are

Table 1.1 Economic Structures and Indigenous Attitudes toward the Extractive Industry

Type of Local Economy	*Characteristics*	*Indigenous Attitudes toward the Extractive Industry*
Subsistence activities (farming, fishing, hunting)	Isolation No access to cash incomes	Pro-extractivist
Subsistence activities coexists with the extractive industry	The population entirely depends or supplements their subsistence activities with jobs in the extractive industry	Pro-extractivist
Viable economy that is threatened by the extractive industry (flourishing agriculture, ecotourism)	Access to cities and broader markets Access to cash incomes Access to information about the extractive industry Low migration	Anti-extractivist

Source: Torres Wong, Marcela. 2018. "Prior Consultation and the Defence of Indigenous Lands in Latin America", In Zurayk Rami, Eckart Woertz and Rachel Bahn (Eds) *Crisis and Conflict in Agriculture*. England: CABI International.

typically associated with this type of economy. When extractive industries threaten the economic activities of indigenous populations, anti-extractivist movements are likely to emerge.[2]

Main sources of indigenous political power

Mobilization capacities in the pro-extractivist indigenous

As will be detailed in the following chapters, prior consultation procedures can work as enablers for pro-extractivist indigenous groups to negotiate significant economic resources with the state and extractive companies. A sector of indigenous rights supporters see in these negotiations a useful mechanism for indigenous peoples to access extractive revenues. However, not all indigenous groups engaging in prior consultations obtain the same results. Chapter 3 shows that compliance of state officials with indigenous economic demands is often dependent upon indigenous peoples' political power and their ability to threaten the viability of extractive projects. Conversely, when indigenous groups are politically weak, state officials are able to obtain consent for extraction without granting economic compensation.

This section underpins the conditions that provide some indigenous groups with political advantage in the face of extractive projects. NGO connections are often pointed out as effective sources of mobilization resources for grassroots movements. In their influential study *Activists beyond borders*, Keck and Sikking emphasize the influence of international advocacy organizations and transnational activism in the defense of human rights and environmental politics in Latin America (Keck and Sikking 1998). Specifically for indigenous movements, scholars find that NGOs significantly shape indigenous political structures and decision-making mechanisms aimed at advancing indigenous territorial rights (Bebbington et al. 2012). Moreover, previous studies on prior consultation procedures find that access to external allies allows indigenous organizations to be better positioned to negotiate with the state (Flemmer and Schilling-Vacaflor 2015:14).

In conflicts concerning natural resources, however, this chapter highlights the essential role of representative indigenous organizations at the local level. Findings demonstrate that involvement of external supporters is neither the only source of mobilization resources, nor does it automatically indicate high levels of indigenous political power. Instead, representative political organizations with extant mechanisms of deliberation and decision-making are prerequisites to develop such capacities. Whereas indigenous political organizing can be spawned by the support of NGO actors, there are other conditions that can lead to similar results. For instance, strong indigenous organizing can emerge from coordinated community responses to specific local needs, not mediated by external resource providers. Chapter 3 illustrates this argument by accounting for diverse types of indigenous organizing. Indigenous political organizations such as the Guaraní in Bolivia and some Amazonian groups in Peru emerged with NGO support, whereas the Yaqui people in Mexico developed strong territorial and political organization since precolonial times, maintaining their political structures over the centuries.

Representative political organizations are essential for indigenous political power as they enable indigenous leaders to mobilize larger groups for the achievement of collective demands. This argument rests upon the theoretical literature on social movements, which shows that preexisting organizing structures work as vehicles to mobilize major waves of protests for collective rights (Gould 1993; McAdam 1999; Trejo 2009). Mobilizing strength, in the case of pro-extractivist groups, enables the indigenous leadership to demonstrate political power *vis-à-vis* state officials when negotiating for resources in prior consultation. Case studies discussed in Chapter 3 illustrate how representative political organizations enable pro-extractivist groups to draw support from nearby communities and exert pressure on the state. In these cases, protestors undertake social mobilization activities to persuade the state and extractive companies to comply with their economic demands.

In addition, representative political organizations generally exhibit strong skills in negotiating with external actors on the use of their natural resources. Over time, indigenous groups have confronted state officials, extractive companies, organized crime groups and other actors attempting to occupy their territories. Consequently, they have had to develop bargaining skills to counteract the negative effects of these incursions, and if possible, obtain financial gains from them. Negotiation skills—especially regarding the main implications of resource extraction and the prices of minerals or hydrocarbons—are key for groups participating in prior consultation procedures to know how much is reasonable to demand. Like mobilization resources, negotiation skills can be obtained with NGO support or through local sources of knowledge. Extraction of oil and gas, for instance, requires sophisticated technology that is inaccessible to average indigenous citizens. The information that indigenous negotiators have about this particular extractive process and the revenues it generates usually comes from their connections to external NGO technicians (Oliver Stella, personal communication, July 31, 2015). The Guaraní in Bolivia, for example, developed negotiating skills over hydrocarbon extraction through connections with NGO experts. The mining industry, on the other hand, is not a new practice for some indigenous groups. In many regions of Latin America, indigenous communities have carried out small-scale mining long before the Spanish conquest. Their knowledge about the process of extraction and the incomes that can be generated from it allows indigenous actors to make reasonable economic demands for relinquishing those resources. Indigenous informal miners operating in the highlands of Bolivia and Peru are an example of this.

Indigenous mobilization capacities and negotiation skills somehow equalize asymmetric power relationships between indigenous organizations, extractive companies and state officials. When indigenous groups are politically powerful, prior consultation is more likely to result in economic benefits for them. One important effect of prior consultation then is that it allows pro-extractivist groups to reach an economic deal. The indigenous leader from Peru, Hugo Llano, argues, however, that if state officials refuse to offer negotiation spaces that are acceptable for indigenous protestors, it will be impossible to solve the conflict; the protesters become unwilling to negotiate, and indigenous leaders can no longer make progress. When conflicts reach this point, the people become furious and will not rest until the project is cancelled (Hugo Llano, personal communication, June 24, 2015).

Politically powerful anti-extractivist indigenous communities

Frequently, indigenous communities opposing extraction face violent state attempts to implement extractive projects. They must unfold far-reaching mobilizing strategies to sustain opposition during several cycles of protest. Unlike the pro-extractivist indigenous aimed at persuading state negotiators, mobilization undertaken by anti-extractivist groups serves to counteract the possibility of state repression. Anti-extractivist protestors must be capable of constructing a defensive discourse, call meetings, overcome internal divisions and enforce local agreements over the majority of community members. As argued earlier, the development of such capacities requires preexisting indigenous organizations with significant credibility *vis-à-vis* the population. This argument echoes research on social mobilization in the developing world showing that without "community resources," sustained opposition movements are unlikely to develop (Carmin 2003; McAdam and Boudet 2010). Accordingly, research on resource-based conflicts in Peru shows the necessity of political organizations that are strongly rooted in local societies in order to achieve the prohibition of the extractive industry activity (Arellano-Yanguas 2011).

Latin America scholars have paid special attention to organizational and coalitional capacities as two conditions allowing protesters to prohibit extractive projects (Arce 2014:23). In this regard, coalitions between indigenous movements and environmental activists are among the most studied by the bulk of literature on indigenous movements (Bebbington et al. 2008; Arellano-Yanguas 2011; Arce 2014). The most emblematic cases of successful anti-extractivist mobilizations led by this type of coalition are the Quilish in 2004 and the Baguazo in 2009, both occurring in Peru. In both cases, indigenous protesters relied on strategic alliances with NGOs and progressive wings of the Catholic Church to articulate an ecological framework and send a message to the government that the indigenous were determined to maintain control of their lands at any cost (Arce 2014). Both cases turned violent, and the state projects were eventually stopped.

While organizational and coalitional capacities are causal mechanisms for the success of this type of protest, this book's findings indicate that these capacities need a local basis to develop. Comparative analysis of mobilization against gas and oil pipeline projects in developing countries shows that opponents are generally able to find ways to sustain mobilization, with or without external resources (McAdam and Boudet 2010). Hence, while alliances with environmental NGOs can contribute to frame the conflict and provide resources for mobilization, these actors are neither necessary nor sufficient to stop extractive projects from going forward. Similar to the argument presented for pro-extractivist indigenous organizations, anti-extractivist indigenous organizations can be built with or without external support. Chapter 4 offers evidence for this argument. Case studies of the Quechua municipality of Chetilla in Peru and the Zapoteca municipality of Capulálpam de Méndez in Mexico illustrate how local leadership, on its own, capably mobilized the citizenry and successfully expelled mining companies. Conversely, Chapter 4 also discusses the cases of the municipalities of Cerro San Pedro in Mexico and Cotabambas and Grau in Peru, where the absence of representative local organizations contributed to the failure of the movement, despite the involvement of NGO supporters.

Furthermore, when anti-extractivist indigenous groups have representative political organizations and develop high levels of mobilization capacities, prior consultation is a detriment to the achievement of their goals.

Chapter 2 evidences the prior consultation bias in favor of extractive industries. Moreover, the chapter shows that in any case are prior consultation procedures mechanisms to manifest indigenous opposition to extractive projects. Moreover, it shows that states use these procedures to create division within indigenous communities (Vargas 2010; Rodriguez-Garavito 2011). Together, these findings suggest that prior consultations can have adverse effects for anti-extractivist movements seeking to prevent hydrocarbon or mining activities within their lands. The cases presented in Chapter 4 support this argument as anti-extractivist communities who were capable of prohibiting mining projects on their lands did not engage in prior consultation procedures (see details in Chapter 4).

Politically weak indigenous communities

As argued earlier, representative political organizations are in many cases a precondition for indigenous political power (whether the indigenous are pro-extractivist or anti-extractivist). Conversely, when these organizations do not exist or are weak, indigenous populations are likely to have low mobilization capacity. Weak indigenous groups can hold anti-extractivist or pro-extractivist attitudes, depending on their socioeconomic characteristics. Viable economies may be present, creating conditions for grievances against mining or oil extraction to emerge. However, this study shows that the lack of mobilization capacities prevents the indigenous from halting extractive projects. Likewise, if viable economic systems are absent, propelling the indigenous to exhibit favorable attitudes toward resource extraction, demobilization prevents them from successfully negotiating significant economic terms with the state.

What conditions weaken or inhibit the formation of representative indigenous organizations? The inability to mobilize broad populations based upon a framework of territoriality is a defining characteristic of a failed indigenous organization. The indigenous population of Latin America rose up to confront neoliberal policies of the 1990s that threatened their control over their community lands. Multicultural policies that affirmed indigenous autonomy rights were implemented in tandem with neoliberal reforms. Such policies provided the language that indigenous peoples would use to rise up when their *de facto* territorial autonomy was threatened (Yashar 2005; Hale 2006). Indigenous movements then used a framework based on territorial autonomy and the right to self-determination to contest state policies affecting their lands. Prerequisites for this, however, were the existence of freedom of association and expression, as well as organizational capacity (Yashar 2005:79).

Indigenous communities that had suffered episodes of sustained political violence were denied the spaces necessary to build collective power, at the same time that preexisting networks were cut off by repressors. This hindered them from the possibility to use the autonomy framework to claim ownership of their territories. Indigenous populations inhabiting the central highlands of Peru illustrate this argument. Political violence from both the Shining Path and the military during the civil war of the 1980s destroyed preexisting community organizing. To date, most mining operations are concentrated in the Peruvian central highlands, which is still marked by severe poverty. Yet indigenous opposition to the state's extractive policies remains weak compared to other parts of the country (Moreno 2014:128). Chapter 4 discusses the cases of the indigenous municipalities of Cotabambas and Grau, located in the central highlands of Peru. A sizeable mining project was implemented across both municipalities, and several NGOs provided support to the indigenous in this case. Yet indigenous populations have been unable to either prohibit the project or negotiate significant economic compensation.

A second factor preventing the establishment of representative political organizations among indigenous groups is the lack of access to communal lands upon which to develop strong organization. Elinor Ostrom shows that the strongest territorial defense is carried out by powerful local organizations that center their mobilization capacities on the collective management of natural resources (Ostrom 1990). However, collective holding of lands and natural resources by indigenous populations is uneven within and across Latin American countries. For instance, the denial of lands rights to the indigenous was broadly spread in Chiapas, Mexico, where agrarian elites escaped the Agrarian Reform (Eisenstadt 2011). This pattern is likely to occur in all places where landowners were able to retain their privileges at the expense of indigenous labor. Chapter 4 presents the case of Cerro San Pedro, where anti-mining mobilization took place yet failed to expel Canadian mining companies operating in this municipality. As is discussed in more detail in the chapter, indigenous political organizations based on long-standing collective land ownership were nonexistent in the case of Cerro San Pedro. Political weakness within local organizations prevented the success of anti-mining mobilization in spite of significant NGO support.

Likewise, indigenous tribes living in the Amazon basin in South America have not been able to establish representative political organizations within their communities. National and international organizations exist to defend Amazonian indigenous territories, and powerful ecological frameworks of the indigenous movement have been articulated with NGO support. Yet, at the local level, the rugged geographic characteristics of the Amazon and the small size and dispersion of the population prevent indigenous territorial consolidation, as well as the emergence of effective mechanisms of territorial management (Oliver Stella, personal communication, July 31, 2015). For these reasons, Amazonian tribes are generally among the most vulnerable when they have to face the implementation of an extractive project. Chapter 3 discusses the cases of the Mosetén in Bolivia, and the Kukama Kukamiria and Capanahua in Peru, all tribes living within Amazonia. The chapter details how the political weakness of the indigenous organizations inhibited these groups from either negotiating significant economic compensation with the state or prohibiting extraction on their lands.

Sometimes politically weak indigenous communities engage in small-scale conflicts against extractive companies. Ecological damage usually triggers social unrest among nearby communities. Violent confrontations may take place, which may result in casualties, but opposition of this type is mostly reactive, and a shift in scale is unlikely to occur. Moreover, extraction activities are rarely stopped. Generally, the most that protesters obtain from small-scale conflicts is to develop clientelistic relationships with mining or oil companies, but without being able to attain substantial compensation for the use of their lands. For instance, in the case of Cotabambas and Grau in Peru discussed in Chapter 4, violent events have taken place and indigenous protesters have been killed. Yet extractive projects are still operating in these municipalities without enabling indigenous communities to negotiate economic compensation to the local population.

One of the main findings of this book is that if indigenous groups are politically weak, it is not relevant for the final outcome if a prior consultation procedure is undertaken or not. If the indigenous are demobilized, it is likely that states will not feel pressured to consult them, and if they do, it will only be a formality to fulfill extant legal mandates. Chapters 3 and 4 show cases illustrating this argument. Demobilized indigenous groups engaging in prior consultation procedures (Chapter 3) obtain the same results as demobilized communities that are not consulted by the state (Chapter 4). In both cases, extraction proceeds without significant economic compensations for the indigenous, and it is irrelevant whether the right to prior consultation is enforced by the state.

Exploring the alliances between NGOs and Latin America's indigenous people

A common presumption associates the involvement of environmental and human rights NGOs with indigenous opposition to extractive industries. Research in this regard shows that NGOs, progressive wings of the Catholic Church, educational institutions and other actors have worked with indigenous populations to provide them with resources to fight the dispossession of their lands (Bebbington et al. 2012). Most salient examples of ethnically centered organizations mediated by alliances with international actors are in Amazonia and El Chaco. As both regions are ecologically fragile, indigenous peoples and their allies frame their grievances in terms of environmental protection, claiming to defend communal lands against degradation caused by resource extraction. The Amazonia and El Chaco regions are shared by several countries in South America. In the Amazon basin, shared by Peru, Bolivia, Colombia, Ecuador and Brazil, organizing of indigenous tribes into federations started in the 1980s. NGO support enabled these federations to gather into national organizations and later into the international organization, COICA, functioning as an umbrella for all indigenous organizations of the Amazon basin (Klima Bundnis 2016). Likewise, the Chaco region, shared by Bolivia, Paraguay and Argentina, is home to a sizable Guaraní population and commands significant NGO resources. These resources enabled the formation of local political organizations named *Asambleas del Pueblo Guaraní* (APGs) or Assemblies of the Guaraní People. National APGs were subsequently formed in each country (Caballero et al. 2010; Ramírez 2016).

In spite of appealing ecological causes attributed to the indigenous in these areas, NGO resources have been insufficient to create sustainable economies that can represent a viable option to the extractive industry. This limits the influence they may have in the formation of indigenous goals in the long term. As will be discussed in detail in the next chapter, hydrocarbon extraction in the Amazon and El Chaco represents one of the few ways the indigenous have to obtain income. Only subsistence economies exist in these areas and are insufficient to cover basic needs of the population. In these regions, ethnic identities are salient and indigenous leaders are skilled in making environmentally based claims. However, Chapter 3 shows that are indigenous communities from the Amazon and El Chaco the ones deriving profits from hydrocarbons. Ironically, the groups catalogued as pro-extractivist indigenous in this book also include groups whose political organizing was mediated by NGOs.

Conversely, Chapter 4 shows that indigenous communities whose political organizations were created without significant NGO support undertake the fiercest ecological defenses. This resonates with Elinor Ostrom's studies in Mexico that demonstrate that communities are capable of self-organizing for sustainable water governance (Pacheco-Vega 2014). Foremost on the list of anti-extractivist organizations are *Rondas Campesinas* in Peru and *Usos y Costumbres* in Mexico. Both serve as political vehicles for social protests. The *Rondas* were born as a communal response to fight crime and insurgency within peasant communities of the Cajamarca region, given the incapacity of the state to guarantee citizen security in rural areas. When ex-president Fujimori came to power and initiated counterinsurgency against the Shining Path, he relied on the *Rondas* to fight rebellion in the countryside. In the context of the civil war, Fujimori faced no obstacles in legalizing these organizations' use of violence to punish criminals. Later, Fujimori included the right of the *Rondas Campesinas* to manage their internal affairs in the Constitution of 1993. Fulfilling justice services in rural towns allowed *Rondas Campesinas*, to proliferate and spread their influence across several parts of the highlands (Gitlitz 2013). Through decades of operation, these organizations accumulated sizable mobilization capacities and credibility among community members. After authoritarian Fujimori left office in 2000, and Cajamarca became the main mining center of Peru, grievances against the American mining company Yanacocha became more salient among peasant communities. *Rondas Campesinas* took the lead in articulating a powerful territorially based framework depicting mining as a threat to water sources and agricultural lands.

Since then, the *Rondas*, in partnership with other social organizations, have led successful mobilizations against billion-dollar projects such as the "Quilish Mountain" in 2004 and "Conga" in 2011. Both projects were intended to expand Yanacocha's gold reserves, yet they were stopped through violent mobilization. According to state official Segundo Pastor, in charge of resource-based conflicts in Peru, even though Cajamarca lacks an indigenous-based identity, *Rondero* culture is strongly rooted in peasant communities, enabling massive responsiveness from the population (Pastor Paredes, personal communication, July 7, 2014). Paradoxically, *Rondas Campesinas* that were born as state allies against terrorist insurgency in the 1980s are now powerful challengers to state authority over their jurisdictions, leading radical anti-mining struggles against the government.

Likewise in Mexico, the gap between the political party system and the indigenous population propelled indigenous municipalities to develop their own customary norms to elect their authorities. Over time, autonomous electoral rules resulted in effective mechanisms of territorial defense (Gerardo Gonzales, personal communication, March 6, 2015). Similar to what Fujimori did with the *Rondas Campesinas* in Cajamarca, electoral self-determination within Oaxaca's indigenous towns was legalized in the 1990s. To counteract the influence of opposition political parties, members of the hegemonic *Partido Revolucionario Institucional* (PRI) or Institutional Revolutionary Party supported implementation of the *Usos y Costumbres* law in 1995, legally enabling indigenous jurisdictions to elect their municipal authorities by whatever means they choose.

This law was thus intended both to allow the PRI to please Oaxaca's indigenous municipalities and to prevent further indigenous rebellions such as that of the Zapatistas (Eisenstadt 2011). However, by eliminating the official political party system within indigenous municipalities, Oaxaca's government might have unintentionally eliminated one important source of divisions among Mexican indigenous communities: political party affiliation (Gustavo Castro, personal communication, March 12, 2015). Based on the services they provide to their people, indigenous authorities that are elected by the *Usos y Costumbres* system are able to accumulate significant amounts of prestige and credibility in the community. This enables political organizations created by *Usos y Costumbres* to organize protests, host meetings and sustain mobilization against interventions that they perceive as a threat to their territories (Salvador Aquino, personal communication, May 15, 2014).

With the government embracing aggressive pro-mining policies in non-traditional areas, powerful indigenous municipalities in Oaxaca have mobilized anti-mining campaigns. Indigenous communities have successfully expelled mining companies from their lands, despite previous approval by the federal government. The framework used was based upon claims that mining threatens water sources and agricultural lands. Examples of this include the Zapoteca municipalities of Capulálpam de Méndez and Magdalena de Teitipac, both located in the state of Oaxaca. The two municipalities are ruled by the *Usos y Costumbres* system, and in 2013, community members expelled Canadian companies seeking to implement gold mines within indigenous territories (*"Comunidades Zapotecas prohíben actividades mineras en sus tierras por 100 años"*).

Legal validation of already-existing indigenous organizations such as *Rondas Campesinas* and *Usos y Costumbres*, by conservative governments in the 1990s, unintentionally provided the indigenous with the resources to build powerful territorially based frameworks to confront controversial mining projects in both countries. These communities see mining as a setback to their quality of life, not a mechanism to improve it. When mining is a risk to collective means of existence, and does not offer replacements that are acceptable for the communities, incentives for anti-extractivist mobilization are reinforced.

Conclusion

This chapter provided analytical tools to understand the complex relationship between indigenous people and the extractive industry. Governments' abandonment of their indigenous citizen manifests through prevailing malnutrition, lack of access to education and health care, and political marginalization among indigenous communities (Due Process of Law Foundation 2015). Economic deprivation prompts many of these groups to see the extractive industry as the most accessible way out of extreme poverty in spite of the ecological risks associated with extractive operations. Conversely, those indigenous communities with more robust economies, connected to bigger cities and markets, and with access to information about the impacts of extractive projects are in a better position to fight the extractive model.

On the other hand, the contrast between indigenous organizations created with NGO support and indigenous organizations created from bottom-up processes shows that the long-standing presence of international supporters does not define indigenous goals. It is likely that NGOs choose to collaborate with the most vulnerable and disadvantaged indigenous groups. However, the advancement of viable economic models that are also ecologically sustainable—even with NGO support—is still a challenging endeavor. Achieving the viability of indigenous economies is critical if environmentalists want to be able to compete with rapid cash disbursements associated with the extractive industry. The evidence presented in this chapter indicates that raising the quality of life of indigenous peoples would be more useful for ecological defense in the long-term than prior consultations.

The next chapter details how governments misuse prior consultation procedures to skip over environmental issues. Chapter 2 shows how governments take advantage of indigenous critical economic situations to mobilize their support for extractive projects. It is for this reason that consultations between state agencies and indigenous communities generally result in indigenous consent to ecologically controversial projects.

Notes

1 Modern mining uses highly sophisticated technology that makes local labor redundant, but it still requires extensive amounts of water and removal of enormous pieces of lands to extract the largest quantity of minerals (O'Huallachain and Matthews 1996).
2 The cases presented in the book emphasize economic conditions present in indigenous territories as one condition explaining indigenous attitudes toward extractive projects. Nonetheless, other factors can explain struggles against mining projects. For instance, the protection of sacred places in the case of the Huichol people in 2011 in Mexico drove their fight against state attempts to implement mining in the Wirikuta territory, which resulted in the cancellation of operations.

References

Arce, Moises. 2014. *Resource Extraction and Protest in Peru.* Pittsburg: University of Pittsburg Press.

Arellano-Yanguas, Javier. 2011. *¿Minería sin fronteras? Conflicto y desarrollo en regiones mineras del Perú.* Lima: IEP.

Bebbington, Anthony, Dani de Haan, and A. Walton. 2008 (Eds.) *Institutional Pathways to Equity: Addressing Inequality Traps.* Washington, DC: World Bank.

Bebbington, Anthony, and Jeffrey Bury. 2009. Confronting the Institutional Challenge for Mining and Sustainability: The Case of Peru. *Proceedings of the National Academy of Sciences* 106(41): 17296–17301.

Bebbington, Anthony, Martin Scurrah and Claudia Bielich. 2012. *Los movimientos sociales y la política de la pobreza en el Perú.* Instituto de Estudios Peruanos, Lima: CEPES.

Brisman, Avi, Nigel Souht, and Rob White. 2015. "Toward a Criminology of Environmental-Conflict Relatioship." In Avi Brisman, Nigel South and Rob White (eds.) *Environmental Crime and Social Conflict. Contemporary and Emerging Issues.* Farnham: Ashgate, 1-38.

Caballero, Gerónimo, Jorge Ramírez Mattos, Victor Villalta, Mario González Lelarge, and Sabino Ruíz. 2010. Buenas Prácticas: Un camino hacia la autodeterminación – Distrito Indígena Guaraní Kaami. Bolivia. Available at: www.bivica.org/upload/autodeterminacion_kaami.pdf (Accessed June 4 2018).

Carmin, Joann. 2003. Resources, Opportunities and Local Environmental Action in the Democratic Transition and Early Consolidation Periods of the Czech Republic. *Environmental Politics* 12(3): 42–64.

Carrington, Kerry, Russel Hogg, and Alison McIntosh. 2015. "The Hidden Injuries of Mining: Frontier Cultural Conflict." In Avi Brisman, Nigel South and Rob White (eds.) *Environmental Crime and Social Conflict: Contemporary and Emerging Issues*. Farnham: Ashgate Publishing Limited, 241–264.

Chirif, Alberto. 2015. "¿Cuál es la situación de los territorios indígenas en la coyuntura actual? Curso taller *Políticas de desarrollo, territorio y consulta previa.*" Organizado por el Fórum Solidaridad Perú, realizado en Tarapoto, 1–3 July. Available at: www.servindi.org/actualidad/134946 (Accessed February 28 2017).

De la Fuente, Aroa. 2013. *La Explotación de los Hidrocarburos y los Minerales en México: Un Análisis Comparativo*. Mexico: Heinrich Boll Stieftung.

Devlin, John, and Nonita Yap. 2008. Contentious Politics in Environmental Assessment: Blocked Projects and Winning Coalitions. *Impact Assessment and Project Appraisal*, 26(1): 17–27. DOI: 10.3152/146155108X279939.

Doyle, Cathal, and Andy Whitmore. 2014. *Indigenous Peoples and the Extractive Sector. Towards a Rights-Respecting Engagement*. Baguio city and London: Tebtebba, Indigenous Peoples Links and Middlesex University.

Due Process of Law Foundation. 2015. *Derecho a la consulta y al consentimiento previo, libre e informado en América Latina*. Washington, DC: DPLF.

Ebus, Bram, and Karly Kuijpers. 2015. "The State-Corporate Tandem Cycling Towards Collision: State-Corporate Harm and the Resource Frontiers of Brazil and Colombia." In Michael J Lynch and Paul B. Stretesky (eds.). *Environmental Crime and Social Conflict. Contemporary and Emerging Issues*. Farnham: Ashgate, 125–152.

Eisenstadt, Todd. 2011. *Politics, Identity, and Mexico's Indigenous Rights Movements*. Cambridge: Cambridge University Press.

Falleti, Tulia, and Thea Riofrancos. 2018. "Endogenous Participation: Strengthening Prior Consultation in Extractive Economies." World Politics. 70(1), 86–121.

Flemmer, Riccarda, and Almut Schilling-Vacaflor. 2015. Unfulfilled Promises of the Consultation Approach: The Limits to Effective Indigenous Participation in Bolivia's and Peru's Extractive Industries. *Third World Quarterly* 37(1), 172–188.

Gitlitz, John. 2013. *Administrando Justicia al Margen del Estado. Las rondas Campesinas de Cajamarca*. Lima: IEP.

Goldstone, Jack, and Charles Tilly. 2001. "Threat (and Opportunity): Popular Action and State Response in the Dynamics of Contentious Action." In Ronald R. Aminzade, Jack A. Goldstone, Doug McAdam, Elizabeth J. Perry, William H. Sewell, Sidney Tarrow, and Charles Tilly (Eds.) *Silence and Voice in the Study of Contentious Politics*. Cambridge, MA: Cambridge University Press, 179–194.

Grindle, Merilee. 2003. "1952 and All That: The Bolivian Revolution in Comparative Perspective." In Pilar Domingo (Ed.) *Proclaiming Revolution: Bolivia in Comparative Perspective*. Cambridge, MA: Harvard University Press, 1–21.

Gould, Roger. 1993. Collective Action and Network Structure. *American Sociological Review* 58(2): 182–196.

Hale, Charles. 2006. *Más que un indio (More Than an Indian): Racial Ambivalence and Neoliberal Multiculturalism in Guatemala*. School of American Research Press: Santa Fe.

Harvey, David. 2003. *The New Imperialism*. Oxford and New York: Oxford University Press.

Hernández, Ursula. 2014. *Vivir la mina. El conflicto minero en San José del Progreso y sus efectos cotidianos en la vida individual y la existencia colectiva. Rupturas, contrastes, reconstrucciones y resistencias*. Oaxaca: CIESAS.

Keck, Margaret, and Kathryn Sikkink. 1998. *Activists beyond Borders: Advocacy Networks in International Politics*. Ithaca, NY: Cornell University Press.
Klima Bundnis. 2016. *COICA*. Available at: www.indigene.de/20.html (Accessed June 4 2018).
McAdam, Doug. 1999. *Political Process and the Development of Black Insurgency 1930-1970*. Chicago, IL: University of Chicago Press.
McAdam, Doug, and Hillary Boudet. 2010. Site Fights: Explaining Opposition to Pipeline Projects in the Developing World. *Sociological Forum* 25(3): 401–427, September.
MMSD. 2002. *Abriendo Brecha. Minería, Minerales y Desarrollo Sustentable*. London: International Institute for Environment and Development y World Business Council for Sustainable Development.
Moreno, Gustavo. 2014. "El Caso Las Bambas." In Ivan Ormachea et al. *Mineria, Conflicto Social y Dialogo*. Lima: ProDialogo.
Milburn, Richard 2015. "Gorillas and guerrillas: environment and conflict in the Democratic Republic of Congo." In Avi Brisman, Nigel South, Rob White (eds). *Environmental Crime and Social Conflict. Contemporary and Emerging Issues*. Aldershot: Ashgate, 57–71.
Mrema, Elizabeth, Carl Bruch, and Jordan Diamond. 2009. *Protecting the Environment during* Armed *Conflict: An Inventory and Analysis of International Law*. Nairobi: United Nations Environment Programme.
O'Huallachain, Breandan, and Richard Matthews. 1996. "Reestructuring of primary industries: technology, labor and corporate strategy and control in the Arizona cooper industry," *Economic Geography*, 72(2), 196–215.
Ostrom, Elinor. 1990. *Governing the Commons: The Evolution of Institutions for Collective Action*. New York: Cambridge University Press.
Pacheco-Vega, Raul. 2014. Ostrom y la gobernanza del agua en México. *Revista Mexicana de Sociología* 15(1) January–March. DOI: 10.22201/iis.01882503p.2014.0.46485.
Pellegrini, Lorenzo, and Marco Ribera. 2012. Consultation, Compensation and Extraction in Bolivia after the 'Left Turn': The Case of Oil Exploration in the North of La Paz Department. *Journal of Latin American Geography* 11(2): 101–118.
Perreault, Tom (Ed). 2014. *Minería, Agua y Justicia Social en los Andes: Experiencias Comparativas de Perú y Bolivia*. La Paz: Justicia Hídrica, Centro de Ecología y Pueblos Andinos; Fundación PIEB.
Ramírez, Eddie. 2016. "Conforman Coordinadora indígena internacional preparatoria para el Encuentro Mundial Chaco 2016." In *El Chaco sin Fronteras*. Available at: www.chacosinfronteras.com/2016/02/28/10546-redeschaco (Accessed June 4 2018).
Roblero, Marin. 2011. *El Despertar de la Serpiente, la Sierra Madre de Chiapas en riesgo: Extracción Minera y Comunidades en Resistencia en Chicomuselos. Master Dissertation for the Autonomous University of Chapingo*. San Cristobal de las Casas, Chiapas. Tarrow Sidney. 1998. *Power in Movement: Social Movements and Contentious Politics*. Cambridge: Cambridge University Press.
The Dialogue. 2015. *Local Conflicts and Natural Resources*. Available at: www.thedialogue.org/wp-content/uploads/2015/05/Local-Conflicts-and-Natural-Resources-FINAL.pdf (Accessed May 29 2016).
Tilly, Charles. 1978. *From Mobilization to Revolution*. Reading, MA: Addison-Weslev.

Trejo, Guillermo. 2009. Religious Competition and Ethnic Mobilization in Latin America: Why the Catholic Church Promotes Indigenous Movements in Mexico. In *American Political Science Review* 103(3), 323–342.

UNDP. 2013. "Indigenous Peoples in Latin America Improve Political Participation, But Women Lag behind, Says UNDP." United Nation Development Programme, May 22. Available at: www.undp.org/content/undp/en/home/presscenter/pressreleases/2013/05/22/pueblos-indigenas-en-america-latina-pese-a-los-avances-en-la-participacion-politica-las-mujeres-son-las-mas-rezagadas-segun-el-pnud.html (Accessed April 8 2018).

UNICEF. 2009. *Atlas Socio-lingüístico de Pueblos Indígenas en América Latina*. Cochabamba: FUNPROEIB Andes. Available at: www.unicef.org/honduras/tomo_1_atlas.pdf (Accessed December 1 2017).

United Nations Department of Public Information. 2010. *State of the World's Indigenous Peoples*. January 14. Available at: www.un.org/esa/socdev/unpfii/documents/SOWIP/press%20package/sowip-press-package-en.pdf (Accessed April 8 2018).

Valcuende del Río, Jose Maria Murtagh, and Klaus Rummenhoeller. 2012. *Turismo y poblaciones indigenas: espacio tiempo y recursos*. Available at: www.ub.edu/geocrit/sn/sn-410.htm (Accessed May 7 2016).

Vargas, Miguel. 2010. *Lecciones Aprendidas sobre la Consulta Previa*. La Paz: CEJIS.

Wise, Holly, and Sokol Shtylla. 2007. *The Role of the Extractive Sector in Expanding Economic Opportunities*. Boston: The Fellows of Harvard College. Available at: www.hks.harvard.edu/m-rcbg/CSRI/publications/report_18_EO%20Extractives%20Final.pdf (Accessed February 2017).

Yashar, Deborah. 2005. *Contesting Citizenship in Latin America. The Rise of Indigenous Movements and the Postliberal Challenge. New York: Cambridge University Press.*

Zavaleta, Mauricio. 2014. *La Batalla por los Recursos Naturales*. Lima: Pontificia Universidad Católica del Perú.

Interviews

Aracely Burguete. "Interview," Torres Wong, Marcela. San Cristóbal de las Casas, Mexico. March 11, 2015.

Gerardo Gonzales. "Interview," Torres Wong, Marcela. San Cristóbal de las Casas, Mexico. March 6, 2015.

Gustavo Castro. "Interview," Torres Wong, Marcela. San Cristóbal de las Casas, Mexico. March 12, 2015.

Hugo Llano. "Interview," Torres Wong, Marcela. Puno, Peru. June 24, 2015.

Oliver Stella. "Interview," Torres Wong, Marcela. Lima, Peru. July 31, 2015.

Pastor Paredes. "Interview," Torres Wong, Marcela. Cajamarca, Peru. July 7, 2014.

Salvador Aquino. "Interview," Torres Wong, Marcela. Oaxaca, Mexico. May 15, 2014.

Chapter 2

Ecological defense or bargaining over indigenous lands?

Introduction

Many of mining and hydrocarbon operations are carried out in territories ancestrally inhabited by indigenous peoples. Under extant international law, including the International Labor Organization Convention 169 or ILO 169 (1989) and the United Nation Declaration of the Rights of Indigenous Peoples (2007), consultation procedures that genuinely seek the free, prior and informed consent of indigenous communities must precede any project attempted on indigenous lands. Overall, the right to prior consultation aims to protect indigenous territories from undesired impacts, as well as to guarantee indigenous peoples the right to have a meaningful and informed participation in the policies that affect them (Due Process of Law Foundation 2011:4).

Even while the protection of the environment was not the main purpose of the right to prior consultation, many environmentalists saw these procedures as useful mechanisms to keep indigenous lands free of industrialized resource extraction. These expectations were in line with studies on deliberative environmental politics showing that public participation in decision making has the potential of producing more environmentally sound policy decisions (Baber and Bartlett 2005). This chapter demonstrates, however, that indigenous participation in prior consultation procedures in three Latin American countries does not serve to put into question the ecological sustainability of extractive industries. On the contrary, prior consultation procedures conducted in the region to date result in systematic indigenous acceptance of mining and hydrocarbon projects. Further, evidence suggests that indigenous communities are in a better position to ban extractive projects when prior consultation does not take place.

Arguably, international and domestic Non-Governmental Organizations (NGOs) advocating for the implementation of prior consultation regimes in Latin America relied on two assumptions. First, and typical of industrialized societies, is that institutions are born strong (Levitsky and Murillo 2013). On the books, prior consultation procedures should include neutral social and environmental impact studies that provide indigenous communities with reliable information over the consequences of accepting extraction. However,

Latin American scholars warn that within an economic model that depends on the export of natural resources, transnational corporations have an increasingly pronounced ability to influence domestic politics (Gudynas 2009). This influence is enhanced by Latin America's weak institutions, which enable governments to non-enforce or selectively enforce legislation according to the interests they have over the matters at stake (O'Donnell 1993; Levitsky and Murillo 2013; Amengual 2016). It should come as no surprise then that the government's implementation of the right to prior consultation does not usually follow international standards, and thereby neutral social and impact assessments are not part of prior consultations. A second assumption probably guiding many NGOs' advocacy campaign is that indigenous peoples are both communitarian and environmentalists. The economic opportunities that extractive projects represent for many indigenous groups determine that many of these groups support mining and hydrocarbon activities (Arellano-Yanguas 2011; Arce 2014).

These two reasons—Latin America's weak institutions and predominant pro-extractivist indigenous stances—contribute to explain why indigenous communities do not use prior consultation procedures to halt extraction. Through the examination of Bolivia, Peru and Mexico—three countries with diverse political and legal settings—this chapter demonstrates that prior consultation outcomes over mining and hydrocarbon operations are similar across countries. In the best-case scenario, these procedures are bargaining tables to negotiate the terms of extraction, instead of spaces to manifest opposition to extractive industries.

Development of the right to prior consultation in Latin America

Whereas the United States and Canada have refused to date to sign ILO Convention 169, 14 out of the 22 states that ratified this international law are Latin American. During the 1990s, most countries in the region formally complied with this international legislation. Domestic implementation of the right to prior consultation, however, did not start until almost two decades later in the subcontinent. Violence between indigenous communities and extractive companies over the control of resource-rich lands skyrocketed during the 2000s commodity boom (Environmental Justice Atlas n.d.). Latin American governments were forced to pass legislation in order to carry out formerly ignored prior consultation procedures.

Currently, Latin America is the region with the greatest legal development of prior consultation regimes (Due Process of Law Foundation 2015). Nearly half of the countries that signed ILO Convention 169 in the 1990s now exhibit some form of legislation regulating the right to prior consultation. Table 2.1 presents a complete list of Latin American countries that have signed ILO Convention 169 and the legal regulation of prior consultation in each country.

Table 2.1 Implementation of Prior Consultation in Latin America

Country (Percent of Indigenous)	*Year of Ratification ILO 169*	*Year of Implementation (Law That Was Passed)*	*PC Over Extractive Industries?*	*Indigenous Veto Power?*
Bolivia (60)	1991	2005 (Law of Hydrocarbons)	Yes	Yes
Peru (40)	1994	2011 (Prior Consultation Law)	Yes	No
Ecuador (30)	1998	1998 Constitution	Yes	No
Mexico (12)	1990	2014 (Law of Hydrocarbons)	Yes	Not defined
Guatemala (40)	1996	No legal implementation	No	Not applicable
Nicaragua (10)	2010	No legal implementation	No	Not applicable
Honduras (7)	1995	No legal implementation	No	Not applicable
Costa Rica (0.6)	1993	No legal implementation	No	Not applicable
Colombia (4)	1991	1998 (Decree 1320)	Yes	No
Venezuela (2.2)	2002	No legal implementation	No	Not applicable
Chile (11)	2008	2009 (Decree 124)	No	No
Brazil (0.4)	2002	No legal implementation	No	Not applicable
Argentina (0.1)	2000	No legal implementation	No	Not applicable
Paraguay (0.2)	1993	No legal implementation	None	Not applicable

Latin American countries did not use the same legislative formula to address the right to prior consultation. Table 2.1 shows wide variation in the way prior consultation was institutionalized. The most progressive legislation incorporated this right into constitutions (Bolivia and Ecuador); some countries passed a framework law to regulate prior consultation procedures (Peru, Chile and Colombia), others only recognized this right through sectoral legislation (Mexico), whereas still others did not implement prior consultation at all. Within the set of countries adopting legal regulations of the right to prior consultation, the legislative spectrum of these initiatives is illustrated in Figure 2.1.

Indigenous movements, prior consultation and government ideology

The bulk of literature in the field of political science attributes social and political transformations to either the strength of the grassroots challengers or the willingness of governments to advance reforms (Rosenberg 1991;

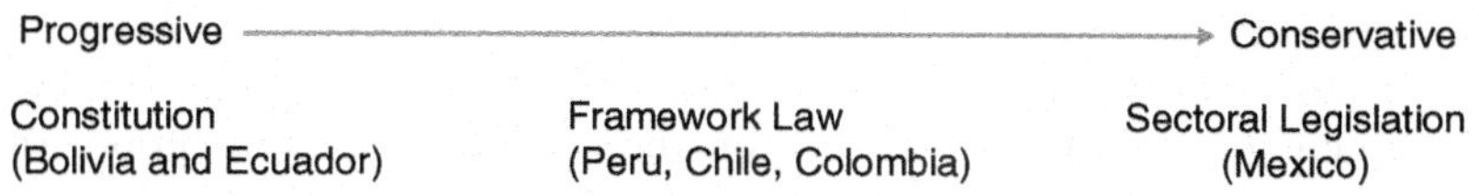

Figure 2.1 Legislative Spectrum.

Source: Torres Wong, Marcela. 2018. "Prior Consultation and the Defence of Indigenous Lands in Latin America," In Zurayk Rami, Eckart Woertz and Rachel Bahn (Eds) *Crisis and Conflict in Agriculture*. England: CABI International.

Cohen and Arato 1992; Epp 1998). Following these studies, differences in prior consultation regimes are explained by the different levels of political influence of indigenous movements in each country and the type of government passing prior consultation legislation. This is supported by subsequent research on contentious politics in the Andes, which demonstrates that constitutional incorporation of the right to prior consultation in Bolivia and Ecuador followed unprecedented indigenous mobilization. Likewise, these constitutional reforms were carried out by governments with progressive ideologies regarding indigenous rights (Yashar 2005; Van Cott 2008; Lucero 2009; Albó 2011). Conversely, in Peru, where indigenous movements are generally weak and governments' ideologies remain conservative, only modest reforms addressing indigenous rights have been introduced (Yashar 2005).

With prior consultation laws now in place in several countries, analysis of institutional outcomes tends to focus on whether prior consultation legislation grants a veto power to indigenous communities (Jaskoski 2013; Due Process of Law Foundation 2015; Greenspan 2015). According to the President of the Inter-American Human Rights Commission, Rose Marie Belle-Antoine, the main problem in the implementation of the right to prior consultation is that while states formally recognize this right, they do so superficially. According to Belle-Antoine and the United Nations special rapporteur on the rights of indigenous peoples Victoria Tauli-Corpuz, indigenous right to give or withhold consent for oil, gas, and mining project development affecting their lands and natural resources is a substantial element of the prior consultation right (Greenspan 2015). States, on the other hand, wish to ensure that norms governing the right to prior consultation explicitly provide that indigenous groups have no right to veto projects on indigenous territories (Due Process of Law Foundation 2011:5). Amid the debate on which should be the scopes of the right to prior consultation, some studies have shown that in cases in which the indigenous response to consultation is binding, results are more beneficial for indigenous groups (Bascopé 2010; Jaskoski 2013).

Based on extant studies, (i) the national influence of indigenous movements, (ii) the ideology of the government in office and (iii) the scope of the right to prior consultation should influence the realization of indigenous rights. Nonetheless, this chapter argues that none of these variables are relevant for explaining prior consultation outcomes. To demonstrate that the economic importance of the extractive industry for both the state and indigenous groups permeates the implementation of prior consultation in Latin America, this work examines Bolivia, Peru and Mexico, three countries with a prominent extractive industry sector and sizable indigenous population. These countries were selected for comparison, in part due to their wide variation across the three key variables: the national influence of indigenous movements, the scope of the right to prior consultation in domestic legislations and the ideology of the government in office. They were also selected due to the rather similar prior consultation outcomes. In none of these cases, prior consultation procedures prevent extractive projects from being implemented. Likewise, "non-enforcement" and "selective enforcement" of prior consultation are equally utilized by governments to soothe the negative effects that this institution might cause on their capacity to further extractive projects.

Applying the variables to the three cases

Indigenous movements in Bolivia have had a much greater influence on national politics than respective movements in Mexico or Peru. Such movements led to the development of one of the most progressive prior consultation systems in all of Latin America, as well as the 2005 election of a leftist indigenous president, Evo Morales. The hydrocarbon industry was nationalized, and indigenous communities living near hydrocarbon reserves were granted veto power over gas and oil extraction. Unprecedented constitutional incorporation of indigenous rights took place, including the right to prior consultation. Such changes led many scholars to argue that Bolivia had become an experimental laboratory for the realization of long-standing indigenous economic and political demands (Eisenstadt 2011).

Peru differs from Bolivia across the three variables outlined earlier. Indigenous mobilization remains weak at the national level, yet conflicts between indigenous communities and extractive companies have increased since the democratic transition in 2001 (Yashar 2005; Paredes 2015). Prior consultation was enacted in 2011, but this did not grant veto power to consulted indigenous populations. Nor was prior consultation added to the Constitution. Neoliberal policies of the 1990s remain in force to this day. Therefore, extractive industries are still in hands of foreign companies.

Mexico also differs from Bolivia and Peru across the variables of interest to this chapter. Indigenous movements have not reached the same level of political salience as in Bolivia, yet ethnic organizing at the local level is stronger than it is in Peru (Yashar 2005; Silva 2009). Ethnic insurgency made it so that indigenous rights were partially regulated through electoral indigenous autonomy. However, prior consultation regimes remain almost completely unimplemented. Unlike the cases of Bolivia and Peru, there is no constitutional mandate or framework law to regulate prior consultation procedures in Mexico despite increasing political violence over control of resource-rich lands. Sectoral legislation exists, yet it does not specify whether the right to prior consultation grants indigenous groups veto power. Neoliberal reforms in Mexico have been in force since the late 1980s. Despite never having been as radical as those in Peru, such reforms expanded under the Peña Nieto government. In 2013, the hydrocarbon industry, formerly under state control, was opened for private oil and gas operators.

The case of Bolivia

National influence of indigenous movements

During the 2000s, indigenous claims upon the rights granted by ILO Convention 169 were common across Latin America. However, in Bolivia, indigenous demands to participate in natural resource policy making grew to national proportions amid economic crisis and mounting social discontent with economic policies in the wake of two major social conflicts. The first such conflict was sparked by the attempted sale of the *Servicio Municipal de Agua Potable y Alcantarillado* (SEMAPA)—the state enterprise in charge of supplying water to Cochabamba—to the Spanish company *Aguas de Tunari*. The Cochabamba "Water War" took place between January and April of 2000, under the presidency of Hugo Banzer (1997–2001), and included a series of protests against the privatization of water. According to the government, selling SEMAPA would result in an improvement in the quality of water provision. However, the sale would also increase the rates paid by Cochabamba's population. Massive mobilization, grounded in a discourse based on ancestral indigenous ownership of natural resources, finally forced the state to withdraw (Albro 2005).

The second event, referred to as the "Gas War," occurred in October of 2003, under the presidency of Sánchez de Lozada (2002–2003). Thousands of Bolivians flocked to the streets to protest the government's decision to export natural gas—which had been in hands of private companies since 1996—through Chile. Protestors claimed that this decision was akin to treason as the government was "giving away" the nation's potential profits to a country that had blocked Bolivia access to the coast. Immediate annulment of this measure, along with nationalization of the hydrocarbon industry, was demanded by a wide range of social organizations (including indigenous organizations and labor unions). Although nationalist demands based on state ownership of this industry were not new in Bolivia, this time, radicalization of protests spread to major cities across the country. The state responded by sending the army to repress protestors in the predominantly indigenous city of El Alto, leaving several dead and injured.

Privatization of state companies and liberalization of the extractive industry were part of the package of neoliberal reforms initiated during the 1990s.

Yet national discontent was articulated through a powerful indigenous-based mobilization, taking the deadly events of El Alto further than previous episodes of social mobilizations. In October of 2003, the government of Sánchez de Lozada was overthrown. Following two years of political uncertainty, union leader Evo Morales was elected in 2005 as the first indigenous president of Bolivia with support from some of the most prominent indigenous organizations. Under Morales's presidency, various neoliberal policies were dismantled. The state took control of Bolivia's sizable hydrocarbon industry, which had been plagued by conflicts between multinational companies and indigenous communities for years. In the mining industry, on the other hand, Morales practically gave *de facto* control of this sector to indigenous mining cooperatives (Espinoza 2010). Since Morales was elected, indigenous opposition to the extractive industry has dissipated. Indigenous groups support state hydrocarbon extraction, and few conflicts exist over mining activities (Observatory of Mining Conflicts in Latin America 2011; Unir Foundation 2015).

The scope of the right to prior consultation

During the period of political instability following the "Gas War," the Bolivian Congress passed a new law declaring that the hydrocarbon industry was to revert to state ownership. Mass social mobilization in the context of the "Gas War" provided indigenous organizations a platform through which to demand that the right to prior consultation be included in the new legislation (Falleti and Riofrancos 2018). Ultimately, the 2005 law afforded indigenous communities the right to be consulted regarding extraction in their lands and explicitly stated that indigenous decisions on extraction must be respected (Article 115 of Hydrocarbon Law 3058). The right to prior consultation was later incorporated into Bolivia's 2009 Constitution, framed as a central mechanism of "participatory democracy" (Articles 30 and 403 of the Political Constitution of Plurinational State of Bolivia, in Spanish *Constitución Política del Estado Plurinacional del Bolivia*).

Yet, within the Bolivian mining industry, the right to prior consultation was not implemented until May of 2014, when a new mining law was approved with the aim of stimulating mining operations. Unlike the progressive hydrocarbon law of 2005, indigenous veto power over mining projects was excluded. Furthermore, although the government is legally obligated to enforce prior consultations before mineral extraction takes place, the 2014 mining law does not mandate consultations in the case of exploration activities. Thus, mining operators have open access to indigenous territories as long as they are only in search of mineral reserves (Madrid 2014:189).

Differences across extractive industries correspond to the different political contexts in which reforms were passed. As of this writing, the Bolivian government is not as enthusiastic about prior consultation as it was in early

2006, when Evo Morales had recently taken office. In addition, the mining industry in Bolivia is not sizable compared to that of hydrocarbons, and there are only a few multinational mining companies operating in this sector. Small- and medium-scale mineral extraction is mostly in the hands of a new generation of miners—organized through mining cooperatives. While these mining operators do not hesitate to identify as indigenous citizens entitled to all possible rights made available by the state, they do not see the point of prior consultation, as they themselves extract the mineral (Espinoza 2010). Furthermore, enduring nationalist feelings regarding mine worker struggles during the Bolivian Revolution of 1952 have validated mining activities in the highlands (Perreault 2014). Today, traditional mining regions lack powerful anti-mining coalitions to demand more substantive recognition of prior consultation procedures (Perreault 2014). For these reasons and despite visible environmental damage caused by the mining industry, indigenous anti-mining movements are not as salient in Bolivia as they are in Peru or Mexico (Madrid 2014). Despite the setback in the regulation of prior consultation within the mining industry, the scope of prior consultation legislation in Bolivia remains one of the most progressive in all of Latin America.

Government ideology

As presidential candidate, leftist indigenous leader Evo Morales promised to protect the *Pachamama* (in English "Mother Earth") from the negative impacts of neoliberal extractivism (Hinojosa 2012). Yet, in light of Bolivia's growing economic dependence on gas exports—hydrocarbons make up 60 percent of Bolivia's total exports—Morales chose to pursue gas extraction as aggressively as former neoliberal governments (Gray Molina 2010; Hinojosa 2012). Unlike those governments before him, however, Morales kept the hydrocarbon industry in the hands of the state as opposed to those of private interests.

Bolivia has the second largest gas reserves in South America after Venezuela and was the first South American exporter of natural gas. Approximately 55 percent of Bolivian territory has been given in concession to the hydrocarbon industry (Perreault 2014). By 2012, gas revenues had become the primary source of income for the Morales government. In the early years of the administration, the government systematically consulted indigenous groups over hydrocarbon projects. Yet neither the Morales government nor indigenous communities viewed prior consultation as a mechanism that could prohibit extraction in practice. In turn, indigenous groups consistently utilized these procedures to negotiate with the state for economic resources (Cedib 2015). Within the mining industry, on the other hand, the fact that indigenous peoples are often miners facilitated state non-enforcement of prior consultation procedures—despite extant constitutional mandate to consult in force since 2009 (Article 239 of the Political Constitution of Bolivia).

Thus, extractivism remains in force in Morales's statist political model. Enforcement of progressive prior consultation procedures did not lead to prohibition of extractive industries, but instead facilitated the expansion of such industries with the approval of indigenous groups. In the last few years, prior consultation has fallen out of favor with the Morales administration. Hydrocarbon prices fell significantly beginning in 2014, and the government now deems prior consultation procedures to be protracted and costly (Correo del Sur 2015). In addition, in 2015, the government lifted prohibitions on hydrocarbon exploration in formerly protected, ecologically significant lands (El Deber 2015).

Indigenous outcomes over the extractive industry

Since 2005, when the right to prior consultation was first included in the hydrocarbon legislation, the Bolivian government has conducted at least 58 prior consultations procedures with indigenous communities living close to gas and oil reserves (Falleti and Riofrancos 2018; Cedib 2015). Although indigenous veto was legally granted and, in theory, indigenous groups could say "no" to extraction, every one of these procedures resulted in indigenous acceptance of the project.[1]. Most of prior consultation procedures over hydrocarbon extraction were carried out with the Guaraní indigenous ethnic group—a sizable, politically skilled and highly mobilized population living in the Chaco region. According to NGO employee Nestor Cuellar of the Peasant Development Research Center (in Spanish *Centro de Investigación y Promoción del Campesinado*), or CIPCA, who has worked with Guarani organizations for many years, prior consultation procedures consist of formal meetings between indigenous leaders and state officials. In a first encounter, state officials offer an economic proposal, as well as possible mechanisms to address environmental damages associated with the proposed extractive project, to indigenous representatives. Afterward, indigenous leaders take these proposals back to their communities and discuss them within their community assemblies. Collective assessment of the state's economic offer results in a counteroffer, which is handed back to state officials in a second meeting, and so on. According to Cuellar, negotiations can last for several months. In many cases, indigenous communities allow operations to begin before an agreement has been reached, as prohibiting extraction is not their ultimate goal. However, in cases in which reaching a final economic settlement takes longer than expected, and the state continues refusing indigenous demands, some groups may begin to adopt mobilization tactics. The blockading of oil wells and roads is a typical means of exerting pressure to force the state to comply with indigenous counteroffers (Néstor Cuellar, personal communication, April 22, 2015).

The fact that none of prior consultation procedures prohibited extraction raised suspicions among both civil society organizations and scholars regarding their validity. Environmentalists criticized these procedures because they were not linked to adequate environmental impact studies (Cedib 2015). They argued that the government strategically used consultation to co-opt indigenous leaders with economic bribes at the expense of ecological harm (Marco Gandarillas, personal communication, April 16, 2015). Yet scholars researching extant prior consultations find that even if extractive projects are always accepted in the end, such procedures are not completely useless to indigenous communities. The case of the Guaraní would demonstrate that consulted indigenous groups do not simply comply with state proposals during prior consultation, but instead block these procedures until projects are made acceptable to them (Bascopé 2010; Flemmer and Schilling-Vacaflor 2015). Moreover, prior consultations can be used to negotiate significant economic rewards for indigenous communities. However, whereas Guaraní territories have benefitted from prior consultation, not all consulted groups receive significant economic rewards. This is the case of the Amazonian Mosetén tribes over the Lliquimuni oil block in 2008. Such consultation resulted in acceptance of the project, yet politically weakened indigenous groups were not able to obtain economic compensation in exchange (see Chapter 3).

Prior consultation, although on the books in Bolivia by 2009, was not implemented over mining projects until June of 2015, when it was used in the indigenous community of Huacuyo located in the Municipality of Antequera, in the Department of Oruro (Mamani 2015). As part of this research, Huacuyo was visited the week after prior consultation was scheduled to take place. There, interviews were carried out with several municipal officials, who stated that they had not yet been informed of any consultation in the area (Municipal employees, personal communication, July 8, 2015). Once in Huacuyo, it was verified that small-scale extraction of minerals was already taking place despite the fact that no prior consultation with the local population had been undertaken. It was also verified that members of the mining cooperative Minera Monserrat Ltda, the company requiring permission to operate in that jurisdiction, were also members of Huacuyo. Such members were extracting the minerals yet were also the indigenous members to be consulted about mineral extraction. Back in Oruro city, the installations of the state office in charge of Mining Affairs (in Spanish *Autoridad Jurisdiccional Administrativa Minera*), or AJAM, were visited to find out why the prior consultation procedure did not occur as was announced in the newspapers. State officials said that due to administrative delays, they had not been able to conduct the procedures yet, but they also said that "prior" consultation was going to be carried out "later" that month. On July 19, 2015, the Bolivian government announced that the first prior consultation over mining had been successfully completed and that mining operations had been approved by the local community of Huacuyo (Paredes 2015).

After nine years of skipping over prior consultation regarding mining projects, the Bolivian government began to systematically apply consultation procedures. No official databases exist in Bolivia detailing the results of these procedures and whether indigenous communities received any compensation for accepting mining projects. Yet a member of the Electoral Tribunal, Jose Exeni, declared that until the end of 2016, 96 prior consultations over mining operations were concluded, all of which resulted in approval (Fuente directa 2016). Still, the numerous consultations undertaken in only one year after the government began to apply these procedures pose serious doubts about their validity. Domestic and international NGOs warn about expeditious consultations and argue that the absence of adequate social and environmental impact studies prevents them from being meaningful tools for political transformation (Due Process of Law Foundation 2011; Cedib 2015).

The case of Peru

National influence of indigenous movements

Unlike Bolivia, influence of indigenous movements in national politics is not salient in Peru. Neoliberal reforms were pursued aggressively under authoritarian president Alberto Fujimori (1990–2000), parallel to the civil war against insurgency movements. Political violence exerted against indigenous populations in the 1990s by both the military and Shining Path rebels closed associational spaces and prevented the emergence of indigenous mobilization (Roberts 1998; Yashar 2005; Silva 2009). Throughout Fujimori's tenure, state-sponsored repression dominated state-society relations and anti-neoliberal mobilization remained weak (Silva 2009:243). Neoliberal policies included the privatization of hundreds of companies, shrinking the state's control over the economy (Cameron and Mauceri 1997). As part of his privatization program, Fujimori privatized formerly state-owned mining industry. Intense exploration for mineral reserves within indigenous community lands was promoted under flexible terms for mining companies (Slack 2009:119). The government afforded multinational companies with flexible environmental standards to develop operations, as well as freedom to choose how they managed their relationships with surrounding communities.

After Peru recommitted to democracy in 2001, discontent with neoliberal policies flourished within rural areas impacted by the mining industry (Ombudsman Office of Peru 2015). To date, perceived lack of local benefit from mining along with ecological damage suffered by indigenous groups as a consequence of mineral extraction has precipitated deadly confrontations between extractive companies, state forces and local communities (Slack 2009:122). The most emblematic such conflict is the case of the Yanacocha mining project—the biggest gold mine in South America—operating in the region of Cajamarca since 1994. Numerous episodes of radical mobilization over gold extraction have taken place in this region. Multimillion-dollar mining projects such as "Cerro Quilish" (2004) and "Conga" (2011) were blocked after violent confrontations between local communities and state forces, preventing the expansion of Yanacocha.

Following Fujimori's resignation in 2000, the hydrocarbon industry was also privatized. Subsequent governments sought to expand the hydrocarbon exploration frontier into the Amazon, engendering social conflicts over this industry as well. The "Baguazo Massacre" detailed in the introduction of this book is among the bloodiest of such conflicts. In 2009, the Peruvian government attempted to advance hydrocarbon extraction by privatizing indigenous communal lands. Amazonian indigenous groups rose up in protest and blocked privatization, 34 people were killed and hundreds were injured.

Unlike the situation in Bolivia, extractive industries are still in hands of multinational companies and neoliberal policies remain in force in spite of numerous deaths associated with resulting clashes (Ombudsman Office of Peru 2015). Today, Peru's mining industry continues to have the most numerous social conflicts in the region, along with Mexico and Colombia (Observatory of Mining Conflicts in Latin America 2011). Social conflicts surrounding the extractive industry, however, remain localized, and only few of them are grounded in indigenous rights rhetoric. Ethnically based mobilization remains weak as indigenous movements neither propel shifts in the national political agenda of the country nor oust presidents, as in Bolivia. Nevertheless, violent indigenous mobilization against both the hydrocarbon and the mining industries frequently stops projects from going forward.[2]

Scope of the right to prior consultation

Legal recognition of the right to prior consultation in Peru did not result from strong indigenous advocacy. Instead, the legalization of this right can be traced to President Ollanta Humala's (2011–2016) reaction to the previous ill-treatment of indigenous people under the government of Alan García (2006–2011) (Paredes 2015). As a candidate, Humala utilized indigenous rights discourse to attract rural votes and promised to end long-standing social inequalities and environmental damage caused by the neoliberal extractivist model. Once in office, he kept his campaign promise by passing a framework prior consultation law. The law explicitly stated that proper prior consultation procedures had to be conducted in advance of any possible impact on indigenous lands (Prior Consultation Framework Law N° 29785). The law was initiated with a symbolic ceremony held in Bagua, Peru, in August of 2011 to commemorate the victims of the Baguazo massacre.

Yet Peruvian prior consultation law did not grant veto power to indigenous communities, and it was not incorporated in the Peruvian constitution. The new legislation generally mandated prior consultation procedures over any type of project to be implemented in indigenous lands (including mining and hydrocarbon projects). The final decision over any consulted measure, however, was left to the state (Article 15 of the Prior Consultation Framework

Law). Thus, as progressive as the prior consultation framework law appears to be in the Peruvian context, it is still conservative in comparison with Bolivia.

Government ideology

Post-Fujimori Peru has witnessed a number of presidential candidates adopt leftist discourse, indigenous rights rhetoric and ecological causes, and then immediately drop such framings in favor of conservative political agendas once elected (Levitsky 2014). Alejandro Toledo's government (2001–2006) deepened Fujimori's economic reforms, supporting existing deregulation of the mining industry and passing a bill to liberalize the hydrocarbons industry in 2002. Alan García (2006–2011) followed a similar path and increased state repression against indigenous protestors. President Ollanta Humala (2011–2016) also abandoned his leftist political agenda aimed at the "great transformation," adopting a neoliberal resource-based model of governance. Finally, in 2016, President Pedro Pablo Kuczynsky took power using the discourse of continuity of the neoliberal model, which was upheld in practice. In Peru, both the hydrocarbon and the mining industries remain dominated by multinational companies. Peru's mining sector is among the most important in Latin America. Mining became the driving force in the country's economy, comprising 60 percent of all Peruvian exports and giving Peru one of the highest concentrations of mining companies in the world (Arce 2014). Peru now occupies a leading position in the global production of gold, coming in sixth, after China, South Africa, the United States, Australia and Canada.

Former president Humala's prior consultation law, passed in 2011, has not made significant impacts over mining conflicts in Peru, and violence did not diminish under Humala's government. This has been due, in part, to strong opposition by economic elites, who were able to delay enforcement of the law until 2013. Yet Humala's own government also played a role in non-enforcement. From 2012 to 2015, the Peruvian government did not consider peasant communities living within the highlands (containing most of the country's mineral reserves) as indigenous peoples (Paredes 2015). Prior consultation was not enforced in the implementation of several large-scale mining projects—such as the "Conga" project (2011), the "Tia Maria" project (2015) and the "Las Bambas" project (2015)—with disastrous results. In such cases, Humala's government refused to consult the population using different legal arguments (it was argued that the highland's population were peasants not indigenous, or that the projects had been initiated before the prior consultation law entered into force). The people did not accept those arguments and engaged in violent protests. Conflicts left several dead and injured in all the cases.

The Peruvian hydrocarbon industry is not economically significant in comparison with the mining industry. Yet several prior consultations have taken place within this sector as numerous ethnic groups inhabit Amazonia, a place where extraction is advanced. As in the case of Bolivia, in Peru's hydrocarbon industry, the indigenous that were consulted approved extraction in their lands.

Indigenous outcomes over the extractive industry

Until the end of 2017, prior consultation regarding hydrocarbon projects has been used a total of 11 times in Peru (Perupetro n.d.). Hydrocarbon projects were accepted by consulted indigenous groups in all 11 cases. Bolivian Guaraní were able to derive economic benefits from prior consultation. Indigenous groups from Peru's Amazon have not been as fortunate (Flemmer and Schilling-Vacaflor 2015). Lacking the negotiation skills and mobilization resources of the Guaraní, these groups have yet to make prior consultation operate in their favor.

Prior consultations in Peru have not represented major obstacles for the advancement of extraction. Consultation procedures usually concluded within the timeframe initially stated by Perupetro, the state agency in charge of enforcing prior consultation protocol. Moreover, only one out of Peru's eleven prior consultations over hydrocarbon projects resulted in substantial state distribution of resources in favor of consulted indigenous communities (Perupetro n.d.). Three Amazonian indigenous groups—the Achuar, Quechuas and Kichwuas—engaging in prior consultation over the implementation of a hydrocarbon project in oil block 192 were able to set the terms in which extraction was to be executed. Even though there is no indigenous veto power in extant Peruvian legislation, these politically skilled indigenous organizations led several waves of protests in parallel with prior consultation, finally forcing the state to comply with their economic demands. In this case, indigenous groups were able to use prior consultation procedure to obtain important compensation (see Chapter 3).

Like in Bolivia, the Peruvian government also delayed prior consultations in the case of mining. As indicated earlier, non-enforcement of this right was systematically used by ex-President Humala to avoid setbacks in important mining projects.[3] However, in September of 2015, Minister of Mining Rosa Maria Ortiz decided to undertake the first ever prior consultation in the highlands of the country. This decision was made two months after a group of journalists broadcasted that two former Ministers had secretly granted 25 mining concessions within indigenous lands. Secret concessions were granted for lands belonging to Quechua communities already recognized as indigenous by the Ministry of Culture. These communities were legally entitled to prior consultation; however, the government failed to uphold such rights, completely skipping over the consultation process (Ojo Público 2015).

Amid these reports, prior consultation with the indigenous community of Parobamba, located in the province of Calca, in the department of Cusco, began on September 8, 2015. Prior consultation included the legal authorization to Canadian mining company, Focus, to build the Aurora mine within Quechua communities. A month after the initiation of the procedure, community members of Parobamba accepted the mining project without negotiating compensation with the state. Questions over the validity of the procedure were immediately posed by several NGOs, which argued that there was not much left to consult about with indigenous members of Parobamba by the time consultation began. According to these sources, the government had already approved environmental impact studies without consulting with communities. Moreover, legal authorization for the use of communal lands had already been granted (CooperAcción 2015).

Prior consultation over mining projects was not implemented until four years after the prior consultation law was approved (2011). It appears that Peruvian "out of time prior consultation" with the communities of Parobamba was carried out to fulfill a legal formality and make up for non-enforcement of prior consultation legislation. Until March of 2017, nine prior consultations followed Parobamba's with the same results (Ministry of Culture n.d.). The opportunity in which consultations are undertaken—after main agreements are made and environmental licenses are approved (Ocampo and Urrutia 2016:182)—prevents them from having a meaningful impact on the way extractive companies carry out mineral extraction.

The case of Mexico

National influence of indigenous movements

Salient ethnically based mobilization exists in Mexico; however, its influence is moderate in comparison with Bolivia's politically powerful indigenous movements. Indigenous mobilization is strong but regionally based, of short duration and limited in its demands (Yashar 2005; Silva 2009). In 1992, President Carlos Salinas (1988–1994) implemented a series of constitutional reforms aimed at liberalizing the economy and diminishing the role of the state as key driver of rural development (Díaz-Polanco 1997:130). The Agrarian Reform was concluded, and existing mechanisms of land distribution, furthered by the Mexican Revolution, were removed. Privatization of *ejidos*, former symbol of communal holding of lands during the revolutionary period, was also legalized.

In Chiapas, discontent with neoliberal policies articulated through an indigenous rights rhetoric reached its peak in 1994 with the Zapatista (EZLN) upheaval. Insurgency targeted social and economic inequalities enhanced by neoliberalism, emphasizing those originated by the 1994 North American Trade Agreement, or NAFTA, signed with the United States and Canada (Antezana 2013). Protestors in Chiapas argued that NAFTA undermined indigenous agricultural production and communal landholding. Rebels claimed that indigenous peoples had the right to autonomy and self-determination and they would no longer follow government laws (Díaz-Polanco 1997:167). Due to the broad international support gathered by the Zapatistas, the government of Ernesto Zedillo (1994–2000) was forced to come to an agreement with the EZLN, with the two parties signing the San Andres Accords in 1996. This agreement laid out constitutional changes specifying the collective rights of indigenous peoples to self-government and autonomy.

Yet, more than two decades after the EZLN upheaval, most agreements reached in the San Andres Accords remain unimplemented. The Chiapas rebellion remained almost completely ineffective arguably because Zapatista rebels did not connect their platform of demands with larger social and political forces in the country (Silva 2009:9). Neoliberal reforms remained in force, and NAFTA was kept intact. In 1996, the government passed a Foreign Investment Law to expand private investment in the mining industry. Further, NAFTA regulations allowed Canadian mining companies to dominate the mining industry of Mexico (Costero 2008).

During the mining boom (2003–2012), the Mexican government sought to enhance the exploration and exploitation of minerals within nontraditional areas, such as the predominantly indigenous states of Chiapas and Oaxaca (Roblero 2011). Indigenous mobilization in several parts of the country has emerged to block controversial mining projects, grounding opposition in ecological causes. In the words of Mexico's ex-federal deputy and current National Commissioner for Dialogue with Indigenous Peoples, Jose Martínez Veloz, "unwanted mining concessions granted to Canadian companies could engender insurgency movements and political violence among indigenous municipalities" (Rodríguez 2014).

Today, Mexico is head in the list of social conflicts over mining activities in Latin America (Observatory of Mining Conflicts in Latin America 2011). These conflicts are usually followed by state repression and violence within indigenous communities. This has been the case of the indigenous municipalities of San José del Progreso in Oaxaca, and Chicomuselos in Chiapas where two activists were killed as a consequence of anti-mining struggles (Roblero 2011; Hernández 2014). Although the impacts of ethnically centered Zapatista insurgency remain limited to some indigenous municipalities of Chiapas, as is the case in Peru, anti-mining movements in Mexico frequently stop mining projects.

Scope of the right to prior consultation

Mexico was the first Latin American country to sign ILO Convention 169, as well as to comply with the indigenous right to prior consultation detailed therein. However, whereas Bolivia first legalized this right in 2005 and Peru passed a framework law in 2011, the Mexican government did not legally incorporate this right until 2014, when President Peña Nieto passed a new hydrocarbon law. The law allowed private investment in the hydrocarbon industry, enabling foreign companies to participate in the sector, which was formerly permitted to state company exclusively. This law also included the right to prior consultation of indigenous communities but only concerning hydrocarbon projects. Unlike Peru's framework law, prior consultation legislation in Mexico is not applied to all cases in which indigenous territories could be at risk. In addition, the inclusion of this right in the hydrocarbon law did not result from strong indigenous coalitions, as had been the case in Bolivia.

Moreover, whereas the inclusion of prior consultation in Bolivia occurred in tandem with the nationalization of the hydrocarbon industry, in Mexico, prior consultation was formalized alongside the allowance of multinational companies in the industry. In addition, the 2014 Mexican law used a participatory language to address indigenous rights yet it did not clearly define indigenous groups' veto power over hydrocarbon projects (The Dialogue 2015:7). In the mining industry, on the other hand, regulation of prior consultation remains absent, and the Mexican government has not conducted any prior consultation procedure in the mining sector.

Government ideology

During the presidency of Miguel de la Madrid (1982–1988), the Mexican government embraced neoliberalism and began to dismantle protectionist policies toward indigenous and peasant communities furthered by the Mexican Revolution. Neoliberal policies were kept in discourse and practice by subsequent presidents. Yet the opening of the economy to foreign investment was gradually carried out (Sacristan 2006), and the privatization of strategic extractive industries followed a slower pace than in the Peruvian case.

Furthermore, corporatist interest articulation in Mexico was not completely dismantled as it was in Peru under the Fujimori regime. The Institutional Revolutionary Party or PRI, governing the country under Peña Nieto (2012–2018), maintained corporatist mechanisms featuring statist-centered political models. Neoliberal economic policies, however, significantly expanded and strengthened. In 2013, the Peña Nieto administration privatized the hydrocarbon industry, central to Mexican nationalism after having remained under state control much longer than in any other country in the region (1938–2013). In the mining industry, on the other hand, foreign investment doubled (Sánchez 2014). Approximately 16 percent of the national territory has been granted to multinational mining companies (De la Fuente 2013).

Although Mexico has a sizable industrialized economy and does not depend on mining and hydrocarbon exports as much as its Latin American counterparts do, both the hydrocarbon and mining industries are crucial to the national economy. Mexico remains the world's top producer of silver. It is among the top ten producers globally of gold, zinc and copper (Bonilla n.d.), and along with Peru, is among the ten most attractive Latin American countries for mining investment (El Economista 2016).

Likewise, over the last two decades, the hydrocarbon industry has been the primary contributor to the national treasury—30 percent of its total income is derived from this sector (Fundar 2013). Since 2014, prior consultation is mandatory for this industry. Until the writing of this book, the government has consulted two hydrocarbon-related projects. As has been seen in both Bolivia and Peru, such procedures resulted in indigenous approval of the project (Secretariat of Energy of Mexico n.d.). Non-enforcement of prior consultation procedures in mining projects, on the other hand, is still used in Mexico.

Indigenous outcomes over the extractive industry

According to the Secretariat of Energy of Mexico or SENER, as of the end of 2017, the Mexican government has completed two prior consultation procedures in the hydrocarbon industry (Secretariat of Energy of Mexico n.d.). The consulted projects were gas pipelines to be built across lands belonging to the Yaqui tribes located in the state of Sonora and the Raramuri people living within the state of Chihuahua. In both cases, indigenous communities ended up complying with the consulted project.[4] Chapter 3 details prior consultation with the Yaqui people which lasted 14 months at the end of which the Mexican government was required to pay 76 million Mexican pesos to indigenous communities in order to advance the project (Daniel Martin, personal communication, February 23, 2016). Long-standing political mobilization and negotiation skills enabled the Yaqui to negotiate important economic compensation with the government. This was the case despite the reality that Mexican legislation is unclear about whether the indigenous have veto power over hydrocarbon projects. Thus, in Mexico, as in Bolivia and Peru, prior consultation led to the acceptance—not the rejection—of hydrocarbon expansion.

While Bolivia and Peru both conducted their first prior consultation procedure within the mining industry in 2015, Mexico has not carried out any consultation within this industry to date. Legislation regulating prior consultations over mining projects does not exist, and the Mexican government continues avoiding its international commitments to ILO Convention 169. Table 2.2 provides a summary of cross-national variation in the three variables discussed in this chapter—influence of indigenous movements in national politics, the scope of the right to prior consultation and political ideology of the government—as well as prior consultation outcomes in the three countries.

Table 2.2 shows that despite wide variation in national variables, prior consultation is implemented rather similarly in Bolivia, Peru and Mexico. As presented in this chapter, non-enforcement of prior consultation procedures within the mining industry has been commonplace in the three countries. In Mexico, the government continues to completely avoid these procedures using the lack of legal regulation as an excuse, whereas in Bolivia and Peru, governments began to apply "expeditious" and "out of time" prior consultations in 2015.

Table 2.2 Summary of Cross-National Variation and Prior Consultation Implementation

National Variables	*Bolivia*	*Peru*	*Mexico*
National influence of indigenous movements	*Far reaching*	*Incipient*	*Moderate*
Type of indigenous actor	Indigenous political party "MAS"	No indigenous party ß indigenous mobilization	Zapatistas (social movement)
Political changes in the aftermath of indigenous upheavals	The indigenous took power in 2006	Reactive political responses to specific conflicts	Electoral autonomy in 1995 and constitutional recognition of indigenous rights in 2006
Scope of the right to prior consultation	*Progressive*	*Moderate*	*Conservative*
Type of domestic legislation	Constitutional recognition Sectorial legislation in mining and hydrocarbons	Framework Law (including mining and hydrocarbons)	Sectoral legislation in hydrocarbons
Indigenous veto	Yes	No	Not defined
Year of implementation	2005	2011	2014
Number of prior consultations until 2017 over hydrocarbon projects	58	11	2
Number of prior consultations until 2016 over mining projects	96	10	0
Government ideology	*Statist*	*Neoliberal*	*Mixed*
Interest articulation	Corporatist	Pluralist	Corporatist
State control of extractive industries	Strong. The hydrocarbons industry is owned by the state. Foreign participation in the mining industry is small	Weak. Both mining and hydrocarbons industries are controlled by private companies	Medium. Mining is private, but the state maintains partial control of the hydrocarbon industry

Implementation of prior consultation	*Bolivia*	*Peru*	*Mexico*
Mining Industry	Non-enforcement until 2015 All consultations resulted in acceptance	Non-enforcement until 2015 All consultations resulted in acceptance	Non-enforcement to the present day
Hydrocarbon Industry	All consultations resulted in acceptance	All consultations resulted in acceptance	All consultations resulted in acceptance

Source: Author's elaboration.

As will be detailed in the case studies presented in Chapters 3 and 4, indigenous opposition to the hydrocarbon industry is frequently milder than it is to the mining industry. A recent study across Colombia, Ecuador, Peru and Bolivia shows that the correlation between growth in mining exports and environmental conflicts is almost perfect (Perez-Rincón et al. 2018). This is consistent with recent research on environmental attitudes in Ecuador showing that environmental concerns are more likely to emerge over mineral extraction than over oil extraction (Eisenstadt and West 2017). Previous research suggests that resource nationalism over hydrocarbons in Mexico and Bolivia (De la Fuente 2013; Perreault 2013), as well as indigenous political weakness within areas of hydrocarbon extraction in Peru (Flemmer and Schilling-Vacaflor 2015), prevents salient anti-extractivist stances in these three countries. In Mexico, social conflicts between indigenous communities and state oil company *Petróleos Mexicanos* (PEMEX) have not been salient over the 70 years of operations by this company (The Dialogue 2015). Similarly, social conflicts between Guaraní communities and state oil company YPFB in Bolivia have been centered over the distribution of resources not over whether extraction is carried out (Falleti and Riofrancos 2018). Finally, in Peru, while social conflicts in the mining sector account for 63 percent of all socio-environmental conflicts going on in the country, conflicts over hydrocarbons represent only 15 percent (Ombudsman Office 2016). This evidence supports the argument that prior consultations over hydrocarbon extraction are more likely to result in agreements between the state and indigenous communities. In the case of Peru, it appears that state agencies selectively enforced these procedures in the hydrocarbon sector where they anticipated that they could reach a deal with indigenous groups. Consistently in Mexico, the government is consulting hydrocarbon-related projects while skipping over consultations over mining.

Why does prior consultation fail to deter extractivism?

Examination of prior consultation practices in Bolivia, Peru and Mexico shows that indigenous banning of extractive industries does not appear possible even under the most progressive legislation. It also suggests that the influence that indigenous movements may have reached on national politics and the ideological background of the government in office are not significant in this regard. These results suggest that even a substantive recognition of the right to prior consultation, such as that of Bolivia that grants veto power to indigenous communities, results in approval of extraction. Likewise, Mirna Cuentas, a prior consultation specialist in this country, argues that indigenous prohibition of extractive projects is unlikely as indigenous organizations know that the prior consultation procedure is designed to obtain their approval (Mirna Cuentas, personal communication, April 8, 2015). Moreover, previous research demonstrated that most indigenous groups do not oppose the extractive industry (Arellano-Yanguas 2011, Arce 2014). Further, some groups are used to negotiate resources with extractive companies (Scurrah and Chaparro 2011; Humphreys-Bebbington 2012). Then, it is no surprise that when offered prior consultation, they use it to negotiate the terms of extractivism, not to oppose extraction.

As such, the following chapters evidence that indigenous communities that are consulted by the state generally have pro-extractivist stances (see Chapters 3). In addition, the weak institutionals that permeate throughout Latin America allow governments to avoid consulting with indigenous population that are more prone to reject extractive projects, which are usually found in the mining industry. Because of this, it is uncommon to see anti-mining groups participating in prior consultation (see Chapter 4).

For many, then, state intermediation through prior consultation does not provide a space to influence a shift in extractive policy, but it validates extractive projects by obtaining formal indigenous approval. Scholars and activists in Southern Mexico acknowledge the limitations of more developed prior consultation legislation in South America, for the advancement of anti-extractivist goals. According to social advocate and professor at the Autonomous University of Chiapas (Universidad Autónoma de Chiapas) Elisa Cruz Rueda,

> Even indigenous organizations oppose a prior consultation law; it would bring more locks than opened doors, the indigenous movement at least in the south-east refuses to a regulation of prior consultation right (...). It has been demonstrated that having more laws does not resolve the problem.
>
> (Elisa Cruz Rueda, personal communication, March 13, 2015)

This chapter has primarily argued that prior consultation is not useful for anti-extractivist indigenous groups as it does not allow space for opposition.

Yet an in-depth analysis of indigenous outcomes over extractive projects in Bolivia, Peru and Mexico also demonstrates that some groups seeking economic resources, catalogued in this book as pro-extractivist indigenous, have benefited economically from these procedures. The next section addresses this topic.

The bargaining nature of prior consultation in Latin America

Economic approaches to indigenous territorial struggles conceptualize them as fights for resources as opposed to struggles over cultural recognition or ecological defense (Otero 2007). In this vein, NGOs aimed at promoting indigenous economic development such as the Organization for the Development of Peasants in Eastern Bolivia (in Spanish *Apoyo para los Campesinos del Oriente Boliviano*), or APCOB, consider prior consultation to be one effective mechanism that indigenous communities have to obtain money and escape poverty (Ysaías Montero, personal communication, April 21, 2015). This book takes the position that economic motives drive most resource-based protests (Arellano-Yanguas 2011; Arce 2014). If the indigenous goal is to profit from the extractive industry, then prior consultation can be a useful mechanism for the realization of indigenous demands.

Who can benefit from prior consultation?

Recall that ten out of the eleven prior consultations carried out over hydrocarbon projects in Peru left the indigenous in the same situation they were in before accepting the extractive project (or worse due to environmental contamination likely to result from hydrocarbon extraction). The next chapter details how prior consultation in the case of the politically weakened Mosetén Amazonian tribe in the Bolivian Amazon did not result in redistribution of state resources to Mosetén communities either. Similarly, "window dressing" consultations over mining projects in Bolivia and Peru were carried out to fulfill a legal formality, yet they did not grant economic resources to consulted indigenous groups. Previous research on prior consultations demonstrates that only those groups that are able to meet important preconditions for political participation are able to engage effectively in consultation procedures (Bascopé 2010; Flemmer and Schilling-Vacaflor 2015). These findings are congruent with previous studies of participatory institutions in Latin America, which conclude that institutional outcomes depend more on specific enabling conditions present within target populations than on the ways these institutions are designed (Avritzer 2009). Yet what conditions enable indigenous groups to benefit economically from prior consultation?

Table 2.3 Outcomes by Politically Powerful Pro-Extractivist Groups

Prior Consultation	*Political Power*	
	Low	*High*
No	Extraction	No Extraction
Yes	Extraction	Extraction Compensation

The previous chapter argued that political power enables indigenous groups to negotiate better economic terms in cases of resource extraction. This is consistent with the bulk of literature on causes of social transformation, emphasizing factors such as mobilization resources and bargaining reputation to obtain better outcomes of existing legislation (Galanter 1974; Rosenberg 1991; Epp 1998). This chapter shows that some indigenous groups within Bolivia, Peru and Mexico obtain similar economic deals from prior consultation procedures. These similarities are found in spite of variation in national political settings and whether prior consultation entails veto power for indigenous peoples. As will be discussed in the case studies presented in Chapter 3, the Guaraní in Bolivia; the Achuar, Kiwchua and Quechua in Peru; and the Yaqui people in Mexico obtained significant economic rewards from prior consultation due to existing mobilization capacities and negotiation skills. Table 2.3 illustrates this argument.

Indigenous political power works as *de facto* veto power for the cases of Peru and Mexico, as state officials are aware that the indigenous can stop (or at least delay) any project in their lands. They are also aware that the reason why politically powerful pro-extractivist indigenous groups agree to participate in prior consultation in the first place is to negotiate economic compensation for the use of their territories. As demonstrated by past research, Latin American governments set prior consultations as spaces of limited participation (Flemmer and Schilling-Vacaflor 2015). However, the political power of the communities that agree "to play the game" can stretch those spaces and set new boundaries: communities are perhaps unable to prohibit extraction but are able to persuade the state to concede more than it would have initially conceded.

This study finds that one limitation of prior consultation procedures as mechanisms of economic redistribution is that they only allow highly mobilized and skilled indigenous groups to benefit from them. Chapter 3 describes cases of strong indigenous communities able to profit from extractive industries through prior consultation. Nonetheless, it also demonstrates that politically weak indigenous population are generally unable to obtain favorable economic terms from prior consultation. In turn, the results

Table 2.4 Outcomes by Politically Weak Indigenous Groups

Prior Consultation	*Political Power*	
	Low	*High*
No	Extraction No compensation	No Extraction No compensation
Yes	Extraction No compensation	Extraction Compensation

Source: Author's elaboration.

that such groups are likely to obtain correspond to predetermined formulas elaborated by state agencies and do not usually involve direct distribution of resources. When the indigenous population is politically weak, it is not determinant whether or not the states conduct prior consultation. Under this condition, if prior consultation is conducted, extraction is likely to occur, without economic compensation for the indigenous. If prior consultation is not conducted, the result will be the same (see Chapter 4). Table 2.4 illustrates this argument.

What changed after prior consultation was implemented?

It is important to point out that prior consultation procedures work as enablers of economic outcomes for pro-extractivist indigenous because they open a space of negotiation between these groups and the state. However, other mechanisms fulfilled this function in the past. For instance, Arellano-Yanguas (2011) finds that two factors increased peasant communities' power to negotiate with multinational mining companies prior to the implementation of prior consultation in Peru. First, Peruvian mining law required companies to reach an agreement with the owners of the land, and second, there was increasing international pressure placed upon extractive companies to obtain "social license"[5] before starting operations. These factors forced mining companies to engage in direct negotiation with local communities, allowing some indigenous groups (the politically strongest) to obtain better prices for selling their lands (Arellano-Yanguas 2011:102).

Arellano-Yanguas also finds that former negotiations between extractive companies and peasant communities over the price of lands led to increased internal divisions among their members (Arellano-Yanguas 2011). Mining companies strategically co-opted local leaders and created clientelistic networks with the population to obtain their approval and advance mining projects (Salas 2008). This form of negotiation between extractive companies and indigenous communities has been replaced by prior consultation, under the premise that the participation of the state entitles a better protection of indigenous interests.

Nevertheless, denounces over division of indigenous members and co-optation of leaders are also found in current prior consultation procedures. Some scholars find that state officials usually use these strategies to obtain consent for projects on consultation, the key difference being that negotiations were previously private (Rodríguez-Garavito et al. 2010; Vargas 2010). Today, prior consultations are public, allowing civil society organizations to participate in these procedures. In addition to providing technical support to indigenous negotiators, NGOs also put pressure on governments to remain accountable to the commitments made during prior consultation. Moreover, whereas extractive companies in the past controlled relevant information over the impacts and profits of resource extraction, state officials must now provide that information to consulted indigenous population (Article 16 of ILO Convention 169).

This parallel between the pre-prior consultation era and the current scenario demonstrates that economic compensation to indigenous peoples in exchange for the ability to carry out extraction within their lands is not new. However, formal prior consultation procedures now enable indigenous communities to access relevant information over the implications of the extractive process. Still, obtaining significant economic compensations depends on indigenous mobilization capacities and negotiation skills.

Research on conditions enabling some groups to perform better in courts shows that regular operation of legal procedures improves their capacity to obtain better results (Galanter 1974) Although Galanter's study focuses on the use of the court system, the influence of his analysis extends to dispute resolution in non-litigation contexts (Hoffmann 2008). By applying the theory of the repeat player to the context of prior consultation, regular indigenous use of these procedures could contribute to build capacity to negotiate better terms in the future. By engaging in these procedures as frequently as possible, "one shotters" indigenous groups could gradually become the resource-rich, well-positioned actors envisioned in Galanter's work. Over time, prior consultation procedures could become focal points through which politically weak indigenous groups organize, get ahead and become powerful operators of the prior consultation system. This is the case of formerly demobilized Maya indigenous communities in the states of Yucatan and Campeche in Mexico. Since 2012, these traditionally "peaceful indigenous groups" have organized politically and actively demanded the government to conduct prior consultation over the production of transgenic soy in their lands by the Monsanto Company (Fundar 2015). In 2015, the Supreme Court of Mexico finally mandated prior consultation with the Maya.

By conceptualizing the right to prior consultation as a bargaining table, this book aims to debunk the legal rights discourse and the culturalist language surrounding this institution. Past research demonstrates that the legalization of rights is usually preceded by episodes of social mobilization, and it is often followed by processes of political negotiation over the scopes of such rights (Rosenberg 1991; Epp 1998; Eisenstadt 2003). Such negotiation processes ultimately define the outcomes of legislation and need to be emphasized. Prior consultation is the new mechanism indigenous peoples have to negotiate resources, now under the control of state agencies. Embracing them as such can help raise awareness among unskilled indigenous communities about the opportunities made available by prior consultation procedures to politically powerful indigenous groups.

Having made this point, the impacts that the commodification of prior consultation might have on indigenous natural environments must not be dismissed. In addition, political division usually following prior consultation along with indigenous engagement in the profits of the extractive industry could accelerate the disappearance of indigenous cultures. In those places where indigenous community values remain, the ancestral ways indigenous groups relate to their lands and natural resources are likely to change as these will no longer be perceived as a necessity for indigenous survival. Without indigenous communities who can to some extent serve as a counterweight to the power of extractive companies, state-corporate control of new resource frontiers will be easier to attain.

Consultations that work for anti-extractivist movements

Recent evidence suggests that anti-extractivist indigenous communities are aware of the prior consultation bias in favor of extractive industries. Today, not only do states strategically decide not to enforce prior consultation when they anticipate complications in obtaining approval, many indigenous communities also refuse to engage in these procedures. In 2016 in Bolivia, for instance, five indigenous groups refused to engage in prior consultation over mining projects on their territories (Fuente directa 2016). More recently, in 2017 in Mexico, the Zoque people in Northern Chiapas withdrew their participation in prior consultation over hydrocarbon operations(Mexican Alliance against Fracking 2017). Similar cases have occurred in Colombia, Ecuador, Argentina, Mexico, Guatemala and Canada where 700,000 people have used internal mechanism of decision-making to vote against mining (Toledo 2015). These cases represent a new movement that proclaims the indigenous right to self-consultation (in Spanish *auto-consulta*) and seeks to counteract the effects of prior consultation. According to Mexican indigenous rights lawyer Orvelin Montiel, indigenous communities "consult themselves" using their native mechanisms of deliberation, which hinders potential internal divisions and co-optation (Orvelin Montiel, personal communication, June 23, 2017). This allows indigenous groups to build collective power and strategic alliances generally enabling them to maintain valuable natural resources in the subsoil (Mining Watch Canada 2012).

Table 2.5 Outcome by Politically Powerful Indigenous Groups in the Absence of Prior Consultation

Prior Consultation	*Political Power*	
	Low	*High*
No	Extraction	No Extraction
Yes	Extraction	Extraction

Source: Author's elaboration.

The success of self-consultations or *auto-consultas* is consistent with the argument presented in this book stating that indigenous political power in combination with non-enforcement of prior consultation procedures enables the prohibition of resource extraction in indigenous lands. As will be shown in Chapter 4, politically powerful indigenous groups use their own consultation mechanisms as part of their set of mobilization resources to build political unity and make community members comply with their anti-extractivist objectives. See Table 2.5.

Conclusion

One of the main arguments of this chapter is that prior consultation is not useful to prevent the expansion of extractive industries into indigenous territories. On the contrary, the evidence presented suggests that prior consultation needs to be absent if the indigenous objective is to prohibit extraction. This is somehow unexpected considering that many environmentalists saw consultation rights as mechanism for ecological defense. Yet Latin American governments implement prior consultation legislation unevenly. The use of diverse strategies, such as denying the existence of indigenous peoples in mineralized areas, not providing specific legislation for prior consultations or skipping over adequate and opportune environmental and social impact assessments, allows governments to overcome potential obstacles for extraction.

A second point the chapter raises is that political power is key for the achievement of indigenous objectives, either if it is to profit from the extractive industry or to prohibit it. Prior consultation might serve as a platform enabling politically powerful indigenous communities to showcase their negotiation skills and reach an economic agreement. If prior consultation is denied, thus eliminating negotiation spaces, powerful pro-extractivist communities may end up stopping projects based upon ecological grounds, despite their willingness in principle to work with the extractive industry. In turn, for anti-extractivist communities to successfully prohibit extractive industries, they need to pursue a strategy of outright confrontation rather than the negotiation inherent to processes of prior consultation. The next chapter examines the contrasting results obtained by politically powerful and weak indigenous groups participating in prior consultation in Bolivia, Peru and Mexico.

Notes

1 Unlike Peru and Mexico, the Bolivian government does not have a database on prior consultation. The information presented in this chapter regarding these procedures was obtained from NGO databases and press releases of state agencies.

2 The Baguazo massacre finally results in government cancellation of decrees seeking to privatize community lands to advance hydrocarbon operations. Likewise, numerous mining projects, such as Conga, Quilish, and Tia Maria, among others, have been canceled due to social conflict.

3 The Peruvian government under the Humala administration continued to weaken environmental safeguards through a law that deprived the environment ministry of jurisdiction over air, soil and water quality standards. It also eliminated the ministry's power to establish nature reserves exempt from mining and oil drilling (Fernandez 2014).

4 By the time fieldwork was completed in Mexico, prior consultation with the Raramuri people had not yet been concluded, and thereby details of this procedure are absent in the book. In the website of state agency of energy SENER, nonetheless, we know that the project was approved.

5 The term refers to the permission given by local communities to extractive companies for operating in their lands.

References

Albó, Xavier. 2011. "Hacia el poder indígena en Ecuador, Perú y Bolivia." In Ana Cecilia Betancur (Ed.) *Movimientos indígenas en América Latina. Resistencia y nuevos modelos de integración*. Copenhague: IWGI, 133–166.

Albro, Robert. 2005. "The Waters is Ours, Carajo! Deep Citizenship in Bolivia's Water War," In June Nash (Ed.) *Social Movements: An Anthropological Reader*. Malden Mass: Blackwell Publishers, 249–271

Amengual, Matthew. 2016. *Politicized Enforcement in Argentina: Labor and Environmental Regulation*. New York: Cambridge University Press.

Antezana, Natalia. 2013. Con inversión extranjera en Pemex, México pierde soberanía gracias al TLCAN. Available at: http://revoluciontrespuntocero.mx/con-inversion-extranjera-en-pemex-mexico-pierde-soberania-gracias-al-tlcan/ (Accessed May 28 2017).

Arce, Moises. 2014. *Resource Extraction and Protest in Peru*. Pittsburg: University of Pittsburg Press.

Arellano-Yanguas, Javier. 2011. *¿Minería sin fronteras? Conflicto y desarrollo en regiones mineras del Perú*. Lima: IEP.

Avritzer, Leonardo. 2009. *Participatory Institutions in Democratic Brazil*. Baltimore: The Johns Hopkins University Press.

Baber, Walter F., and Robert V. Bartlett. 2005. *Deliberative Environmental Politics. Democracy and Ecological Rationality*. Cambridge: MIT Press.

Bascopé, Ivan. 2010. *Lecciones aprendidas sobre la Consulta Previa.* La Paz: CEJIS.

Bolivia. Political Constitution of Bolivia. "Constitución Política del Estado Plurinacional de Bolivia. Available at: www.harmonywithnatureun.org/content/documents/159Bolivia%20Consitucion.pdf (Accessed November 09 2016).

Bonilla, Armando. n.d. Diez países con mayor producción de plata. Available at www.conacytprensa.mx/index.php/diez-mas/2010-diez-paises-con-mayor-produccion-de-plata (Accessed November 11 2017).

Cameron, Maxwell, and Philp Mauceri. 1997. *The Peruvian Labyrinth.* Pennsylvania: The Pennsylvania State University Press.

Cedib. 2015. Consulta Previa. Available at: www.Cedib.org/tag/consulta-previa/, last (Accessed November 09 2016).

Constitución Política del Estado Plurinacional de Bolivia. 2009. Available at www.cervantesvirtual.com/obra/constitucion-politica-del-estado-plurinacional-de-bolivia-promulgada-el-9-de-febrero-2009/ (Accessed April 09 2018).

CooperAcción. 2015. Caso Las Bambas. Available at: http://cooperaccion.org.pe/main/images/Descargas-Otros_copy/Las%20Bambas%20-%20informe%20ocm.pdf (Accessed August 30 2016).

Correo del Sur. 2015. Evo dice que se pierde mucho tiempo en las consultas. Available at: http://correodelsur.com/politica/20150713_evo-en-la-consulta-previa-se-pierde-mucho-tiempo.html (Accessed July 06 2015).

Costero, Cecilia. 2008. *Internacionalización Económica, Historia y Conflicto Ambiental en la Minería. El caso de Minera San Xavier.* San Luis Potos: El Colegio de San Luis.

De la Fuente, Aroa. 2013. *La explotación de los Hidrocarburos y los Minerales en México: un Análisis Comparativo.* Mexico: Heinrich Boll Stieftung.

Díaz-Polanco, Héctor. 1997. *La Rebelión Zapatista y la Autonomía.* Mexico: Siglo Veintiuno Editores.

Due Process of Law Foundation. 2011. El derecho a la consulta libre, previa e informada de los pueblos indígenas. La situación de Bolivia, Colombia, Ecuador y Perú. Available at: www.dplf.org/sites/default/files/1301596126.pdf (Accessed January 28 2018).

Due Process of Law Foundation. 2015. *Derecho a la consulta y al consentimiento previo, libre e informado en América Latina.* Washington, DC: DPLF.

Eisenstadt, Todd. 2003. Thinking Outside the (ballot) Box: Informal Electoral Institutions and Mexico's Political Opening. *Latin American Politics and Society* 45: 25–54.

Eisenstadt, Todd. 2011. *Politics, Identity, and Mexico's Indigenous Rights Movements.* Cambridge: Cambridge University Press.

Eisenstadt, Todd, and Karleen West. 2017. Public Opinion, Vulnerability, and Living with Extraction on Ecuador's Oil Frontier: Where the Debate between Development and Environmentalism Gets Personal. *Comparative Politics* 49(2): 231–251.

El Deber 2015. Decretos Petroleros y Regresividad Normativa. Available at: http://ftp.eldeber.com.bo/opinion/decretos-petroleros-y-regresividad-normativa.html (Accessed June 13 2016).

El Economista. 2016. México de los más atractivos para inversión minera en AL. Available at: www.eleconomista.com.mx/empresas/Mexico-de-los-mas-atractivos-para-inversion-minera-en-AL-20160309-0116.html (Accessed May 23 2017).

Environmental Justice Atlas. n.d. Available at: https://ejatlas.org/ (Accessed April 06 2018).

Epp, Charles. 1998. *The Rights Revolution: Lawyers, Activists and Supreme Courts in Comparative Perspective.* Chicago, IL: Chicago University Press.

Espinoza, Jorge. 2010. *Minería Boliviana. Su realidad.* La Paz: Plural.

Falleti, Tulia, and Thea Riofrancos. 2018. "Endogenous Participation: Strengthening Prior Consultation in Extractive Economies." *World Politics* 70(1): 86–121.

Flemmer, Riccarda, and Almut Schilling-Vacaflor. 2015. Unfulfilled Promises of the Consultation Approach: The Limits to Effective Indigenous Participation in Bolivia's and Peru's Extractive Industries. *Third World Quarterly* 37(1): 172–188.

Fuente directa. 2016. En un año, el OEP acompañó 165 procesos de consultas previas en minería. Available at: http://fuentedirecta.oep.org.bo/noticia/en-un-ano-el-oep-acompano-165-procesos-de-consultas-previas-en-mineria/ (Accessed October 13 2016).

Fundar. 2015. La SCJN frente a los pueblos indígenas: oportunidad histórica para proteger los DDHH del pueblo maya y detener el avance de la soya transgénica. Available at: http://fundar.org.mx/la-scjn-frente-a-los-pueblos-indigenas-oportunidad-historica-para-proteger-los-ddhh-del-pueblo-maya-y-detener-el-avance-de-la-soya-transgenica/ (Accessed November 16 2016).

Galanter, Marc. 1974. Why the "Haves" Come out Ahead: Speculations on the Limits of Legal Change. *Law & Society Review.* 9(1): 95–160. Litigation and Dispute Processing: Part One (Autumn, 1974).

Gray, George. 2010. The Challenge of Progressive Change under Evo Morales. In Kurt Weyland (Ed.) *Leftist Governments in Latin America: Successes and Shortcomings.* New York: Cambridge University Press, 140–179.

Greenspan, Emily. 2015. The right to say "No": Indigenous rights experts weigh in on community consent. *The politics of poverty,* available at: politicsofpoverty.oxfamamerica.org/2015/08/the-right-to-say-no-indigenous-rights-experts-weigh-in-on-community-consent (Accessed June 4 2018).

Gudynas, Eduardo. 2009. Diez tesis urgentes sobre el nuevo extractivismo. Contextos y demandas bajo el progresismo sudamericano actual. *"Extractivismo, política y sociedad".* November 2009. Quito: CAAP (Centro Andino de Acción Popular) and CLAES (Centro Latino Americano de Ecología Social) 187–225.

Hernández, Ursula. 2014. *Vivir la mina. El conflicto minero en San José del Progreso y sus efectos cotidianos en la vida individual y la existencia colectiva. Rupturas, contrastes, reconstrucciones y resistencias.* Oaxaca: CIESAS.

Hinojosa, Leonith (Ed.). 2012. Gas y desarrollo. *Dinámicas territoriales rurales en Tarija, Bolivia.* La Paz, Bolivia: Fundación Tierra–CERDET.

Hoffmann, Elizabeth. 2008. The "Haves" and "Have-Nots" within the Organization. *Law and Contemporary Problems.* 71: 53.

Humphreys-Bebbington, Denisse. 2012. Las tensiones Estado-Indigenas debido a la expansion de la industria hidrocarburifere en el Chaco boloviano.

Hydrocarbon Law of Bolivia. "Ley de Hidrocarburos 3058." Text Retrieved from www.ine.gob.bo/indicadoresddhh/archivos/alimentacion/nal/Ley%20N%C2%BA%203058.pdf, last (Accessed November 09 2016).

Jaskoski, Maiah. 2013. "The Local Politics of Project Approvals in the Peruvian Mining and Bolivian Gas Sectors" Paper Presented at APSA Conference. September 1st of 2013.

Levitsky, Steven. 2014. Elecciones y Tarados. *La Republica.* October 4, 2014. Available at: from www.infolatam.com/2014/10/05/elecciones-y-tarados/ (Accessed May 14 2017).

Levitsky, Steven, and Maria Victoria Murillo. 2013. Building Institutions on Weak Foundations: Lessons from Latin America. *Journal of Democracy* 24(2): 93–107.

Lucero, Jose Antonio. 2009. "Decades Lost and Won: Indigenous Movements and Multicultural Neoliberalism in the Andes." In John Burdick, Phillips Oxhorn and Roberts Kenneth (Eds.) *Beyond Neoliberalism in Latin America: Societies and Politics at the Crossroads*. New York: Palgrave Macmillan, 63–81.

Madrid, Emilio. 2014. "Challapata: Resistencia communal a la desposesion de la mineria" In Thomas Perreault (Ed.) *Mineria, Agua y Justicia Social en los Andes*. La Paz: PIEB, 81–99.

Mamani, Lidia. "Hoy arranca la primera consulta previa" *Página Siete* June 14, 2015, Available at: www.paginasiete.bo/economia/2015/6/15/arranca-primera-consulta-previa-para-explotacion-minera-59984.html (Accessed May 4 2016).

Mexican Alliance Against Fracking. 2017. Defensa del territorio Zoque Chiapas. Available at: www.nofrackingmexico.org/defensa-del-territorio-zoque-chiapas/ (Accessed April 10 2018).

Mining Watch Canada. 2012. Local Votes and Mining in the Americas. Available at: http://miningwatch.ca/blog/2012/5/14/local-votes-and-mining-americas (Accessed November 15 2016).

Ministry of Culture. n.d. Consulta Previa. Available at: http://consultaprevia.cultura.gob.pe/ (Accessed April 10 2018).

O'Donnell, Guillermo. 1993. "On the State, Democratization and Some Conceptual Problems: A Latin American View with Glances at Some Postcommunist Countries." *World Development* 21(8): 1355–1369.

Observatory of Mining Conflicts in Latin America. 2011. Mining Conflicts in Latin America. Available at: www.conflictosmineros.net/ (Accessed December 2 2017).

Ocampo, Diego, and Isabel Urrutia. 2016. "La implementación de la consulta en el sector minero: una mirada a los primeros procesos." In Karina Vargas (coord.) (Ed.) *La implementación del derecho a la consulta previa en Perú*. Lima: Cooperación Alemana.

Ojo Público. 2015. Los secretos mineros detrás de la lista de comunidades indígenas del Perú. Available at: http://ojo-Público.com/77/los-secretos-detras-de-la-lista-decomunidades-indigenas-del-peru (Accessed May 19 2016).

Ombudsman Office 2016. Reporte de Conflictos Sociales N° 154. Available at: www.defensoria.gob.pe/modules/Downloads/conflictos/2017/Reporte-Mensual-de-Conflictos-Sociales-N-154--Diciembre-2016.pdf (Accessed April 10 2018).

Ombudsman Office of Peru. 2015. Monthly Report of Social Conflicts (September of 2015). Available at: www.defensoria.gob.pe/modules/Downloads/conflictos/2015/Reporte-Mensual-de-Conflictos-Sociales-N--139-Septiembre-2015.pdf (Accessed November 09 2016).

Otero, Gerardo. 2007. "Class or Identity Politics? A False Dichotomy." *International Journal of Comparative Sociology* 48(1): 73–80.

Paredes, Jimena. 2015. Realizan la primera consulta previa minera, *La Razón July 18 of 2015*. Availabe at: www.la-razon.com/economia/AJAM-realizan-primera-consulta-previa-minera_0_2309769016.html (Accessed February 22 2017).

Paredes, Maritza. 2015. "Transnational Networks Acting from Below: Indigenous Prior Consultation and the Peruvian Paradox." Paper Presented at Lasa Conference. San Juan, May 27–30.

Perez-Rincón, Mario Alejandro, Julieth Vargas, and Zulma Crespo-Marín. 2018. "Trends in Social Metabolism and Environmental Conflicts in Four Andean Countries from 1970 to 2013." *Sustainability Science* 13(3): 635–648.

Perreault, Tom. 2013. "Nature and Nation: The Territorial Logics of Hydrocarbon Governance in Bolivia." In Anthony Bebbington and Jeffrey Bury (Eds.) *Subterranean Struggles: New Geographies of Extractive Industries in Latin America*. Austin: University of Texas Press, 67–90.

Perreault, Tom (Ed). 2014. *Mineria, agua y justicia social en los andes: experiencias comparativas de Perú y Bolivia*. La Paz: Justicia Hídrica, Centro de Ecología y Pueblos Andinos; Fundación PIEB.

Perupetro. n.d. Database on Prior Consultation in Peru. Available at: www.consultasindigenas.org/ (Accessed November 07 2016).

Prior Consultation Framework Law of Peru. n.d. "Ley del Derecho a la Consulta Previa a los Pueblos Indígenas u Originarios Reconocido en el Convenio 169 de la Organización Internacional del Trabajo (OIT)." Available at: www.minem.gob.pe/minem/archivos/Ley%2029785%20Consulta%20Previa%20pdf.pdf (Accessed November 09 2016).

Roberts, Kenneth. 1998. *Deepening Democracy? The Modern Left and Social Movements in Chile and Peru*. Stanford: Stanford University Press.

Roblero, Marin. 2011. El Despertar de la Serpiente, la Sierra Madre de Chiapas en riesgo: Extracción Minera y Comunidades en Resistencia en Chicomuselos. Master Dissertation for the Autonomous University of Chapingo. San Cristobal de las Casas, Chiapas.

Rodríguez, Oscar. 2014. Existen focos rojos por concesiones mineras. Available at: www.remamx.org/2014/03/existen-focos-rojos-por-concesiones-mineras-en-oaxaca/ (Accessed April 08 2018).

Rodríguez-Garavito, César, M. Morris, N. Orduz, and P. Buriticá. 2010. *La consulta previa a pueblos indígenas: los estándares del derecho internacional*. Bogotá: Universidad de los Andes.

Rosenberg, Gerard. 1991. *The Hollow Hope. Can Courts Bring About Social Change?* Chicago: Chicago University Press.

Sacristan, Emilio. 2006. Las privatizaciones en México. Available at: www.ejournal.unam.mx/ecu/ecunam9/ecunam0904.pdf (Accessed January 28 2017).

Salas, Guillermo. 2008. *Dinámica social y minería. Familias pastoras de puna y la presencia del proyecto Antamina (1997–2002)*. Lima: IEP.

Sánchez, Axel. 2014. Mineras extranjeras duplican inversiones pese a más impuestos, El Financiero. Available at: www.elfinanciero.com.mx/empresas/mineras-extranjeras-duplican-inversiones-pese-a-mas-impuestos (Accessed May 5 2018).

Scurrah, Martin, and Anahi Chaparro. 2011. "Estrategias indígenas, gobernanza territorial e industrias extractivas en la Amazonia peruana," Presented in the Congress "Desarrollo territorial y extractivismo: luchas y alternativas en la región andina" at the Bartolomé de las Casas center. Cusco, November 7, 2011.

Secretariat of Energy of Mexico. n.d. *Consulta previa a comunidades y pueblos indígenas*. Available at: www.gob.mx/cms/uploads/attachment/file/273192/consultaLibre2.pdf (Accessed April 8 2018).

Silva, Eduardo. 2009. *Challenging Neoliberalism in Latin America*. New York: Cambridge University Press.

Slack, Keith. 2009. "Digging Out From Neoliberalism: Responses to Environmental (Mis) Governance of the Mining Sector in Latin America" In John Burdick, Phillips Oxhorn and Roberts Kenneth (Eds.) *Beyond Neoliberalism in Latin America: Societies and Politics at the Crossroads.* New York: Palgrave Macmillan, 117–134. The Dialogue. 2015. Local Conflicts and Natural Resources. Available at: www.thedialogue.org/wp-content/uploads/2015/05/Local-Conflicts-and-Natural Resources-FINAL.pdf (Accessed May 29, 2016).

Toledo, Zarai. 2015. Zaraí Toledo escribe sobre Tambogrande, Hernando de Soto y lo que pasa después del no a la minería. Available at: http://utero.pe/2015/08/07/zarai-toledo-escribe-sobretambogrande-hernando-de-soto-y-lo-que-pasa-despues-del-no-a-la-mineria/ (Accessed May 19 2015).

Unir Foundation. 2015. Conflictos de Tierra y Recursos Naturlaes en Bolivia. *Doce Quarterly Newsletter* (Boletín Trimestral) 1(3).

Van Cott, Donna Lee. 2008. *Radical Democracy in the Andes.* New York: Cambridge University Press.

Vargas, Miguel. 2010. *Lecciones Aprendidas sobre la Consulta Previa.* La Paz: CEJIS.

Yashar, Deborah. 2005. *Contesting Citizenship in Latin America. The Rise of Indigenous Movements and the Postliberal Challenge. New York: Cambridge University Press.*

Interviews

Daniel Martin, "Interview," Torres Wong, Marcela. Ciudad de México. February 23 of 2016.

Elisa Cruz Rueda, "Interview," Torres Wong, Marcela. San Cristobal de las Casas, México. March 13 of 2015.

Marco Gandarillas, "Interview," Torres Wong, Marcela. Cochabamba, Bolivia. April 16 of 2015.

Mirna Cuentas, "Interview," Torres Wong, Marcela. La Paz, Bolivia. April 8 of 2015.

Municipal employees, "Interview," Torres Wong, Marcela. Oruro, Bolivia. July 8 of 2015.

Néstor Cuellar, "Interview," Torres Wong, Marcela. Camiri, Bolivia. April 22 of 2015.

Orvelin Montiel, "Interview," Torres Wong, Marcela. Ciudad de México. June 23 of 2017.

Ysaías Montero, "Interview," Torres Wong, Marcela. Santa Cruz, Bolivia. April 21 of 2015.

Chapter 3

Rights do not matter, political power does

Introduction

The commodification of indigenous territories can be framed as an unintended consequence of the implementation of the right to prior consultation or as an opportunity for indigenous peoples to escape poverty. This chapter explores the connection between prior consultation procedures and indigenous access to extractive revenues. As argued throughout this book, the application of prior consultation is not useful to deter extractive projects, yet these procedures are not completely useless to indigenous communities. By examining five indigenous municipalities across Bolivia, Peru and Mexico, the chapter shows that some indigenous groups negotiate significant economic compensation in exchange for allowing extraction. In this context, prior consultation serves as a negotiation platform for indigenous leaders to present some of their economic demands.

The chapter begins with an examination of prior consultation in the context of highly mobilized, politically powerful indigenous groups, all of whom benefited from the consultation procedure. Analyses demonstrate that using strategic mobilization in tandem with prior consultation negotiations, the Guaraní from Takovo Mora (Bolivia), the Achuar, Kiwchua and Quechua from Andoas (Peru), and the Yaqui from Sonora (Mexico) were able to persuade their respective governments to accept their economic demands. Likely, the state awarded economic resources to consulted groups as a preventive measure to stave off project delays or blockages that may have resulted from indigenous opposition. The chapter continues with an examination of the outcomes of prior consultation in the context of politically weak indigenous peoples. Prior consultation procedures conducted with the Mosetén tribes in La Paz (Bolivia) and the Kukama Kukamiria and Capanahua in Loreto (Peru) did not result in economic compensation for the consulted communities. Arguably, these groups did not represent serious risks to the state and thereby were incapable to set the terms of negotiation.

Using a green criminological perspective, the chapter considers the environmental and political impacts that economic negotiations have on indigenous territories and political organizations. Prior consultations are reshaping indigenous movements´goals regarding the protection of their territories. The cases examined in this chapter show indigenous groups willing to accept projects, yet concerns over the environment also existed. Nevertheless, consultation procedures have come to replace indigenous movements´demands over the prevention of environmental harm with demands over economic compensation. Nevertheless, the improvement of living conditions in impoverished indigenous communities does not necessarily follow indigenous access to extractive resources. Furthermore, profund political divisions within indigenous organizations often result from prior consultation procedures.

Prior consultation with powerful indigenous groups

The Guaraní and gas extraction in El Chaco, in Bolivia

From 2007 through the end of 2017, the government of Evo Morales carried out 58 prior consultation procedures over hydrocarbon projects (Falleti and Riofrancos 2018). The majority of these prior consultations were carried out with indigenous communities belonging to the Guaraní ethnic group. The Guaraní inhabit the El Chaco region in Eastern Bolivia, a place where all of Bolivia's gas reserves are found. Politically powerful Guaraní communities have used prior consultation procedures as spaces to negotiate the terms of gas extraction with the state, obtaining remarkable economic outcomes (Bascopé 2010).

The Guaraní are the third largest indigenous group in Bolivia, after the Quechua and the Aymara. They are settled agriculturalists and rely on semi-subsistence-based farming, hunting, fishing and the gathering of wild plants and fruits (Perreault 2008). Guaraní communities exhibit hierarchical political organization and have well-established mechanisms of deliberation and decision-making (Alcides Vadillo, personal communication, April 19, 2015). At the end of the 19th century, the Guaraní were forced to work as semi-slaves in the estates of powerful rancher elites for nearly a century. International resources to indigenous peoples during the 1980s created the conditions necessary for the liberation and subsequent political organization of the Guaraní people.

The Guaraní joined the rest of the indigenous tribes from the lowlands of Bolivia and organized through the Indigenous Organization of the Bolivian East (in Spanish *Comunidades Indígenas del Oriente Boliviano*), or CIDOB, in 1982. CIDOB was created with the assistance of the Organization for the Support of the Indigenous Peasant of the Bolivian East (is Spanish *Apoyo para el Campesino-Indígena del Oriente Boliviano*), or APCOB, the Research Center to Develop Bolivian Peasants (in Spanish *Centro de Investigación y Promoción del Campesinado*), or CIPCA, and progressive wings of the Catholic Church. In 1987, also with the support of such organizations, the Guaraní created the General Assembly of the Guaraní People (in Spanish *Asamblea General del*

Pueblo Guaraní), or APG. The APG began to aggregate all Guaraní communities of Bolivia while simultaneously initiating a process of internal organizational strengthening. As a result of this process, the APG's political system has reached notable convening and coordination powers *vis-à-vis* Guaraní communities, along with high levels of political representation (Albó 1990; Caurey 2015). Today, Guaraní people are grouped in 17 territories under the legal category of Indigenous Original Territories, or TIOCs, each with their own subnational APGs politically subordinated to national APG.

Extraction of hydrocarbons is not new for the Guaraní, and such activity dates back to the period of dominance under the estate system (Marco Gandarillas, personal communication, April 16, 2015). Guaraní organizing structures and political goals, then, were shaped by their ongoing experiences with hydrocarbons operations (Humphreys-Bebbington 2012:138). As local APGs started claiming lands enriched with sizable gas reserves, violent confrontation between these communities and extractive operators began.

Guaraní leaders have substantial experience negotiating with oil extractivists. During the neoliberal period between 1996 and 2005, the state did not control the hydrocarbon industry, prior consultation was not yet in place, and negotiation between multinational oil companies and indigenous leaders was informal and contentious. The Guaraní were forced to develop all sorts of disruptive tactics, such as blockades to oil wells, protests and the kidnapping of employees, in order to advance their demands in the face of extractivists. Long-standing connections with Non-governmental organization (NGO) experts provided the Guaraní access to sophisticated knowledge regarding hydrocarbon impacts and revenues. The Guaraní became knowledgeable in the use of ethnically centered and ecological discourses to their benefit as well as in development projects that could be implemented with extractive resources. In the mid-1990s, the government legalized Guaraní territory in the form of Indigenous Original Territories or TIOCs. This granted the Guaraní with their first legal tool with which to confront extractive companies and demand economic compensation for operating on their lands (Néstor Cuellar, person communication, April 22, 2015).

With the establishment of prior consultation in 2007, extant tools were enhanced, allowing indigenous actors to gain more leverage *vis-à-vis* the extractive process (Bascopé 2010). From then on, each time the state attempted to execute a hydrocarbon-related project on any of 17 Guaraní TIOCs, the state oil company of Bolivia (in Spanish *Yacimientos Petrolíferos y Fiscales de Bolivia*), or YPFB, had to formally consult with the APGs in advance.

Prior consultation and the Rio Grande liquid separation plant: an example

Takovo Mora is a Guaraní TIOC located in the municipality of Cabezas, in the Department of Santa Cruz, within the El Chaco region. The population of this TIOC has engaged in several episodes of social mobilization over hydrocarbon operations carried out in their lands. One of these episodes is illustrated by the conflict over the construction of the Río Grande plant which resulted in prior consultation and subsequent distribution of economic resources toward Takovo Mora.

Takovo Mora was legally created in 1997 and has a small population numbering around 2,041 inhabitants (Takovo 2012). It is politically organized through its local Assembly of the Guaraní People of Takovo Mora, or APG-TM, and subordinated to the national APG. As in most Guaraní territories, the people of Takovo Mora rely heavily on subsistence farming and fishing activities. However, the subsistence economy is incapable of providing for the basic needs of most Guaraní Takovo Mora families; thus, many have to seek temporary jobs outside their communities to access cash incomes (Takovo 2012). In 1999, a sizable hydrocarbon reserve, "El Dorado," was discovered within Takovo Mora territory, prompting APG-TM to demand as many prior consultation procedures as possible in order to obtain economic resources from state oil company YPFB.

In 2011, the government decided to build a liquid separation plant, dubbed Río Grande, within Takovo Mora to process 5.6 million cubic meters of natural gas per day. The plant would allow the state to meet domestic gas demands while generating a revenue of approximately 350 million dollars per year (Jornadanet.com 2012). While Bolivian legislation mandated that prior consultation take place in advance of the project's start, consultation with the APG-TM was not immediately undertaken. Instead, the environmental license for the project was approved without the consent of the Guaraní population.

The APG-TM rejected the environmental authorization, arguing that several ecological damages that would result from the Río Grande plant had not been considered. The APG-TM then called a General Assembly meeting to discuss the implications of the plant. The Guaraní leaders invited state officials from the Ministry of Hydrocarbons and Energy and the Ministry of Environment and Water to join them; however, state representatives did not attend.

In January of 2012, the APG-TM decided to occupy the sites in which the plant was being built. Guaraní members seized state facilities and forced company employees to stop operations and leave. As *mburuvicha* Higinio Coca, the head political leader of Takovo Mora, explained,

> We made several attempts to talk to the government, but they forced us take forceful measures and now we will occupy these lands until the authorities show up. This will continue until the state is opened to a dialog with us.
>
> (Quispe 2012)

The central demand of the APG-TM was to have a prior consultation procedure. Adolfo Chávez—then-president of CIDOB, who compelled the government to acknowledge indigenous demands (Quispe 2012)—backed up Coca's arguments.

A week later, a governmental commission headed by Juan Sosa, Minister of Hydrocarbons and Energy, met with Guaraní protestors in the hopes of settling the dispute. The government finally agreed to carry out prior consultation and reach indigenous consent regarding the Río Grande plant (Lazcano 2012). After this event, the indigenous abandoned the installations of the plant, allowing the company to proceed with construction activities. Prior consultation was started the next day and lasted for another week. Seventy detrimental environmental impacts of the Río Grande plant were identified, 18 of which were argued to directly impact Takovo Mora. An agreement regarding the project was reached in April of 2012 in the town of Iguazurenda, Santa Cruz. Initially, the Guaraní demanded compensation of ten million bolivianos if the project were to move forward, whereas the state offered just four million (Lazcano 2012). After several rounds of negotiation, both parties finally settled upon seven million bolivianos (equivalent to one million dollars) to be paid to the APG-TM in compensation for social environmental damages associated with the Río Grande plant.

After negotiations were made public, Gerson Rojas, manager of the Río Grande plant, highlighted that the Guaraní always showed willingness to reach a deal and that this helped YPFB to advance the project (Los Tiempos 2012). In other words, the Guaraní never actually sought to prevent the plant from moving forward; they just wanted proper economic compensation. This is evidenced by the fact that construction of the Rio Grande plant resumed immediately after the state agreed to consult with the APG-TM. By the time the final agreement was reached, more than half of the plant had already been built.

On November 20, 2012, the Bolivian government disbursed seven million bolivianos to the APG-TM, fulfilling the state's prior consultation commitment. This money would serve to fund seven human development projects, eight economic and productive development projects, and three projects on indigenous organizational strengthening. In its first year of operation, the Río Grande Plant produced a profit of 149 million dollars from the production and sale of liquefied petroleum gas (Ministerio de Comunicación Bolivia 2014).

The case of Takovo Mora's prior consultation procedure over the Río Grande plant is only one among many illustrating how mobilization capacities of Guaraní political organizations serve to equalize power relationships between the indigenous, the state and extractive companies. This case shows how strategic mobilization tactics used by indigenous groups, along with formal consultation procedures, served to tip the balance in favor of indigenous negotiators. Likewise, the case demonstrates that although the Guaraní had the right to veto extractive projects according to Bolivian prior consultation legislation, this was never their objective. The logic of prior consultation procedures for both the indigenous and the state was to negotiate extractive terms. Today, however, the Morales government is less willing to comply with extant legal obligations to consult indigenous populations. State repression of indigenous protestors demanding prior consultation in El Chaco has increased.

Indigenous tribes and oil extraction in the Peruvian Amazon

From 2012 through the end of 2017, the government completed 11 prior consultation procedures within the hydrocarbon sector. All such consultations were carried out with indigenous tribes inhabiting the Amazonian region, a place where hydrocarbon extraction is furthered in Peru. Yet given the political weakness of most Amazonian groups, these procedures have not had substantial effects on the way indigenous communities engage with the extractive industry (Flemmer and Schilling-Vacaflor 2015). Of the 11 prior consultations, only one resulted in significant economic compensation to Amazonian tribes. This proved to be an exceptional case involving politically powerful communities.

Unlike the sizeable and unified Guaraní ethnicity in Bolivia, indigenous Amazonian communities in Peru are divided among 65 different ethnicities. They are small in size and geographically isolated. Most of these tribes are dependent upon subsistence farming, hunting, fishing and gathering (Cossío et al. 2014). Extreme conditions of Amazonian environments allowed the indigenous to resist Western invasion longer than other indigenous groups, yet these conditions also prevented Amazonian indigenous from developing functioning communication channels. The Political Association of Indigenous Ethnicities of the Peruvian Amazon (in Spanish *Asociación Interétnica de Desarrollo de la Selva Peruana*), or AIDESEP, was created in 1980 to defend Amazonian tribes against territorial dispossession. However, the geographical dispersion of the numerous ethnicities living in the Amazon forest inhibits this organization from consolidating political representation of Amazonian tribes. Organizational structures remain weak as indigenous organizations are often not recognized as representative or are unknown to many communities (Flemmer and Schilling-Vacaflor 2015).

There are some places in the Amazon, however, where strong indigenous organizations exist. Many NGOs have built strong partnerships with some indigenous groups in the hopes of preventing deforestation and preserving biodiversity. In areas in which NGOs concentrate their activities, international supporters focus on pressuring the government to respect indigenous rights, redress past harms caused to the environment and halt the expansion of the extractive industry (Amazon Watch 2015). One NGO enclave can be found in the province of Datem del Marañon, within the Department of Loreto, located in the heart of Peru's Amazonia (Bebbington et al. 2012). Since the 1990s, organizations such as the US Amazon Watch, Peru's *Racimos de Ungurahui* and Spain's *Levante en Marcha*, among others, have contributed to the strengthening of indigenous organizational capacities (Bebbington et al. 2012). Over time, the indigenous of Datem del Marañon have developed well-established political organizations. Thereby indigenous leaders can mobilize the support of local communities using a discourse grounded in the defense of ancestral territories.

The hydrocarbon industry is not new in Datem del Marañon. Oil block 192 (formerly named Block 1-AB), the biggest oil producer in Peru, has been active in the province since 1970, under the control of the American company Occidental Petroleum Corporation, or OXY. Similar to the Guaraní in Bolivia, indigenous political organizing in this province has been shaped by indigenous interaction with oil companies (Bebbington et al. 2012). Environmental disasters and exploitation of indigenous labor have frequently triggered indigenous protests, complicating the extractive process on numerous occasions (Congreso de la República del Perú 2015).

Oil spills in 2006 and 2013 prompted indigenous communities to rise up and take over installations of the Argentinean oil company Pluspetrol, which has controlled the oil block since 2001. As a result, the Peruvian government and Pluspetrol were forced to negotiate with the indigenous in order to mitigate ecological impacts of the oil spills (Bebbington et al. 2012; Amazon Watch 2015).

Prior consultation over oil block 192: the state must do it!

In 2015, the contract between the Peruvian state and PLUSPETROL governing oil block 192 came to an end. A new process to find another operator had to be made. The new legislative framework in force since 2012, however, mandated that prior consultation with indigenous communities had to be carried out in advance. Oil block 192 is located in the municipality of Andoas, one of the seven districts in Datem del Marañon. The indigenous population in Andoas totals 10,522 and is comprised of three different ethnicities: Achuar, Quechua and Kiwchua. These groups are organized politically into three indigenous federations: Fediquep (created in 1998), Feconaco (created in 1991) and Feconat (created in 1991). Such federations are affiliated politically with national organization AIDESEP.

Like most Amazonian groups, indigenous communities in Andoas are primarily dependent upon subsistence activities. Oil companies have caused significant ecological damage in Andoas, while, at the same time, they have been one of the few sources of cash incomes available for indigenous people. Payoffs made by Pluspetrol to either compensate for negative environmental impacts of industrial activities or in the form of salaries for temporary employment of community members exemplify this relationship. Given the economic importance of this block, the incoming oil company had to begin operations as soon as possible. The state decided to formally consult with indigenous organizations before the conclusion of the contract with Pluspetrol. The indigenous organizations of Andoas saw prior consultation as an opportunity to negotiate new terms for extractive operations in oil block 192.

Prior consultation began on May 19, 2015. The state agency in charge of conducting the procedure was Perupetro, the company also in charge of allocating hydrocarbon concessions to the best-qualified oil companies. Perupetro decided to consult with the three indigenous organizations representing the communities living close to extraction sites—Fediquep, Feconaco and Feconat—separately. These organizations had experience negotiating with oil companies since the 1990s. By the time they engaged in prior consultation with Perupetro, they already had plenty of experience bringing forth demands of economic compensation to make up for ecological damages caused by industrial activity (Scurrah and Chaparro 2011).

In prior consultation meetings held in the month of July 2015, indigenous representatives requested the creation of an endowment fund to be directly administered by the indigenous and financed with the production of oil block 192. Indigenous leaders also asked for state representatives to improve education and health services, as well as to create jobs for local communities. According to indigenous leaders, the state had not taken any measures in the past to remediate environmental damage, and they were not willing to allow a history of environmental degradation to repeat itself. In this vein, indigenous leaders said that the fund would be used to compensate for past and future environmental impacts of extraction, and to improve living conditions of indigenous citizens (Servindi 2015a).

Peruvian state officials initially questioned the viability of an indigenous administered endowment fund. Unlike prior consultations in Bolivia, prior consultation in Peru had never precipitated economic compensation for the consulted group. Renato Baluarte, then-official of the Ministry of Energy and Mines, required some time to assess such a demand. This was not well received by the 50 indigenous leaders attending prior consultation meetings. The leaders decided to suspend the procedure until the state came to a decision over the economic fund. Before abandoning the meetings, the indigenous warned the state that they were not willing to allow oil extraction to proceed if the economic fund was not agreed. Indigenous female leader Magdalena Chino publicly declared that "If the state does not accept our demands, we, men and women, are coming back to our lands and we are going to mobilize." These declarations were backed up by Henderson Rengifo, president of the national indigenous organization AIDESEP, who declared, "The state is imposing terms and negotiating hastily. This attitude does not inspire confidence among indigenous communities" (Puinamudt 2015).

On August 14, 2015, after several months of negotiations, the state finally agreed to create the indigenous fund. This decision, catalogued as historic by Vice Minister of Culture, Patricia Balbuena, mandated that 0.75 percent of total audited oil production (one million dollars per year) would be paid to the 13 indigenous communities living in the vicinity of oil block 192. The fund was to be managed by indigenous organizations, without any intervention from state agencies (Andina 2015).

Indigenous mobilization continued after the announcement of this decision. Two of the consulted federations, Fediquep and Feconaco, were not satisfied with the yearly payment of one million dollars. They said that they would return to their communities to communicate the state offer to their people and make a decision about whether to accept it. Indigenous leaders also said that they will continue fighting until the state fulfills its commitments over environmental redress and compensation (Servindi 2015b). Notwithstanding disagreements over the amount of money to be distributed through the fund, prior consultation was formally concluded and final acts were signed. Divisions between the indigenous federations participating in prior consultation, however, were deepened as some of them refused to sign the agreement acts (La República 2015).

A couple of days later, Perupetro allocated oil block 192 to the Canadian company Pacific Stratus Energy. This allocation was made through a process of direct negotiation and granted for a period of two years. The decision unleashed new conflicts with indigenous communities. Past negative experiences with foreign companies, such as OXY and PLUSPETROL, prompted indigenous organizations to reject Pacific Stratus Energy. In addition, indigenous communities of Andoas demanded a contract for hydrocarbon operations that lasted at least 30 years, considering that they were to receive one million dollars yearly for the economic fund.

The conflict spread to Iquitos, capital city of the department of Loreto. Drawing upon regional state authorities, such as the governor of Loreto and other municipal mayors, the General Confederation of Workers (in Spanish *Confederación General de Trabajadores*) and the Patriotic Front of Loreto (in Spanish *Frente Patriótico de Loreto*), both of whom also opposed the Canadian company, the indigenous launched a 24-hour strike on August 24, 2015. The strike paralyzed Iquitos. The governor of Loreto, Fernando Meléndez, said to the press that neither indigenous organizations nor the rest of Loreto's population was against oil extraction. However, he noted that they rejected Pacific Stratus and demanded that the state company Petroperu operate the block (La República 2015).

Officials from the Ministry of Economy said that Petroperu lacked technical capacities necessary to take control of block 192 (Gestión 2015a). Along these lines, Pedro Cateriano, then-president of the Cabinet of Ministers, stressed that granting Petroperu control of block 192 would undermine foreign investment in the country (Gestión 2015b). Likewise, Minister of

Energy and Mines, Rosa Maria Ortíz, publicly asked indigenous organizations to reconsider their demands, as they could lose what they had already accomplished through prior consultation (Radio nacional 2015). Protests intensified, however, and a 48-hour strike was announced. In parallel, thousands of indigenous protestors seized facilities and airdromes nearby oil block 192 (Amazon Watch 2015). On September 3, 2015, the Peruvian Congress accepted protestors' demands and authorized the state company Petroperu to replace Pluspetrol in the operation of oil block 192 (El Comercio 2015).

In spite of discontent of some indigenous organizations regarding the amount of the endowment fund, the economic outcomes of prior consultation regarding oil block 192 and further state operation of this block are remarkable in the Peruvian context. Indigenous mobilization capacities operated as *de facto* veto power, as Peruvian prior consultation legislation does not grant indigenous rights to veto. The Peruvian government, however, was persuaded that oil extraction in block 192 would only proceed speedily and peacefully with indigenous approval.

The Peruvian hydrocarbon industry has been in hands of private companies since the 1990s. The state has been absent from most extraction areas and foreign oil companies, and indigenous communities have negotiated directly over the implications of extractive operations. Yet this relationship has been contentious, and violent conflicts—such as the Baguazo Massacre in 2009—have erupted over hydrocarbon activities. Prior consultation over oil block 192 demonstrates that meaningful economic agreements can be reached with indigenous communities even while a formal veto power to indigenous communities has been denied by Peruvian legislators. Yet, given the organizational weakness of most indigenous peoples in the Amazon, today this case is exceptional.

The Yaqui people and gas transportation in the Mexican desert

From 2013 through the end of 2015, the government of Enrique Peña Nieto has completed only one prior consultation procedure over hydrocarbon projects. This procedure was carried out in the Southeast Sonora desert (located in the border with the United States), inhabited by nine indigenous ethnicities. Prior consultation was conducted with the Yaqui indigenous people over the construction of a gas pipeline that would cross Yaqui territories. Through this procedure, highly mobilized Yaqui communities advanced significant economic compensation and political concessions from the government.

The Yaqui are the largest indigenous group in the Sonora state. Yet, unlike Guaraní or Amazonian tribes, Yaqui members do not live off subsistence agriculture or fishing activities. Most of Yaqui communities currently obtain cash incomes from renting their lands to farmers in Ciudad Obregon (Colaboración Cívica 2016). This ethnic group has a long-standing reputation of political mobilization. The Yaqui resisted the influence of Spanish colonizers and the Catholic Church during the colonial period, as well as land dispossession attempted by the Porfirio Díaz government at the end of the 19th century (Memoria Política de México n.d.). The political impact of Yaqui struggles led President Lázaro Cárdenas to legally recognize Yaqui ownership of their lands and political self-government in the form of *Usos y Costumbres*, as early as 1940 (De la Maza 2004). However, the implementation of Yaqui territorial rights was discontinued by following administrations. Over decades, the Yaqui continued to mobilize toward the legalization of the lands that were compromised in Cárdenas's decrees.

At the end of the 1980s, the Mexican government launched a project to develop the Yaqui agricultural economy. Outstanding economic funding and logistic support toward this indigenous group, however, failed to boost an agricultural industry within Yaqui territories. In turn, indigenous communities began to rent their lands as a means to access cash incomes (De la Maza 2004). Furthermore, a new generation of Yaqui professionals emerged in the aftermath of state development policies. Today, Yaqui leaders are known for not using intermediaries in political negotiations held with the government; indigenous authorities negotiate directly with the President of Mexico or the governor of Sonora. When Yaqui demands are not attended to in a reasonable period, the Yaqui use strategic forceful measures, such as interrupting traffic to the United States, taking control of state offices and blockading the water supply for Sonora's cities (De la Maza 2004:1127).

In 2010, the state attempted to build the Independencia Aqueduct in Yaqui territories that would take water from the Yaqui River to Hermosillo city. The Yaqui authorities perceived that this measure would threaten the main water source available for indigenous communities. Through the use of social and political action, the Yaqui were able to mobilize the support of several civil society organizations and some state agencies. In 2012, the Supreme Court of Mexico ordered the government to stop the aqueduct, upon the argument that prior consultation with indigenous communities had not taken place. However, as of the writing of this book, the government had not completed prior consultation, and the water from the Yaqui River continued to be taken to Hermosillo contravening legal mandates (Centro Mexicano de Derecho Ambiental or CEMDA 2015).

Prior consultation over the Sonora gas pipeline

In 2014, the government decided to construct a gas pipeline, dubbed the Sonora gas pipeline, to transport gas from the United States to Mexico's main power plants. This gas pipeline would cross Yaqui territories, and the state announced that it would conduct prior consultation with indigenous communities in advance. Prior consultation with the Yaqui over the Sonora pipeline, however, overlapped with social mobilization carried out by this group against the Independencia Aqueduct.

The Yaqui people are spread across three different municipalities Guaymas, Bacum and Cajeme, all of them located in the Sonora state. This population totals 33,000 and is divided in eight different jurisdictions, each ruled by their own political authorities elected through the Usos y Costumbres system. The government sought to build the gas pipeline across 500 miles, crossing through the states of Sonora, Sinaloa and Chihuahua. By the end of 2016, the pipeline would carry approximately 770 million cubic feet of natural gas per day, meeting ten percent of domestic gas demand. Indigenous leaders were aware of theeconomic potential of the project and its importance for the government (Adrián Hernández, personal communication, February 23, 2016). The Yaqui thus engaged in prior consultation with the aim of negotiating with the state over the allocation of economic benefits.

Prior consultation began in July of 2014. The state agency in charge of conducting the procedure was the Secretariat of Energy or SENER. Given that the Yaqui were divided in eight territories, SENER decided to consult indigenous communities separately. Prior consultation meetings were followed by intense negotiations over the amount of money demanded by Yaqui leaders. At this stage, only SENER, IEnova (the company hired to build the gas pipeline) and Yaqui authorities were allowed (Daniel Martín, personal communication, February 23, 2016).

SENER initially offered the Yaqui 36 million Mexican pesos in compensation for the gas pipeline (equivalent of approximately two million dollars). Through negotiations, the Yaqui were able to raise the amount to 76 million Mexican pesos (equivalent of four million dollars) (Adrián Hernández, personal communication, February 23, 2016). In the words of a Yaqui leader, "The obstacles in prior consultation were mostly economic, it was hard to negotiate with the company. We had to make some concessions because the goal was to reach an agreement" (Centro de Colaboración Cívica 2016). Of eight Yaqui groups, only one was not satisfied with the result of negotiations and refused to sign the final act. However, as the other seven groups accepted, SENER concluded the procedure upon majoritarian indigenous approval of the project. The government committed to paying half of the 76 million Mexican pesos in November of 2015 and the other half by the time the construction of the gas pipeline was finished. Both parts agreed that funds were going to be administered by Yaqui leaders according to their custumary norms. The Yaqui chose to distribute the money equally among the eight communities and agreed that each group would use funds to cover its most urgent needs. Simultaneously to prior consultation over the Sonora gas pipeline, the Yaqui had continued to protest against the Independencia Aqueduct. In May of 2015, the Yaqui undertook mobilization in 23 states of the country culminating in a demonstration in Mexico City, demanding cancellation of the Independencia project (Al momento 2015). Two Yaqui leaders, Mario Luna and Fernando Jiménez, were arrested in the midst of protests and despite denunciations made by Amnesty International over the alleged criminalization of opposition to the aqueduct (Masde131 2015). Although the conflict over the Independencia Aqueduct was not included in the government's official records on prior consultation, the freedom of Luna and Jiménez might have been an additional element of negotiation. Some Yaqui authorities explicitly addressed this issue in prior consultation meetings and offered to approve the gas pipeline in exchange for the release of their leaders (Centro de Colaboración Cívica 2016). Formally, the freedom of Yaqui prisoners was never offered by the state. Yet, after prior consultation concluded with an agreement in September of 2015, the Yaqui activists were finally discharged (Gutiérrez 2015).

The Mexican government was persuaded that the Yaqui had sufficient capacities to obstruct projects intended within their lands (Daniel Martín, personal communication, February 23, 2016). Through prior consultation, powerful Yaqui communities were able to advance political goals as well as economic demands. In turn, the unavailability of this procedure in the case of the Independencia Aqueduct exemplifies the limits of this institution. Independencia jeopardizes Yaqui's access to water, and it could damage the quality of their agricultural lands which the Yaqui rent to foreigners. This activity represents the Yaqui's main source of income; therefore, indigenous approval of the aqueduct is less likely to be reached.

Similar to the case of Amazonian tribes living nearby oil block 192 in Peru, the case of the Yaqui shows how indigenous political strength can operate as veto power even when indigenous rights to veto are not clearly defined in Mexican legislation. Moreover, this case shows that prior consultation can be used by the indigenous to negotiate economic resources, as well as political demands. With the new energetic reform put in place in Mexico since 2013, private oil operators have begun to enter into the hydrocarbon sector. Likely, the Mexican government will use prior consultation to replace old forms of resource distribution to nearby communities, which were formerly carried out by state oil company PEMEX.

Weak indigenous groups and window dressing prior consultation

The Kukama Kukamiria and the Capanahua and oil block 164

In January of 2014, the Peruvian government sought to expand the hydrocarbon industry by awarding concessions of seven new oil blocks within Amazonia to be operated by the best-qualified oil companies. Through these concessions, the government expected an investment of 450 million dollars for each block (Gestión 2014). One of these oil blocks—oil block 164—was located across the provinces of Requena and Ucayali, in the department of Loreto. Indigenous communities from the Kukama Kukamiria and the

Capanahua ethnic groups inhabit these two provinces. According to Peruvian legislation, Perupetro had to conduct prior consultation.

The Kukama Kukamiria and the Capanahua are among the smallest indigenous groups in Peru, and they do not concentrate in one single province. The Kukama Kukamiria (spread across six different provinces) number around 20,000 people, whereas the Capanahua (found in two provinces) are comprised of 588 individuals (Database of the Peruvian Ministry of Culture). Members from both tribes still live off subsistence fishing, agriculture and hunting, yet they have lost much of their indigenous identity. Only a few still speak the indigenous language of their corresponding ethnic groups, as they live in areas mostly inhabited by non-indigenous members (mestizos). To avoid discrimination from predominantly mestizo population, the Kukama Kukamiria and the Capanahua do not identify as indigenous (Ministerio de Cultura n.d.). Furthermore, most members belonging to these groups are not organized politically. They are not affiliated with any indigenous organization in Requena or Ucayali, or with national Amazonian organization AIDESEP.

Prior consultation procedure over oil block 164 initiated on June 13, 2014 and concluded on September 9 of the same year. According to the information available on the website of Perupetro, the procedure followed the timeline determined in the Consultation Plan elaborated by this agency. Perupetro determined that 2,249 people, divided into 12 communities, were to be consulted. Of all these communities, only one had a political affiliation with the Indigenous Association for the Conservation of the Peruvian Amazon (in Spanish *Asociación Indígena de Conservacion de la Selva Peruana*), or Asincosep. To ensure that the Kukama Kukamiria and the Capanahua were politically represented through an indigenous organization, Perupetro asked the Federation of Native Communities of Requena (in Spanish *Federación de Comunidades Nativas de la Provincia de Requena*), or Feconapre, to participate in the consultation. Feconapre accepted to participate and was included in the consultation procedure even while none of the consulted communities was affiliated with this federation.

Eleven indigenous representatives, six from the Kukama Kukamiria group and five from the Capanahua, attended Perupetro's consultation meetings. Indigenous leaders were provided with proper interpreters in both indigenous languages. State officials from agencies in charge of overseeing indigenous affairs, such as the Ministry of Culture and the Ombudsman office, also participated to guarantee that indigenous rights were respected. Unlike indigenous federations in Datem del Marañón (examined earlier), Asincosep (created in 2007) and Feconapre (created in 2013) were fairly young. These organizations lacked experience in the negotiation of agreements. Hydrocarbon extraction was new for the Kukama Kukamiria and the Capanahua, for which these groups had no previous experience with extractive operations either. Moreover, indigenous rights NGOs were not involved in the consultation procedure, probably because Requena and Ucayali are not predominantly indigenous provinces.

After several informational sessions, indigenous representatives were asked to express their concerns and proposals over the hydrocarbon project. Indigenous leaders generally referred to the urgency of improving living conditions within their communities. Likewise, indigenous representatives expressed that indigenous people should receive a share of the incomes generated by oil extraction. Perupetro registered indigenous requirements in a prior consultation act and committed to communicate these demands to the corresponding state agencies.

Indigenous representatives also requested the improvement of health care, education and transportation. Such demands, although included in the prior consultation act, were classified as "not related to the consulted measure" (see page 10 of the Final Consultation Act over oil block 164). In addition, indigenous organizations expressed concerns about potential environmental impacts associated with hydrocarbon extraction. Specifications on potential ecological damage, however, were missing as were proposals for environmental protection. In this regard, Perupetro committed to supervise extractive operations and to verify that extractive processes follow legal environmental standards (Perupetro 2014). With regard to job opportunities, the indigenous asked Perupetro that the oil company taking control of oil block 164 hire indigenous labor. Perupetro committed to inform the new oil company about the priority of hiring indigenous community members (Perupetro 2014).

Stipulations on an indigenous quota, types of jobs that should be available for the indigenous or labor conditions, however, were missing from the prior consultation act.

Unlike prior consultation over oil block 192 examined earlier, none of the indigenous demands presented in this case were framed as a condition to allow the hydrocarbon concession to move forward. Perupetro complied with the legal mandate to address and register all the questions, concerns and suggestions of indigenous communities (Article 14 of the Prior Consultation Law). However, Perupetro only committed to transmit indigenous proposals to the corresponding state agencies and to send copies of such communications back to indigenous leaders (Perupetro 2014). A transfer of money was not pledged for the Kukama Kukamiria and the Capanahua as it was for the Achuar, Kiwchua and Quechua. The prior consultation over block 164 ended according to schedule without conflicts or setbacks (Perupetro 2014). In the words of the anthropologist and state official in charge of supervising this procedure, Oliver Stella,

> The Kukama Kukamiria leaders felt that they had no right to be in the prior consultation procedure. They did not really feel indigenous, instead they identified with the mestizo identity." On the other hand, the Capanahua were almost invisible during the meetings as this group has suffered discrimination from non-indigenous population in Requena, for years.
>
> (Oliver Stella, personal communication, July 31, 2015)

The lack of representative political organizations prevented the 11 indigenous leaders who participated in the consultation procedure from presenting their demands strongly and persuasively. Indigenous representatives made important requests, such as an economic fund, job opportunities, health care and education services. Ye, they lacked the political strength to compel Perupetro to address such requests. Feconapre did not represent the consulted population, and Asincosep only represented one of the 13 communities included in the consultation. Moreover, both organizations were politically unexperienced.

In the end, the Kukama Kukamiria and the Capanahua complied with predetermined formulas typically used by Perupetro in prior consultation procedures. On November 25, 2014, two months after the prior consultation over block 164 was officially concluded, the Peruvian government authorized the hydrocarbon concession. This case shows the inability of the state to make of prior consultation a mechanism of resource distribution that is available to all indigenous groups.

The Mosetén and the Lliquimuni oil block in Northern La Paz, Bolivia

In August of 2008, governments of Bolivia and Venezuela created the oil Company Petroandina—a joint Venture between Bolivian State Oil Company *Yacimientos Petrolíferos Fiscales Bolivianos*, or YPFB, and Venezuelan State Oil Company *Petróleos de Venezuela S.A.*, or PDVSA. This agreement included an investment of 600 million dollars to exploit hydrocarbons in Northern La Paz in Bolivia. The hydrocarbon project dubbed Lliquimuni covered part of the indigenous territory belonging to the Mosetén ethnic group. According to Bolivian legislation, prior consultation had to be conducted with this group before the project began.

The Mosetén people inhabit the Mosetén TIOC, located in the province of Sud Yungas, in the department of La Paz, in Bolivia's Amazonia. The Mosetén are a small group, numbering only 2,000 people (Bolivian Census 2012). Yet they were among the first Amazonian groups to organize politically through the Organization of the Mosetén People (in Spanish *Organización del Pueblo Indígena Mosetén*), or OPIM, in 1994. OPIM was created with NGO support, as part of the umbrella organization of indigenous people of Northern La Paz, or CPILAP, and also affiliated with the national indigenous organization CIDOB.

In the beginning, OPIM developed a sophisticated political organization, different levels of decision-making and effective mechanisms of coordination between the eight communities that compose the Mosetén TIOC. In the 1990s, Mosetén organizational capacity enabled this group to achieve legal recognition of the Mosetén Territory (Bascopé 2010:62). Yet OPIM's inability to put forth viable economic models for new generations of Mosetén members progressively undermined its representative capacities (Herbas and Patiño 2010). Traditionally the Mosetén lived off subsistence fishing, hunting and farming; however, these activities were insufficient to cover indigenous basic needs. Over the last decade, the control that OPIM had over the Mosetén TIOC has been increasingly weakened by the presence of timber companies. OPIM attempted to prohibit timber extraction within the Mosetén territory yet failed to do so as young Mosetén individuals have engaged in this activity with the expectation of incrementing their income (Biblioteca virtual de pueblos indígenas n.d.).

By the time the Lliquimuni hydrocarbon project was launched, OPIM was politically weakened (Ribera 2013). Moreover, the project was announced in the context of the then-recent nationalization of the hydrocarbon industry. Citizen expectations over the oil reserves potentially contained in the Lliquimuni block were high, and "resource nationalism" was at its peak. The state agency in charge of undertaking prior consultation with the Mosetén was the Ministry of Hydrocarbons and Energy, or MHE. Due to the magnitude of the enterprise and the diversity of actors involved (other types of communities also overlapped with the oil block), MHE decided to conduct prior consultations with each group, separately.

Initially, MHE determined that OPIM would represent the Mosetén people in the consultation procedure. Unlike the Guaraní APGs in El Chaco, OPIM had no experience in negotiating profits produced by hydrocarbon extraction. OPIM used preliminary prior consultation meetings to demand lands, not money, in compensation for extractive activities (Bascopé 2010:72). In the end, however, OPIM failed to obtain any form of compensation from the state.

After preliminary meetings concluded, MHE excluded OPIM and engaged in prior consultation directly with indigenous communities. In addition, the state included non-indigenous groups or *colonizadores* in prior consultation meetings. The *colonizadores* saw in the hydrocarbon project a source of employment and sought to avoid all possible delays caused by consultation procedures (Bascopé 2010:67). Division among indigenous members deepened as some groups demanded that the state consulted with OPIM, while other groups supported the *colonizadores* stance (Bascopé 2010:81). Amid increasing indigenous polarization and before prior consultation concluded, oil company Petroandina entered into the Mosetén territory with the intention of starting operations. Simultaneously, the government accused indigenous political organization CPILAP (on which the OPIM depended politically) of conspiring with the US Development Agency (USAID) to sabotage state projects (La Jornada 2012).

OPIM and CPILAP denounced irregularities in prior consultation; however, these denunciations did not have substantial impacts on the continuity of the Lliquimuni project. Most of Mosetén communities complied with hydrocarbon activities upon the promises of the government to provide health care, education and infrastructure, among others (Bascopé 2010:74–75). The Bolivian government announced that prior consultation with indigenous people had concluded successfully. However, unlike the case of the Guaraní, economic compensation for the Mosetén did not result from prior consultation. Exploration of the Lliquimuni block began amid criticism from some NGOs over alleged irregularities in the consultation procedure (CEDLA 2011).

While the Mosetén had a well-established political organization and functioning mechanisms of decision-making, the organizational capacity of OPIM had decreased in the years previous to the Lliquimuni project. OPIM had become less capable of controlling the activities developed in Mosetén lands, as well as enforcing its decisions over resource allocation. Moreover, the agriculturally based development model offered by OPIM had lost credibility over illegal extraction of timber. This was worsened by the entrance of Petroandina into Mosetén territories raising indigenous expectations of finding jobs in the oil company. With a discredited CPILAP, the capacity that OPIM could have to convene meetings with broader indigenous groups and call for strikes and protests, practically disappeared (Ribera 2013).

Currently, the Lliquimuni block has a potential of 10 million barrels of oil and 153 million cubic feet of natural gas. At the same time, this project represents the expansion of the hydrocarbon frontier toward Amazonia, a region formerly prohibited for extractive operations in Bolivia (Zegada 2015). The Mosetén ended up divided between pro-PETROANDINA SAM and pro-OPIM groups, and OPIM lost almost all of its representative capacities after prior consultation over the Lliquimuni block was completed (Bascopé 2010; CEDLA 2011; Ribera 2013).

The case of the Mosetén in Bolivia demonstrates that resource distribution through prior consultation is uneven in this country as is the case in Peru. While the majority of Bolivia's prior consultations have delivered resources to consulted groups, this was because consultations were carried out with politically powerful Guaraní organizations. Politically weaker indigenous groups, such as the Mosetén, do not seem to benefit from prior consultation in the same way, despite indigenous rights to veto in Bolivia's legislation, progressive government ideology and influential indigenous movements.

Comparative analysis of the cases

Chapter 2 argued that national variables such as national political influence of indigenous movements (NIIM), the scope of the right to prior consultation (SPC) and the political ideology of the government (GI) do not account for variation in prior consultation outcomes over extractive projects. Chapter 1, on the other hand, indicated that the type of indigenous organization (TIO)—mediated by NGO resources or created from bottom-up processes—is not

Table 3.1 Type of Indigenous Group, Political Power and Outcomes

Cases	*Type of Indigenous Group*	*Political Power*	*Prior Consultation*	*Indigenous Outcome*
Guaraní, Takovo Mora	Pro-extractivist (economy based on subsistence farming and fishing)	High mobilization capacities (representative APG indigenous organizations)	Yes	One million dollars in exchange for allowing the construction of the separation plant
Achuar, Kiwchua and Quechua	Pro-extractivist (economy based on subsistence farming and fishing)	High mobilization capacities (representative indigenous federations)	Yes	One million dollars per year of extractive operations
Yaqui	Pro-extractivist (economy based on the leasing of agricultural land)	High mobilization capacities (representative Usos Usos y Costumbres organizations)	Yes	Four million dollars for allowing the gas pipeline to cross Yaqui lands
Mosetén	Pro-extractivist (economy based on subsistence farming and fishing)	Low mobilization capacities (unrepresentative indigenous organizations)	Yes	No compensation
Kukama Kukamiria and Capananua	Pro-extractivist (economy based on subsistence farming and fishing)	Low mobilization capacities (unrepresentative indigenous federations)	Yes	No compensation

Source: Author's elaboration.

Table 3.2 Table A

Cases	*IPP*	*PC*	*NIIM*	*SPC*	*GI*	*TIO*	*SP*	*Outcome*
1	High	Yes	S	P	P	N	S	Extraction with compensation
2	High	Yes	W	M	C	N	S	Extraction with compensation
3	High	Yes	M	C	M	B	L	Extraction with compensation
4	Low	Yes	W	M	C	N	S	Extraction
5	Low	Yes	M	C	M	B	S	Extraction

IPP = Indigenous political power
High, Low
PCP = Enforcement of prior consultation
Yes, No
NIIM = National Political Influence of Indigenous Movements
Strong (S), Moderate (M), Weak (W)
SPC = Scope of prior consultation
Progressive (P), Moderate (M), Conservative (C)
GI = Government ideology
Progressive (P), Moderate (M), Conservative (C)
TIO = Type of indigenous organization
NGO founded (N), bottom-up organizing (B)
SP = Size of the population
Smaller than 30,000 (S), larger than 30,000 (L)
Source: Author's elaboration.

the best predictor of indigenous outcomes over the extractive industry. Table 3.2 shows all logically possible combinations of the aforementioned variables including indigenous political power (IPP) and prior consultation procedures (PCP), the two variables specified in this chapter as conditions explaining indigenous outcomes over the extractive industry.

The cases presented in this chapter demonstrate that similar prior consultation outcomes are found across countries in spite of variation in national political influence of indigenous movements (NIIM), the scope of the right to prior consultation (SPC) and the political ideology of the government (GI). Likewise, the cases exhibit wide variation in types of indigenous organizations. This variable, however, does not appear to account for case results either. As has been demonstrated throughout this chapter, different degrees of IPP, combined with enforcement of PCP are what lead to different indigenous economic outcomes over the implementation of extractive projects.

I

An additional variable that varies widely across cases, yet does not lead to different levels of IPP, is the size of the indigenous population (SP). The indigenous populations examined here range in size from 2,000 to 33,000 people; nevertheless, size was not determinant for the levels of political power found in each case.

The trade-off between economic redistribution and environmental harm

This chapter presents five cases of indigenous groups seeking to negotiate a cut of the profits produced by extractive industries. As indicated in Chapter 2, one of the main factors accounting for pro-extractivist attitudes among the indigenous is whether they lack viable local economies that are potentially threatened by industrialized resource extraction. When this is the case, the extractive industry represents an opportunity for the indigenous to make a living or to maximize extant incomes. Ecological concerns in these cases play a secondary role to indigenous groups, as the primary mobilizing goal is likely to be the redistribution of economic resources.

The hydrocarbon industry has been present in El Chaco for over a hundred years. Thus, there is long-standing coexistence between oil companies and Guaraní people. Moreover, indigenous communities have learned to supplement their subsistence economies with the resources obtained from negotiations with oil companies. Likewise, many indigenous communities in the Amazon of Bolivia and Peru still depend upon subsistence agriculture, fishing and hunting. As of today, these activities are not sufficient to cover indigenous basic needs and do not offer indigenous communities access to cash incomes either. In the absence of another source of revenue, some community members are forced to engage in any economic activity available to them in order to make a living (e.g. illegal resource extraction, temporary migration to urban centers in search of jobs). Hydrocarbon extraction, in all these cases, represents a viable source of revenue. The Yaqui people in Mexico, in turn, do not depend upon subsistence activities and can access cash by renting their lands. The construction of the Sonora gas pipeline did not represent a major threat to Yaqui livelihoods, but instead was seen as an opportunity to negotiate with the state.

In all the cases explored in this chapter, pro-extractivist indigenous groups engaged in prior consultation with the state, but only some of them were able to negotiate significant economic compensation. As detailed in Chapter 2, prior consultation procedures are spaces for negotiation between indigenous groups and the state. These procedures allowed most politically skilled indigenous negotiators in Takovo Mora (Bolivia), Andoas (Peru) and Sonora (Mexico) to present their demands, receive offers from state officials, make counteroffers and eventually reach an agreement.

Nevertheless, the cases show that negotiations between state officials and indigenous leaders focused mainly over economic compensation. Indigenous concerns over environmental damages were almost completely replaced by discussions over the amount of money to be paid in exchange for extraction.

Deforestation and oil spills, however, are the most common ecological disasters attributed to hydrocarbon extraction. In addition, the construction of roads, airports and other facilities built by extractive companies to develop operations have the additional effect of facilitating illegal extraction and trade of natural resources (Davide 2007). Still, the cases studied here do not evidence the adoption of significant environmental provisions; measures for preventing oil spills or illegal logging, for instance, are not specified in the agreements following prior consultations.

Chapter 1 argued that indigenous groups must have sufficient political power to present demands persuasively and forcefully. Representative political organizations at the local level were emphasized as preconditions of such capacity. To participate in negotiations with the state, Guaraní communities of Takovo Mora relied on well-established and hierarchical APG political organizations. Similarly, the Achuar, Kichwua and Quechua tribes from the Peruvian Amazon participated in prior consultation through politically skilled indigenous federations Fediquep, Feconaco and Feconat. Likewise, the Yaqui engaged in prior consultation through long-standing and well-reputed *Usos y Costumbres* indigenous representatives. In all these cases, indigenous political organizations had significant credibility *vis-à-vis* community members, enabling them to call for protests, persuade the population to confront extractive companies and lead several cycles of mobilization. Such mobilization capacities operated as *de facto* veto power that culminated with the advancement of indigenous economic goals. In turn, state agencieswere able to further extractive projects with the approval of indigenous peoples, yet governments had to compensate the communities in exchange.

Another negative effect of prior consultation agreements is indigenous political division. The Guaraní in Bolivia accuse the government of Morales of using intimidation and bribes to divide indigenous leaders over the exploitation of hydrocarbons. As a result, most important indigenous organizations in the lowlands of Bolivia such as CIDOB and APG struggle to survive in a context of weakened political leaderships. Similarly, in the case of Amazonian tribes in Peru's Amazon, indigenous organizations split after prior consultation ended. Some of the organizations did not agree with the economic terms set over oil extraction in block 192 and abandoned negotiations, while the other groups accepted and signed agreements with the government. Likewise, one of the seven Yaqui communities did not agree with the construction of the gas pipeline. Confrontations between community members in this case turned violent leaving one dead and several injured (El Universal 2016).

Furthermore, there is no certainty yet regarding the improvement of living conditions in indigenous communities resulting from indigenous access to extractive resources. Frequently, prior consultation funds are misused by indigenous organizations, which often lack the technical capacity to develop projects that deliver long-lasting benefits for their communities (Néstor

Cuellar, personal communication, April 2015). The Yaqui in Mexico are known for having a solid political class with strong negotiation capacities *vis-à-vis* the government. Yet studies show that these political leaders do not always have the ability of addressing main economic and social problems faced by community members (De la Maza 2004:82). On the other hand, some Guaraní leaders in Bolivia have been involved in several scandals for alleged misuse of prior consultation economic resources to their personal benefit (El Periódico 2016).

Returning to the cases of the Kukama Kukamiria and Capanahua (Peru), and the Mosetén (Bolivia) exemplifies the condition of political weakness. These two studies show failing cases of indigenous negotiation of extractive resources. Indigenous organizations, such as OPIM in Bolivia and Feconapre in Peru, did not represent the interests of the majority of consulted communities. Many of Mosetén, Kukama Kukamiria and Capanahua members looked for a rapid implementation of hydrocarbon projects as they saw extractive companies as potential sources of employment and wealth creation. These groups engaged in prior consultation with their respective governments; however, they were not able to advance their economic objectives. The Kukama Kukamiria and the Capanahua in the Peruvian Amazon live in lands occupied by non-indigenous populations. Neither of these groups self-identify as indigenous, nor do they claim indigenous territorial rights. Moreover, as these groups are not affiliated with indigenous political organizations, they lack the conditions necessary to construct territorially based discourses and coalitions. The Mosetén in Bolivia, in turn, organize through the ethnically centered OPIM and had their indigenous territories legalized in the 1990s. However, the incapacity of OPIM to put forth viable economic models for indigenous communities diminished its ability of aggregating indigenous interests into a territorially based political project. Over the years, its control of the Mosetén territory was significantly undermined.

The incapacity to negotiate economic compensation for complying with extraction places these groups at a disadvantage compared to politically powerful indigenous organizations. As exemplified by these cases, political weakness frequently overlaps with disconnection from economic markets and insufficient incomes. Extractive projects create opportunities for nearby communities in the form of temporary jobs, local businesses to cover demands of services by company workers and infrastructure built to facilitate extractive activities (Bebbington et al. 2013:256).

In spite of potential economic growth associated with these industries, existing literature documents that the economic flow that emerges around the extractive projectstends to disappear after operations conclude (Wise and Shtylla 2007). Indigenous labor is typically hired for low-skilled employment and is poorly paid, and businesses created to satisfy the demands of extractive companies usually close after the companies abandon extraction sites (International Labor Organization). Moreover, indigenous groups living in isolated regions are often left at the mercy of potential environmental damages associated with the extractive industry (Bebbington et al. 2013). These communities generally lack political connections and economic means to present their grievances to broader audiences. What is perhaps worse, prior consultation with indigenous populations in "non-traditional" extractive areas may contribute to pushing the extractive industry deeper into ecologically fragile regions such as the Amazon.

Conclusion

Prior consultation procedures are useful for indigenous groups seeking profits from resource extraction, catalogued in previous chapters as pro-extractivist indigenous. They are also useful in that they might allow the state to implement projects within a more peaceful political scenario. Politically powerful indigenous groups frequently engage in small-scale conflicts and disruptive mobilizing strategies to pressure governments to comply with their demands. The level of violence involved in these cases, however, is not high in comparison with cases in which negotiation spaces are denied (see Chapter 4). Systematic enforcement of prior consultation procedures—still not offered through Latin American countries—would likely contribute to diminish the violence sparkled by extractive projects when the indigenous driver is access to extractive revenues. However, the evidence presented here shows that divisions and further weakening of indigenous political organizations usually follow prior consultation negotiations and can be a source on internal violence. Moreover, there is not evidence that the resources distributed through prior consultations are actually used to raise the quality of life among indigenous communities. This undermines the credibility of direct forms of economic compensation in exchange for extraction.

On the other hand, prior consultations with politically weak indigenous groups reinforce the uneven resource distribution typical of economic models based on primary commodity exports. The Kukama Kukamiria and the Capanahua, and the Mosetén in the Peruvian and Bolivian Amazon represent the worst-case scenario for indigenous peoples. They live in poor economic conditions, isolated from broader markets and indigenous political organizations. Yet economic improvement for these groups has not followed prior consultations.

Finally, the economic use given to prior consultation has not been helpful for indigenous movements opposing extractive projects. The next chapter shows that anti-extractivist indigenous groups in Bolivia, Peru and Mexico are still able to prohibit extraction within their lands. However, Chapter 4 shows that while political power is also needed to achieve this goal, indigenous protesters must operate in the absence of prior consultation in order to succeed.

References

Al momento. 2015. Llega al DF caravana Yaqui por el agua. Available at: www.almomento.mx/llega-al-df-caravana-Yaqui-por-el-agua/ (Accessed April 27 2016).

Albó, Xavier. 1990. Los Guaraní-Chiriguanos 3. La comunidad hoy. *Cuaderno de investigación* 32. CIPCA: La Paz-Bolivia.

Amazon Watch. 2015. Block 192: Government in Disarray; Indigenous Indignant. Available at: http://amazonwatch.org/news/2015/0907-block-192-government-in-disarray-indigenous-indignant (Accessed April 25 2016).

Andina. 2015. Califican de histórico el fondo social de Lote 192 para comunidades nativas de Loreto. Available at: www.andina.com.pe/agencia/noticia-califican-historico-fondo-social-lote-192-para-comunidades-nativas-loreto-571637.aspx (Accessed April 25 2016).

Bascopé, Ivan. 2010. *Lecciones aprendidas sobre la Consulta Previa.* La Paz: CEJIS.

Bebbington, Anthony, Martin Scurrah, and Claudia Bielich. 2012. *Los movimientos sociales y la política de la pobreza en el Perú.* Instituto de Estudios Peruanos, Lima: CEPES.

Bebbington, Anthony, Denise Humphreys-Bebbington, Leonith Hinojosa, Maria Luisa Burneo, and Jeffrey Bury. 2013. "Anatomies of Conflict: Social Mobilization and New Political Ecologies of the Andes." In Anthony Bebbington and Jeffrey Bury (Eds.) *Subterranean Struggles: New Geographies of Extractive Industries in Latin America.* Austin: University of Texas Press.Biblioteca virtual de pueblos indígenas. n.d. *Mosetén.* Available at: http://pueblosindigenas.bvsp.org.bo/php/level.php?lang=es&component=50&item=26 (Accessed May 10 2017).

Caurey, Elias. 2015. Asamblea del Pueblo Guaraní. Un breve repaso a su historia. Available at: arakuaarenda.org/panel/wp-content/uploads/2018/02/Asamblea-del-Pueblo-Guaraní.-Elias-Caurey.pdf (Accessed June 5 2018).

CEDLA. 2011. Temas Urgentes para el Debate: Consulta Previa Indígena y Análisis Ambiental de la Política Petrolera. Available at: www.Cedla.org/sites/default/files/Boletin%20energ%C3%A9tico%201.pdf (Accessed November 6 2016).

Centro de Colaboración Cívica. 2016. *Aproximaciones Consulta Indígena.* [unpublished] Report. Ciudad de México.

Centro Mexicano de Derecho Ambiental (CEMDA). 2015. Pide CIDH al Estado Mexicano medidas cautelares por el caso de la Tribu Yaqui. May 21. Available at: www.cemda.org.mx/pide-comision-interamericana-de-derechos-humanos-al-estado-mexicano-medidas-cautelares-por-el-caso-de-la-tribu-yaqui/ (Accessed April 8 2018).

Congreso de la República del Perú. 2015. Opinion over bills 4726/2015-CR, 4749/2015-CR and 4750/2015-CR, September 09. Available at: www2.congreso.gob.pe/sicr/comisiones/2011/com2011enemin.nsf/551cad89731f6b070525790e0079695e/a24618e81fb88f9805257ed10003116f/$FILE/DictamenObservacionAutografaLote192.pdf (Accessed April 8 2018).

Cossío, Rosa, Mary Menton, Peter Cronkleton, and Anne Larson. 2014. *Community Forest Management in the Peruvian Amazon.* Indonesia: Center for International Forestry Research. DOI: 10.17528/cifor/004426.

Davide, Giacomo. 2007. *Roads, Development and Deforestation: A Review.* Washington, DC: World Bank.

De la Maza. 2004. Gobierno Indígena y Política Social. Los Yaquis de Sonora, México (1989–2003). Available at: www.aacademica.org/v.congreso.chileno.de.antropologia/148.pdf (Accessed April 5 2017).

El Comercio. 2015. Lote 192: Congreso aprueba que Petro-Perú opere el pozo, September 4. Available at: https://elcomercio.pe/politica/congreso/lote-192-congreso-aprueba-petro-peru-opere-pozo-207294 (Accessed April 8 2018).

El Periódico. 2016. Guaranís denuncian la desaparición de 6.5 millones de dólares. Available at: http://elperiodico-digital.com/2016/04/19/Guaraníes-denuncian-la-desaparicion-de-65-millones-de-dolares-de-la-apg/ (Accessed June 23 2017).

El Universal. 2016. Riña entre Yaquis deja un muerto, tres heridos y 12 autos incendiados, October 21. Available at: www.eluniversal.com.mx/articulo/estados/2016/10/21/rina-entre-yaquis-deja-un-muerto-tres-heridos-y-12-autos-incendiados (Accessed April 10 2018).

Flemmer, Riccarda, and Almut Schilling-Vacaflor. 2015. "Unfulfilled Promises of the Consultation Approach: The Limitations to Effective Indigenous Participation in Bolivia's and Peru's Extractive Industries." Paper presented at the *Alacip Conference*. Lima, July 22–24.

Gestión. 2014. Perupetro adjudicará siete lotes petroleros en selva peruana en agosto. December 15. Available at: https://gestion.pe/economia/Perupetro-adjudicara-siete-lotes-petroleros-selva-peruana-agosto-86886 (Accessed April 9 2018).

Gestión. 2015a. ¿Por qué Petroperu no opera lote 192? August 25. Available at: https://gestion.pe/economia/Petroperu-opera-lote-192-98209 (Accessed April 8 2018).

Gestión 2015b. Premier Cateriano: Gabinete mantiene posición de que Petroperú no opere el Lote 192, September 13. Available at: https://gestion.pe/economia/premier-cateriano-gabinete-mantiene-posicion-Petroperu-opere-lote-192-99815 (Accessed August 1 2016).

Gutiérrez, Ulises. 2015. Liberan al líder Yaqui Mario Luna. September 23. Available at: http://jornadabc.mx/tijuana/23-09-2015/liberan-al-lider-yaqui-mario-luna (Accessed April 9 2018).

Herbas, Amparo, and Marco Patiño. 2010. *Derechos indígenas y gestión territorial: el ejercicio de las TCOs de Lomerío, Mosetén y Chacobo-Pacahuara*. Santa Cruz: PIEB.

Humphreys-Bebbington, Denisse. 2012. "Las tensiones Estado-Indigenas debido a la expansion de la industria hidrocarburifere en el Chaco boloviano." In Leonith Hinojosa (Ed.) *Gas y Desarrollo. Dinamicas Territoriales Rurales en Tarija-Bolivia*. La Paz: Fundacion Tierra, 131-150.

Jornadanet.com. 2012. La planta Río Grande generará $us. 350 millones, April 3. Available at: www.jornadanet.com/n.php?a=75473-1 (Accessed 23, August 2017).

La Jornada. 2012. Arremete Evo Morales contra economía verde, nueva forma de colonialismo. June 22. Available at: www.jornada.unam.mx/2012/06/22/mundo/028n1mun (Accessed April 7 2018).

La República. 2015. Loreto exige Lote 192 para PetroPero. August 12. Available at: http://larepublica.pe/impresa/economia/398051-loreto-exige-lote-192-para-Petroperu (Accessed May 18 2016).

Lazcano, Miguel. 2012. Río Grande tiene vía libre tras acuerdo con Guaraníes. *La Razón*. April 11. Available at: http://la-razon.com/index.php?_url=/economia/Rio-Grande-libre-acuerdo-Guaraníes_0_1594040620.html (Accessed April 8 2018).

Los Tiempos. 2012. Por 7 millones de bolivianos YPFB y APG Takovo Mora acuerdan compensación. April 11. Available at: www.Cedib.org/bp/a12/04/h/agua34.html (Accessed November 8 2016).

Masde131. 2015. Tras liberación de Mario Luna, sigue cancelar el acueducto independencia: tribu *Yaqui*. Availabe at: www.cgtchiapas.org/noticias/tras-liberacion-mario-luna-sigue-cancelar-acueducto-independencia-tribu-yaqui (Accessed April 27 2016).

Memoria Política de México. n.d. Sublevación de los yaquis; las compañías deslindadoras extranjeras los despojan, valiéndose de la ley de deslinde de terrenos baldíos. Available at: www.memoriapoliticademexico.org/Efemerides/7/31071899.html (Accessed November 8 2016).

Ministerio de Comunicación Bolivia. 2014. Takovo Mora inaugura su sede con recursos de compensación por impacto socioambiental. Availabe at: www.comunicacion.gob.bo/?q=20140809/16311 (Accessed November 9 2016).

Ministerio de Cultura Perú. n.d. Pueblo Kukama Kukamiria, http://bdpi.cultura.gob.pe/sites/default/files/Kukama%20Kukamiria.pdf (Accessed April 8 2018).

Perreault, Tom. 2008. "Natural Gas, Indigenous Mobilization and the Bolivian State: Identities, Conflict and Cohesion." Programme Paper 12. United Nations Research Institute for Social Development.

Perupetro. 2014. Prior consultation act oil block 164. Available at: www.PERUPETRO.com.pe/wps/wcm/connect/97f3729f-acab-43cb-b034-61a33d7f37d8/ACTA+DE+LA+CONSULTA+PREVIA+DEL+LOTE+164+-+Requena.pdf?MOD=AJPERES (Accessed June 9 2016).

Perupetro. 2015. Prior consultation act oil block 192. Available at: www.PERUPETRO.com.pe/wps/wcm/connect/be48d229-754f-48ca-92e3-75afbb09487f/Acta+de+Consulta+Previa+Lote+192+-+Alto+Pastaza.pdf?MOD=AJPERES&Acta%20Consulta%20Previa%20Lote%20192%20-%20Alto%20Pastaza (Accessed June 9 2016).

Puinamudt. 2015. No podemos retornar a un diálogo de sordos: Apus envían carta a Humala sobre el lote 192. Available at: http://observatoriopetrolero.org/no-podemos-retornar-a-un-dialogo-de-sordos-apus-envian-carta-a-humala-sobre-el-lote-192/ (Accessed September 21 2016).

Quispe, Aline. 2012. Guaraníes de Takovo Mora toman predios. *La Razón*. January 21. Available at: www.la-razon.com/economia/Guaraníes-Takovo-Mora-toman-predios_0_1545445493.html (Accessed April 8 2018).

Radio nacional. 2015. Ortiz: Es un acto de responsabilidad que Lote 192 no deje de producir en beneficio de Loreto. August 25. Available at: www.radionacional.com.pe/informa/politica/ortiz-es-un-acto-de-responsabilidad-que-lote-192-no-deje-de-producir-en-beneficio-de-loreto (Accessed July 24 2016).

Ribera, Marco Octavio. 2013. *Conflictos indígenas e hidrocarburos en el nortede la paz: situación de la OPIM, CPILAP, CRTM*. La Paz. Lidema.

Scurrah, Martin, and Anahi Chaparro. 2011. Estrategias indígenas, gobernanza territorial e industrias extractivas en la Amazonia peruana. Presented in the Congress "*Desarrollo territorial y extractivismo: luchas y alternativas en la región andina*" at the Bartolomé de las Casas center. Cusco, November 7.

Servindi 2015a. Nativos sobre Lote 192: No permitiremos que se repita la misma historia de impunidad y muerte. Available at: www.servindi.org/node/56727 (Accessed April 25 2016).

Servindi. 2015b. Lote 192: Estado nuevamente se burla de indígenas y crea escenario fraudulento. Available at: www.servindi.org/actualidad/137541 (Accessed April 25 2016).

Takovo, Mora. 2012. Nuestra experiencia en procesos de consulta asamblea del pueblo Guaraní capitanía takovo-mora febrero de 2012. Available at: https://vdocuments.mx/nuestra-experiencia-en-procesos-de-consulta-asamblea-del-pueblo-Guaraní-capitania-takovo-mora-febrero-de-2012-.html (Accessed November 8 2016).

Wise, Holly, and Sokol Shtylla. 2007. *The Role of the Extractive Sector in Expanding Economic Opportunities*. Boston: The Fellows of Harvard College. Available at: www.hks.harvard.edu/m-rcbg/CSRI/publications/report_18_EO%20Extractives%20Final.pdf (Accessed April 11 2017).

Zegada, Alejandro. 2015. Lliquimuni marca expansión de frontera hidrocarburífera en Bolivia. January 5. Available at: www.elpaisonline.com/index.php/2013-01-15-14-16-26/centrales/item/154257-lliquimuni-marca-expansion-de-frontera-hidrocarburifera-en-bolivia (Accessed June 13 2016).

Interviews

Adrián Hernández, "Interview," Torres Wong, Marcela. Ciudad de México. February 23, 2016.

Alcides Vadillo, "Interview," Torres Wong, Marcela. Santa Cruz, Bolivia. April 19, 2015.

Daniel Martín, "Interview," Torres Wong, Marcela. Ciudad de México, February, 23 of 2016.

Marco Gandarillas, "Interview," Torres Wong, Marcela. Cochabamba, Bolivia. April 16, 2015.

Néstor Cuellar, "Interview," Torres Wong, Marcela. Camiri, Bolivia. April 22, 2015.

Oliver Stella, "Interview," Torres Wong, Marcela. Lima, Peru. July 31 of 2015.

Chapter 4

There is nothing to consult here!

Introduction

The modern mining industry is associated with devastating impacts on the quality of agricultural lands and water sources. Previous studies demonstrate that people living close to mineral extraction sites are more prone to manifest environmental concerns than groups living close to hydrocarbon-related operations (Eisenstadt and West 2017). In this regard, scholars show that in several countries in Latin America, there is a perfect correlation between mining operations and social conflict (Pérez et al. 2018). Widespread perceptions about community opposition to mining projects might have created incentives for governments to skip over prior consultation procedures. An example of this could be that while Bolivia and Peru have recently began to consult mining projects, Mexico continues to non-enforce prior consultations within the mining industry.

This chapter explores the combination of state non-enforcement of prior consultation with different levels of indigenous political power. The first part of the chapter examines the cases of politically powerful indigenous organizations from the municipalities of Challapata (Bolivia), San Esteban de Chetilla (Peru) and Capulálpam de Méndez (Mexico), all cases where mining was attempted yet there were no prior consultations. Contrary to state expectations, avoiding consultation procedures in these cases did not preclude local resistance. The indigenous groups mobilized broad support across the population to oppose mining operations that were alleged to threaten local water sources finally banning extractive activities within their lands.

The second part of the chapter explores the combination of politically weak indigenous groups operating in the absence of prior consultation procedures. In these cases, although episodes of protests took place, the state advanced extraction without granting direct economic compensation for indigenous groups. Political organizations in the municipalities of Corocoro (Bolivia), Cotabambas and Grau (Peru), and Cerro San Pedro (Mexico) were unable to mobilize support from indigenous residents to their anti-mining mobilizations. The chapter concludes with a reflection on the limitations and opportunities created by the implementation of the right to prior consultation in Latin America.

Powerful indigenous communities do not need prior consultation

The anti-mining movement in Challapata, Bolivia

Challapata is located in the province of Abaroa, in the department of Oruro, in the Bolivian highlands. In the 1990s, the population of this municipality was part of a powerful anti-mining movement, contrasting with most pro-mining communities that define the region of Oruro. Today, Challapata figures as the only indigenous municipality prohibiting mineral extraction in its jurisdiction, due to widespread fear of water contamination.

The municipality of Challapata has 27,046 inhabitants, the majority of whom belong to the Quechua indigenous ethnicity and speak the Quechua language (National Census of Bolivia 2012). Challapata is politically organized into a municipal council, headed by a mayor. The municipal authority is elected every five years and legally adheres to the state political rules. At the same time, the population is organized into the ayllu system, an ancestral model of indigenous political organization still in force in some parts of the Andes. The ayllu in Challapata is headed by a Cacique elected through a Community Assembly (*Asamblea Comunal*) every year, and in charge of solving main political and economic issues faced by community members (Alanes and Condarco 2005). In 1961, the Bolivian government carried out the building of the Tacagua dam, intended to improve water provision and develop the cattle and agriculture industry in Challapata. Following this, a third type of political organization was created. Several ayllu members organized into an Irrigators Association (in Spanish *Asociación de Regantes*) with the aim to administer the use of the dam and assign water ships to indigenous users.

Over time, the effective management of the Tacagua dam gave the Irrigators Association significant credibility *vis-à-vis* indigenous communities (Emilio Madrid, personal communication, April 13, 2015). Challapata's optimum soil conditions for agriculture and its proximity to the capital city of Oruro, only two hours away, and to the department of Potosí, three hours away using the Potosí-Oruro highway, boosted the cattle-raising and agriculture industries. The economy of the municipality flourished, the population no longer is dependent on subsistence activities, and the quality of life is good (Madrid 2014:92). Basic services are mostly covered, communication services such as internet and radio are present, and agrarian careers are available for the youth (Limbert Sánchez, personal communication, July 7, 2015).

A handful of governmental institutions, Non-governmental organizations (NGOs) and research centers opened offices in Challapata to support the agricultural development of the municipality (Alanes and Condarco 2005:37). Challapata now exports quinoa, barley, cheese, milk and meat, providing employment to 4,000 families (Madrid 2014). In 2003, Challapata was granted the title of capital of agriculture, farming and dairy industries of Western Bolivia (Madrid 2014). These economic conditions make of Challapata an outlier within the highlands of Oruro where the population generally needs to migrate in search of employment that they usually find in mining centers.

The conflict: "There is nothing to consult here"

In 1993, the government of Sánchez de Lozada authorized the mining consortium EmusaOrvana—formed by Bolivian and Canadian companies—to exploit mineral reserves lying the Achachucani Mountains of Challapata. Without consulting with the population, this consortium had been seeking for minerals since 1990. As a result of exploration activities, Emusa-Orvana predicted to find 51.6 million tons of metallic minerals, containing 2.3 million ounces of gold, using the open-pit exploitation technique (Madrid 2014: 92). However, the plan would have located the mine pit close to the Tacagua dam, raising concerns within the Irrigators Association about possible impacts on their use of water.

Droughts are common in the department of Oruro, and many localities have problems with insufficient water provision. Moreover, community leaders in Challapata knew that the Switzerland Mining company Glencore operating relatively close to this municipality consumed large amounts of this resource for the development of extractive operations (Madrid 2014). The perception that mining projects would jeopardize control of the Tacagua dam—the productive base of the Challapata's economy—rapidly spread among the population. The bulk of indigenous ayllus comprising the territories within the municipality, under the lead of the Irrigators Association, decided to evict Emusa-Orvana. Indigenous users of the Tacagua dam were able to get support from neighboring populations, culminating in a large-scale, three-month mobilization against the mining company. During the months of January and February 1994, protestors blockaded the highway connecting the departments of Oruro and Potosí. This measure impeded the free transit of the population and interrupted commerce between these two regions, finally prompting the government to suspend mining activities (Madrid 2014: 93).

Again in 2007, now with the approval of the Morales government, the Canadian company Castillian Resources attempted to reinitiate exploration activities in Challapata. The population blockaded the Oruro-Potosí highway as it had done in 1994. In addition, protestors received support from the Governor of Oruro who passed a resolution banning mining companies within Challapata. Castillian Resources was forbidden to operate; however, the sizable revenues the project would have likely earned prompted the mining company to continue searching for mechanisms to obtain indigenous approval.

In the following years, Castillian Resources undertook publicity campaigns advertising the advantages of mining. In addition to the revenues for the state and the creation of jobs and infrastructure in Challapata, the company advertised the use of sophisticated technology that would avoid contamination

(Madrid 2014: 93). However, the influential Irrigators Association had successfully convinced water users that mining activities would inevitably contaminate the Tacagua dam (Madrid 2014:95). According to NGO employee Limbert Sánchez, the anti-mining movement in Challapata received support from various civil society organizations; however, the main mobilizing structure was the Irrigators Association (Limbert Sánchez, personal communication, July 7, 2015). In February of 2011, main ayllu authorities and other indigenous organizations operating in the region called a General Assembly to ratify their rejection to mineral extraction. These authorities grounded their decision in their adscription to the indigenous ayllu system and the indigenous rule over Challapata.

A resolution was approved in this General Assembly, stating that the Native Indigenous People of Bolivia *(Pueblos Indígenas Originarios)* prohibited the mining industry with the ultimate goal of protecting Mother Earth (Ribera 2013:79). Subnational authorities of the Oruro department, the National Council of Ayllus and Markas of the Qullasuyu (*Consejo Nacional de Ayllus y Markas del Qullasuyo*) or CONAMAQ, and environmental NGOs supported the indigenous anti-mining stance. The resolution of the General Assembly was later handed to President Evo Morales in a symbolic ceremony during his visit to the municipality (Observatory of Mining Conflicts in Latin America n.d.; Madrid 2014). To maintain control of the Tacagua dam, ayllu leaders strategically grounded their opposition to mining in their attachment to ancestral lands and indigenous political authority over their territories (Emilio Madrid, personal communication, April 13, 2015). Castillian Resources was not able to further the project which remains suspended as of the completion of this book.

The right to prior consultation was not offered by the government. Neither was such a right demanded by Challapatan organizations. In the words of the anthropologist Emilio Madrid, "The ayllus did not want to be consulted as they had already agreed in their General Assembly that they did not want the mine" (Emilio Madrid, personal communication, April 13, 2015). Implicitly, prior consultation was perceived as a means of negotiation, and the Irrigators Association was not willing to trade ongoing profits of their agricultural economy for uncertain benefits from the mining industry. The successful anti-mining movement of Challapata is depicted by ecological NGOs as sustained indigenous rejection of the mining industry, in defense of water (CEPA 2011). Ultimately, the potential threat that mining represented to flourishing local economies was the main driver of the opposition.

The case of Challapata demonstrates that anti-mining movements, uncommon in Bolivia's highlands, emerge when viable local economies are threatened by the mining industry. This case also exemplifies how indigenous institutions, such as the General Assembly of Native Indigenous Peoples in Challapata, were useful to prohibit mining operations. This corroborates the evidence presented in Chapter 3 showing that while prior consultation cannot channel anti-extractivist demands, native deliberation and decision-making mechanisms typical of representative indigenous political organizations are valuable tools for anti-extractivist movements.

The anti-mining municipality of San Esteban de Chetilla, Peru

The municipality of San Esteban de Chetilla, or Chetilla, is located in the province of Cajamarca, in the department of Cajamarca, in the Peruvian highlands. The population of Chetilla is known for opposing to the implementation of mining activities on their lands, in spite of being located within the largest mining department of Peru. Upon the discourse that water is more valuable than gold, political authorities in Chetilla reject the mining industry as they perceive that it will cause greater ecological damages than it will bring forth economic development for local communities.

The population of Chetilla totals 4,296 (National Institute of Statistics of Peru 2014), the majority of which speaks the Quechua language. Yet Chetillans do not identify with ethnically centered identities, and instead, they self-identify as peasants. Chetilla is politically organized into a municipal council headed by a mayor. The municipal authority is elected every four years through state election rules. Simultaneously, Chetilla is a peasant community ruled by a traditional type of political authority, elected through customary norms. The peasant political organization is comprised of a Community Assembly—in charge of political and economic affairs—and a *Rondas Campesinas* justice system—in charge of punishing local crime in the absence of state provision of justice. The Community Assembly and the *Rondas Campesinas* are strongly rooted in Chetilla due to the effectiveness of their practices for the benefit of the people. For this reason, municipal authorities generally coordinate their decisions with traditional community leaders.

In Chetilla, the quality of life is still low in comparison with neighboring municipalities. Basic services such as education and health care are not completely covered. The population depends on agriculture and cattle raising for the most part, and nearly half of the total agricultural production in Chetilla is for self-consumption. In 1995, traditional and municipal authorities together organized the work of community member for the construction of the road that now connects Chetilla with Cajamarca city, capital of the department and main urban center of the region. This road enabled the population access to cash incomes by facilitating the trade of agricultural products in broader markets. For this reason, Chetillans do not have to migrate to other cities in search of jobs (Asociación para el Desarrollo Rural de Cajamarca 2004). Likewise in 2000, joint efforts of both types of political authorities guided the construction of a hydroelectric that now provides electricity to the population at minimum cost (La Rotativa 2013).

Access to water is critical for Chetilla's agriculturally based economy as well as for the functioning of its hydroelectric. The proximity to Cajamarca city, where a powerful anti-mining movement exists, allowed Chetillans contact with the discourse over the negative impacts that the mining industry has on waters sources. Cajamarca has the largest reserve of gold in South America which is controlled by the American mining company Yanacocha since 1994. Environmental disasters attributed to Yanacocha, as well as the numerous conflicts between the company and adjacent communities, have influenced radical anti-mining attitudes in Chetilla. The fact that poverty prevails among peasant communities in Cajamarca after 22 years of gold extraction (National Institute of Statistics of Peru 2014) prevents the population from believing that they will benefit from this activity.

Community opposition to the expansion of mining into Chetilla

In 2003, the Peruvian government granted the Canadian Shield company mining concession over the Colpayoc Mountain located within Chetilla's lands. Preliminary studies carried out by the company predicted findings of over 313,000 ounces of gold, using the open-pit exploitation technique (Enlace 2014). Yet exploration activities were initiated without consulting with the people. In a Community Assembly, traditional authorities decided to send Rondas Campesinas members to capture the engineers working in the Colpayoc. In an interview with Aníbal Ramírez, then-member of the municipal council, he recounts that without permitting any form of negotiation, hundreds of community members caught the engineers and gathered in the main square. In the presence of community members, the leaders burned the engineers' mining equipment, took away their shoes and some of their clothing, and expelled them from the municipality (Aníbal Ramírez, personal communication, July 16, 2014).

Again in 2009, the same company, under the name of Estrella Gold Peru, sent employees to Chetilla to resume exploration activities in the Colpayoc yet they obtained the same hostile treatment. Estrella Gold Peru withdrew the project in 2013 arguing that "social costs" were too high and that local conditions had to change in order to advance mining operations (Enlace 2014). In an interview, Abel Tafur, Justice of the Peace and community leader of Chetilla, said, "We know that there is a lot of gold underneath our lands and we know that eventually it will be taken away, but while we are here we will try to impede it" (Abel Tafur, personal communication, July 15, 2014). In 2014, the company sold its mining concession to the Australian mining company Wild Acre; however, this company was also forced to postpone operations (Enlace 2014).

In the words of an indigenous rights lawyer in Cajamarca, Henry Alcántara, "Violent confrontations with mining employees over the last years have defined Chetilla as a radical anti-mining municipality" (Henry Alcántara, personal communication, July 7, 2014). Foreigners having the appearance of engineers or who seem to be related to the mining industry are not allowed in the municipality. Municipal mayors of Chetilla support the anti-mining stance of traditional authorities. Former mayor, Israel Mendoza, was affiliated with the APRA party, headed by the then-president Alan García, who had a strong pro-mining agenda for Cajamarca. However, Mendoza remained accountable for the community decision of not allowing mining in Chetilla and participated in anti-mining mobilizations held in Cajamarca city along with the rest of Chetillans. Likewise, current municipal mayor, Augusto Iglesias, campaigned as an anti-mining activist and then said in a private interview, "In Chetilla you have to be against mining, if the people saw me talking to a mining employee they may kill me" (Augusto Iglesias, personal communication, July 20, 2014). In 2013, the Regional Government of Cajamarca validated Chetilla's anti-mining stance and initiated actions to promote the industry of tourism as an economic alternative to the extractive industry (Regional Government of Cajamarca 2013).

As of the writing of this chapter, Chetilla's mineral reserves remain unexploited. The Peruvian government refuses to conduct prior consultation in the department of Cajamarca, despite numerous episodes of violent anti-mining mobilization witnessed in the last decade. People in this region do not identify with indigenous identities, and demands for prior consultation are not salient. However, by relying on their customary mechanisms of decision-making, the political leadership in Chetilla managed to prohibit extraction more than once.

Social conflicts and violence over mining projects are common in Peru, which along with Mexico heads the list of mining conflicts in Latin America (Observatory of Mining Conflicts in Latin America n.d.). While most of these conflicts involve pro-extractivist communities seeking a share of extractive resources (Arellano-Yanguas 2011), Chetilla is an example of an anti-extractivist community. Chetilla is catalogued as a poor municipality; however, the proximity to the discredited Yanacocha mining project has led traditional and municipal authorities to perceive that the damages associated with the mining industry are greater than its potential benefits, creating conditions for radical anti-mining attitudes.

Ecological mobilization in Capulálpam de Méndez, Mexico

Capulálpam de Méndez is an indigenous municipality located in the Sierra de Juárez, in the state of Oaxaca, in Southern Mexico. In 2006, municipal authorities in Capulálpam de Méndez initiated a legal and political battle to prohibit the restart of mining activities, even while the municipality had been an important mining center until the 1990s. Residents of Capulálpam de Méndez based their decision on the defense of water sources and the protection of ecologically harmonious indigenous livelihood.

The population of Capulálpam de Méndez totals 3,000 and ascribes to the Zapoteca ethnic group, although the majority of people speak Spanish, and only a few still speak the Zapoteca language (National Institute of Ecology 2007). The population is politically organized into a municipal council headed by a president; however, in the mid-1990s, residents of this municipality decided to convert to the *Usos y Costumbres* municipal system. Since then, the population no longer abides by state rules to elect municipal authorities. Instead, such authorities are elected through customary norms and are accountable to a Community Assembly (Municipal council of Sustainable rural development 2009). Although formally municipal authorities are part of the state, such authorities do not receive a salary for the work they perform, which contributes to enhancing the credibility of this form of political organization *vis-à-vis* the local population.

Capulálpam de Méndez is known as an extremely closed municipality. This means that state officials from outside the town or any other type of external actor do not participate in the decision-making of the community. In the words of the anthropologist and community member of Capulálpam de Méndez Salvador Aquino, "By keeping their political organization prohibited to foreigners, state officials and NGOs, local authorities have built a strong deliberation system, highly responsive to community demands" (Salvador Aquino, personal communication, June 12, 2014).

In comparison with adjacent indigenous municipalities, Capulálpam de Méndez demonstrates high levels of economic development. The quality of life is good, and main basic needs, such as functioning education and healthcare systems, are available for the population (Bray and Merino 2004: 153;; Madrid 2014). The majority of residents do not live off subsistence activities; neither do they have to migrate to other cities in search of jobs (Municipal council of Sustainable rural development 2009; Ramirez 2013). Historically, the municipality of Capulálpam de Méndez was a mining center. Mineral extraction existed since 1775 and was the main employment source. However, extractive activities came to a halt in the 1990s, and a sector of the population composed of the sons and daughters of former mining workers was left with the perception that mining companies had exploited indigenous labor. Moreover, the drying of former water sources was attributed to mining operations (Aquino 2011; Ramírez 2013). Political authorities then looked for new sources of incomes and turned their efforts to the sustainable use of forest resources and the industry of ecotourism in the 2000s (Municipal council of Sustainable rural development 2009).

The municipality is well connected to important urban centers, only two hours away from Oaxaca, capital city of the state. This connectivity has facilitated the trade of local products in broader markets, as well as the flourishing of tourism. Communally centered attitudes expressed in the *Usos y Costumbres* political organization were translated to new economies based on the conservation and sustainable use of environmental resources. Municipal authorities decided to create new businesses to receive foreign tourists, which are owned by the community. Like municipal authorities, tourism operators in Capulálpam de Méndez are appointed through the *cargo* system and do not get paid for their work. Utilities generated by communal businesses are used for the provision of social services for the population (National Institute of Ecology 2007).

"Communitarian ecological tourism" and environmentally conscious attitudes among community members have come to define the identity of Capulálpam de Méndez (see website of Capulálpam de Méndez). Likewise, municipal authorities encourage the preservation of customary values. Although they welcome tourism, community leaders advise to keep foreign tourists under supervision, to avoid "contamination of the residents' livelihood" (young member of Capulálpam de Méndez, personal communication, June 10, 2014).

Ecological opposition to reactivation of the mining industry

In 2002, the Mexican government granted the Canadian company Continuum Resources rights for exploration and exploitation of silver and gold in lands that were part of Capulálpam de Méndez. Studies carried out by the company showed that sizable amounts of these valuable minerals still existed in the area, which could be extracted using the open-pit technique (Environmental Justice Atlas n.d.). In the beginning, Continuum Resources operated in locations outside of the municipality. However, over the years, the company started exploring areas that were close to spring water sources. This preoccupied municipal authorities, bringing out tensions between the population and mining employees (ANAA 2011; Aquino 2011).

In 2005, municipal authorities filed a complaint against the government's decision to authorize mineral extraction in Capulálpam de Méndez. The arguments used to question the legality of the mining project were that the indigenous population had not been consulted about mining concession and that mining activities were producing damage to the environment. The lack of state response prompted indigenous communities to adopt forceful measures, which included seizing mining company offices, cutting off mine access to employees and state officials, and blockading of the highway connecting Capulálpam de Méndez with Oaxaca City (ANAA 2011; Aquino 2011; Mraz Bartra 2013).

Municipal authorities mobilized support from neighboring municipalities also ruled by the *Usos y Costumbres* system, based on the argument that contamination of water sources would impact them as well. In addition, some deputies of the state of Oaxaca also joined Capulálpam de Méndez's anti-mining movement (Mraz Bartra 2013:81). Several cycles of protests took place in the cities of Oaxaca and Mexico, demanding the eviction of Continuum Resources, the restitution of communal lands and economic compensation for the ecological damage caused by exploration activities (Aquino 2011; Mraz Bartra 2013).

The Federal Environmental Office (*Procuraduría Federal de Protección al Ambiente*), or PROFEPA, was finally persuaded to inspect mining company operations. The agency verified that ecological damages had been caused by mining activities and suspended the mining project (La Jornada 2013). Continuum Resources withdrew operations and sold its concession to the Canadian mining company Sundance Resources. Today, Capulálpam de Méndez remains free of mining, although it is still unknown whether Sundance will reactivate operations in the future. Yet municipal authorities have publicly stated that mineral extraction will not be allowed within their lands (La Jornada 2013).

Prior consultation was demanded by municipal authorities of Capulálpam de Méndez; however, the government did not enforce this right. State agencies remained unresponsive to indigenous complaints over ecological damage until the anti-mining mobilization grew bigger persuading federal agency PROFEPA to enforce environmental legislation. Ecologically centered organizations and anti-mining movements in other parts of Mexico use Capulálpam de Méndez as an example of successful indigenous protection of Mother Nature (Movement M4 2012). The existence of a viable local economy centered in the preservation of environmental resources created conditions for municipal authorities to oppose to mining.

The case of Capulálpam de Méndez shows how emerging ecotourism industry creates incentives for indigenous opposition to mining projects. Mining conflicts in Mexico are the most numerous in Latin America and often involve violence (Observatory of Mining Conflicts in Latin America n.d.). In this case, however, anti-mining mobilization was somehow peaceful, and indigenous leaders used the law in tandem with social mobilization. A combination of viable economic model with representative political organization at the local level contributed to deliver anti-extractivist results through non-violent means.

Weak indigenous communities and the absence of prior consultation

The municipality of Corocoro in Bolivia

Corocoro is the capital of Bolivia's Pacaje Province, in the department of La Paz. It is also home to the biggest copper-mining project in the country, and even while the government committed to conducting prior consultation with the indigenous population of this city before beginning the extraction process, this commitment was not fulfilled. The project was implemented, but the terms of extraction were not negotiated with indigenous representatives.

Corocoro is inhabited by 10,647 people of Aymaran descent, half of which still speak the Aymara language (National Census of Bolivia 2012). The city is organized into a municipal council headed by a municipal mayor, who is elected every four years through the state election rules. At the same time, Corocoro is part of the indigenous territory Jach'a Suyu Pakajaqi or JSP (Vargas 2010). JSP is ruled by the ayllu political model, headed by Mallku leaders. The reconstitution of the ayllu political authority in JSP, however, was not as successful as it was in Mallku Khota (Emilio Madrid, personal communication, June 23, 2015).

Historically, Corocoro's primary industry and source of employment has been mining. When the state mining company COMIBOL took control of the Corocoro mine in the aftermath of the 1952 Bolivian revolution, the political and economic participation of mine workers in the extractive process was enhanced (Vargas 2010:99). The formation of a strong, politically active mine worker identity along with unionization became the most powerful mobilization forces during the three decades that COMIBOL operated in the city. Falling mineral prices prompted mining activities to come to a halt in 1985. COMIBOL abandoned Corocoro, and miners subsequently migrated to other cities in search of jobs (La Patria 2011).

Corocoro became a "ghost town" in contrast to the vibrant society that defined the city at the peak of the mining boom. The local economy shifted to agro-mining, and the population that remained in Corocoro engaged in subsistence agriculture, cattle ranching and small-scale mining activities (Emilio Madrid, personal communication, June 23, 2015). Still, Corocoro lived with its glorious mining past, and municipal authorities constantly demanded that the central government resume mining operations (Duran 2017).

The Corocoro hydrometallurgy and the unfulfilled promise of prior consultation

High mineral prices in the 2000s created the conditions for the reactivation of the Corocoro copper mine. In June of 2008, the Morales government formed a joint venture between COMIBOL and the Korean Resources Corporation, or KORES, to implement a hydrometallurgical project in Corocoro. Preliminary studies estimated that the mine would produce 30 to 50 thousand tons of copper per year (Madrid et al. 2012). The companies announced the investment of $210 million dollars to develop the project using the open-pit exploitation technique (Eju 2009). This announcement raised the expectations in Corocoro for those that saw the mining project as an opportunity to revive the city and for those who had left Corocoro in search of jobs and wished to return (El Diario 2009). Similarly, the National Federation of Miner Unions of Bolivia supported the government initiative with the understanding that reactivation of mining activities would create jobs for unemployed mine workers (La Patria 2009).

Yet the Mallkus of JSP demanded that a prior consultation procedure with indigenous ayllus be conducted before the project was implemented. Indigenous leaders used ecological arguments to question the viability of the

Corocoro mine, alleging that the contamination of rivers and agricultural lands would damage indigenous livelihoods (Vargas 2010). However, according to Emilio Madrid, who researched the conflict, JSP did not seek prior consultation to prohibit mining but to negotiate economic benefits with the government (Emilio Madrid, personal communication, June 23, 2015). The Mallkus demands for prior consultation gained leverage as the recently ratified 2009 Bolivian Constitution included this indigenous right as a central component of participatory democracy. The Bolivian Congress supported JSP and compelled the Ministry of Mining and COMIBOL to comply with the prior consultation legislation. JSP also received support from the national indigenous organization CONAMAQ and from other civil society organizations (Vargas 2010)

The Morales government agreed to conduct prior consultation and initiated a consultation plan. However, this plan suffered continual delays while mining operations were furthered by COMIBOL (Vargas 2010:116). JSP authorities accused the state of violating indigenous rights and organized several demonstrations denouncing the project. Indigenous groups supported by CONAMAQ adopted forceful measures to compel the government to consult with them. Mining activities were prohibited for 48 hours, and the riverbed, which had been altered by COMIBOL to enable mining activities, was restored by the indigenous. Protestors claimed that the project would contaminate the environment, and furthermore, it would not create jobs for the local people as most workers came from outside Corocoro (La Patria 2009).

However, as indigenous voices gained salience, contradictions within the ayllu leadership became more pronounced. The Mallku Evaristo Condori, an indigenous leader from Pacajes Province, publicly disregarded the necessity of prior consultation. Condori added that CONAMAQ did not have authority within the province of Pacajes, as it functioned as an NGO and its members had not been elected by the indigenous people (Eju2009). Likewise, mining and agricultural unions of Corocoro intervened in the conflict in support of the government, undermining representative capacities of JSP (Emilio Madrid, personal communication, June 23, 2015). Mining unions accused JSP leaders of conspiring with foreign NGOs and right-wing parties with the aim of sabotaging the Morales government. The pro-mining sectors violently confronted indigenous protestors; they took control of the sites in which COMIBOL was operating and prohibited JSP access to these locations (Vargas 2010).

COMIBOL formally started the mining project in October of 2009 despite JSP discontent and broad criticism from civil society organizations (Vargas 2010). The government drew on the support of mining unions to evade prior consultation, while maintaining an official story that a consultation plan was in progress (Madrid et al. 2012). In another attempt to advance prior consultation, JSP and CONAMAQ supporters cut the city's water access. However, COMIBOL engaged in private negotiations with some of the community leaders that were still mobilized, obtaining their permission to begin mining operations (Mineria de Bolivia 2009; Vargas 2010). JSP authorities accused the state of attempting to buy the support of indigenous leaders; however, these accusations did not have a broader impact on the residents of the city.

In the fall of 2016, the government had not consulted with JSP regarding the hydrometallurgical project. Despite this violation to extant legal mandates, COMIBOL was able to further operations without major complications. Exploration activities estimated that the mineral reserves of Corocoro represented over 8,000 million dollars (Lazcano 2012). Exploitation operations began in 2013, and by the end of 2014, Corocoro had generated 11 million dollars for Bolivia, with a monthly production of 170 tons of copper. These results surpassed initial expectations of the government who initiated plans to expand the geographic scope of the mine (Eabolivia.com 2014). In turn, the League for the Defense of the Environment (*Liga de Defensa del Medio Ambiente*), or LIDEMA, has warned about the insufficient provision of water for Corocoro as a result of mining operations (Eju 2012). However, as new jobs have become available for the population and new businesses have been created to provide services to mining employees, anti-mining coalitions remain weak. Today, mining unions remain the most prominent form of political organization in this city.

Corocoro illustrates how political organizations that are different from unionization are unlikely to prevail in places where the mining industry is prominent. In these cases, demands for prior consultation based on indigenous territorial rights do not seem to have effect on the broader population or the government. In mining centers, such as Corocoro, most negotiations over mining do not take place before mining projects are implemented, which is the logic of prior consultation. In turn, negotiations between miners and the company focus on labor rights and take place once mining operations begin.

The "Las Bambas" mining project in Apurímac, Peru

Cotabambas and Grau are two provinces of the department of Apurímac in the central highlands of Peru. Las Bambas is located within these two provinces and is deemed to be the biggest copper project in the country. Indigenous discontent with the distribution of extractive resources, however, has caused deadly conflicts in the last two years. Yet such conflicts have neither impacted the continuity of the project nor have they changed the distribution terms in favor of local communities.

There are 79,486 people living in Cotabambas and Grau (National Institute of Statistics 2014), and nearly 90 percent of them speak Quechua (Servindi 2012). However, the people in Apurímac do not identify with indigenous identities. Instead, the population self-identifies as peasants. Cotabambas and

Grau are ruled by municipal authorities, comprised of a municipal council and a mayor, who are elected every four years according to Peruvian election rules. Simultaneously, the indigenous population is distributed in various peasant communities, which are politically organized through Directorates (*Juntas Directivas*), headed by a president.

High levels of distrust define the relationship between peasant communities and municipal authorities in Apurímac (Moreno 2014). Likewise, communally based forms of political organization remain weak in comparison with other parts of the Andes. The department of Apurímac was among the most heavily impacted by the civil war between the Peruvian government and the Shining Path during the 1980s and 1990s. Moreover, the provinces of Cotabambas and Grau were sites of occupation by insurgency forces for the recruitment and training of rebels (Moreno 2014:128). By the time the civil war came to a halt in the mid-1990s, local political organizations had practically disappeared. Associational spaces and trans-community networks were suppressed by repression either by state forces or by terrorist attackers (Yashar 2005:79).

Apurímac remains one of the poorest region in Peru (National Institute Statistics of Peru 2013). Sizable mineral reserves in this part of the country have attracted several mining companies to the region. Mining operations were sporadically developed before the 1990s offering temporary employment for local communities. In the absence of mining companies, the population lives from agro-mining, combining subsistence agriculture and cattle raising with the small-scale extraction of gold. Extreme geographic conditions and the difficult access to urban centers and capital cities, however, prevent the integration of the population to broader economic markets, as well as access to basic services such as education, health care and infrastructure (Ministry of Health of Peru 2005).

Xstrata copper and the Las Bambas mining project

Through a Public Contest in 2004, the Peruvian government granted the Swiss-Australian mining company Xstrata Copper rights to explore for minerals in Cotabambas and Grau. The terms of this contest required that a portion of the payment made by the mining company be directed to local communities potentially impacted by the project. Xstrata Copper offered the government 121 million dollars for the right to develop Las Bambas project. Forty-five million dollars would be deducted from this amount to develop the provinces where mining operations would take place.

By 2004, social conflicts over mining projects had proliferated within Peru. In response, the then-government of Alejandro Toledo launched a set of reforms to redistribute mining profits to local communities more rapidly and effectively. As part of these reforms, a Trust Fund was created with the payment made by Xstrata Copper to improve living conditions in nearby communities. The administration of this Trust Fund was given to the state agency Proinversión. In the context of these new redistributive reforms, the announcement of the mining project raised the economic expectations of the people from Cotabambas and Grau.

Before the implementation of the project, Xstrata Copper and the government undertook several informational workshops with peasant communities with the aim of addressing local concerns over mining activities. Important NGOs such as OXFAM and Coper-Acción were also invited to participate in these workshops. Tensions during informational sessions, however, reflected the discontent among some subnational politicians of Apurímac over the economic terms of Las Bambas. Regional and municipal mayors attempted to change the mining resources distribution stated by the central state and demanded that the total investment of Xstrata Copper be directed to Apurímac. In addition, these politicians demanded the removal of Proinvesión from the administration of the Trust Fund.

Subnational politicians were able to mobilize sporadic support of peasant communities in Cotabambas, Grau and other provinces of Apurimac. In 2005, several episodes of short-term protests took place. However, peasant communities' distrust of their political authorities prevented far-reaching impacts of these mobilizations. Peasant communities perceived that subnational politicians in the form of municipal mayors and regional presidents, as well as NGO actors, were opportunists attempting to frighten people about the impacts of mining with the purpose of advancing their own political goals (Moreno 2014). Neither the increment in the economic distribution toward Apurímac nor the removal of Proinversión from the administration of the Las Bambas Trust Fund was achieved. The mining project moved forward according to the terms stated by the central government.

In 2005, Xstrata Copper initiated exploration activities in Cotabambas and Grau. By 2010, the company estimated a production of 400 thousand tons of copper per year. Xstrata Copper announced that these findings met the expectations of the company and initiated exploitation activities using the open-pit technique. Xstrata Copper announced an investment of 4,200 million dollars in Las Bambas making of this project one of the most profitable in Peru (El Economista 2010). In 2009, the government created the Social Fund of Las Bambas Project (*Fondo Social Las Bambas*), or Fosbam, to replace the former Trust Fund. With this measure, subnational political authorities of Apurímac and representatives of Xstrata Copper were placed as the new administrators of Fosbam. In 2011, new protests over the distribution of mining profits took place, prompting short-term solutions by the state to peace protestors. Still, tensions continued to mount, and some authorities in Apurímac argued that local communities did not oppose mining; however, more effective mechanisms of negotiation were needed to prevent further conflicts (Segovia 2013:16–17).

By 2012, Xstrata Copper had invested nearly 50 million dollars in local development (Gestión 2012). Yet the population of Apurímac still perceived that the distribution of mining resources was unfair. In 2014, Xstrata Copper sold the project to the Chinese consortium headed by the company MMG for 5,850 million dollars. In 2015, a new conflict took place in Cotabambas and Grau. This time, protestors opposed to operative changes made by MMG as these changes were not consulted with local communities and were alleged to have negative impacts on the environment. Protests intensified and spread to other provinces in Apurímac resulting in three people killed, several injured and the following military occupation of Cotabambas (El Comercio 2016). Sporadic episodes of violence took place in the aftermath of this event. In the fall of 2016, military forces had not abandoned the area, and a solution to the conflict had not been reached.

In 2004, the government did not conduct prior consultation with local communities over Las Bambas mining project. Neither was a consultation conducted over operative changes made by MMG in 2015. By this omission, the Peruvian government violated extant prior consultation legislation in force since 2012, but most importantly, the state lost an opportunity of reaching a satisfactory agreement with increasingly discontent peasant communities. The mechanisms of resource distribution stated by the government in the mid-2000s were created from the top-down. Local politicians were incapable of changing that distribution during the first years of Las Bambas. The interaction between Xstrata Copper and indigenous communities over 12 years of mining operations, however, seems to have created conditions for new forms of political mobilization (Moreno 2014). Environmental discourse—never used in Apurímac before—could now articulate local discontent over the distribution of extractive resources more effectively, as is the case in other parts of Peru.

The case of Las Bambas shows that mobilization capacities among indigenous populations can increase over time. In Peru, expectations about mining resources, as well as recent prior consultation legislation, have triggered conflict in places such as Apurímac where indigenous communities remained politically weak. Yet the government's reluctance to enforce prior consultation procedures over million-dollar mining projects such as Las Bambas could hinder negotiations and trigger conflict. While this remains the case, the use of violence by indigenous protestors and the state—often observed in Peru's mining industry—is unlikely to decrease.

The anti-mining movement in San Luis Potosí, Mexico

Cerro San Pedro is a municipality located in the state of San Luis Potosí in North Central Mexico. In 2007, a social movement emerged in the capital city of San Luis Potosí to prohibit the implementation of mining activities within Cerro San Pedro. The anti-mining movement used the historical value of this municipality along with environmental causes to oppose to the mining company San Xavier seeking to operate in Cerro San Pedro. Protestors drew broad support from national and international civil society organizations. Yet, after several years of social and legal action undertaken to compel the state to withdraw the mining project, extraction moved forward.

The population of Cerro San Pedro totals 3,404; however, less than 100 people actually live in this municipality (Peña and Herrera 2008:129). Indigenous roots from the Guachichil ethnic group are found in Cerro San Pedro; however, locals neither ascribe to an indigenous identity nor do they speak an indigenous language. The population is politically organized into a municipal council, headed by a president, elected every three years through the state election rules. There is a second type of political organization based on the property of *Ejido* lands, comprised of an *Ejido* board (*Junta Ejidal*), in charge of solving land-related affairs. However, this form of organization is not salient in Cerro San Pedro in comparison with other parts of Mexico, as a land-based economy never developed (Gamez 2008).

Owners of *Ejido* communal lands do not live in Cerro San Pedro, and although they keep the formal property of lands, they only come to this municipality for recreational purposes (to spend the weekends and visit friends). The families residing in this municipality practice subsistence agriculture, cattle rising and the small-scale extraction of gold. These activities, however, are supplement of incomes produced by employment sources generally found outside the municipality.

Historically, Cerro San Pedro was a mining center. This locality was discovered by Spanish colonizers at the end of the 16th century, and since then, the mining industry was the main source of employment for locals and foreigners. Unionization was the prevailing form of political organization until 1948 when the American Smelting and Refinery Company (ASARCO) closed operations and the majority of the population abandoned Cerro San Pedro in search of jobs. Some people migrated to the United States, whereas a big portion of ex-miners found employment in the city of San Luis Potosí, only 45 minutes away from Cerro San Pedro. The social fabric in this municipality was torn apart, and the city was reduced to a "ghost village" only inhabited by a handful of families (Peña and Herrera 2008). From the 1950s to the 1990s, local families saw several mining companies attempting to resume operations in Cerro San Pedro; however, after exploring the area, those companies usually found that existing mineral deposits were not economically viable (Gamez 2008).

The environmental movement against mining in San Luis Potosí

In 1995, the mining company San Xavier, owned by the Canadian company New Gold, initiated exploration activities in Cerro San Pedro. Through the use of the open-pit exploitation technique, the company predicted to extract 1.2 million ounces of gold and 47 million ounces of silver. For security purposes, the use of this extraction method required the company to move the whole town to a different location as well as to demolish some of the 16th-century historical buildings. This announcement preoccupied a sector of civil society in San Luis Potosí.

The environmentalist organization Pro-Ecological San Luis Potosí (*Pro-San Luis Ecológico*) was the first to demonstrate opposition to mining activities. Pro-Ecological San Luis questioned the validity of the environmental impact report presented by San Xavier and demanded independent scientific studies. A second organization, dubbed the Board for the Defense of Cerro San Pedro (*Patronato Pro Defensa de Cerro San Pedro*), also opposed the mining project. This organization was comprised of *Ejido* owners and other members of Cerro San Pedro that no longer lived in the area but were frequent visitors of the municipality. In 1997, pro-ecological San Luis and the Board for the defense of Cerro San Pedro used legal resources to demonstrate the historical value of the municipality that would make mining operations unviable (Peña and Herrera 2008:175).

Yet San Xavier had already reached an agreement with the residents of Cerro San Pedro over the use of *Ejido* lands. These lands, although they were not legally owned by the residents, were used by local families with the permission of *Ejido* owners (living in San Luis Potosí). The families living in Cerro San Pedro immediately accepted the mining project as it represented a source of employment within their hometown. In addition to job opportunities, the company offered these families a new town with modern infrastructure and better living conditions. For this sector living off subsistence activities, there was not much to defend from the mining industry (Francisco Peña, personal communication, February 13, 2015).

A legal battle began between *Ejido* owners and San Xavier over the validity of the agreements reached with local families. The then-municipal president of Cerro San Pedro, Baltazar Loredo, supported anti-mining groups and refused to give San Xavier the municipal permission to operate. Loredo was found dead in March of 1998, and although the police said he had committed suicide, the events behind his death remained unclear (Peña and Herrera 2008:176). The local press associated the strange conditions in Loredo's death with his anti-mining stance, which contributed to increase protests against San Xavier.

A coalition dubbed the Broad Opposition Front (*Frente Amplio Opositor*), or FAO was formed to prevent San Xavier from operating in Cerro San Pedro. FAO drew support from important international organizations such as UNESCO, Greenpeace, Canadian anti-mining activists, Mexican intellectuals, local artists and university students. FAO activists undertook a series of protest events in the streets of San Luis Potosí and in front of the Embassy of Canada, demanding the cancellation of the mining project. Peaceful forms of protest such as festivals and forums were also held to raise environmental awareness in the population of San Luis Potosí. However, when environmental activists attempted to access the mine with the aim of distributing flyers that advocated for the suspension of the project, they were violently repelled by company employees. Tensions between anti-mining and pro-mining sectors increased after this event.

In a visit to San Luis Potosí in 2004, then-president Vicente Fox expressed his support to the San Xavier project. Fox suggested that municipal authorities in Cerro San Pedro should authorize mining operations as these represented ecologically responsible foreign investment and job opportunities for the people (Peña and Herrera 2008). Finally in 2006, the Secretary of Environment and Natural Resources (*Secretaría de Medio Ambiente y Recursos Naturales*), or SEMARNAT, authorized the Canadian company to operate. SEMARNAT argued that San Xavier had addressed the environmental concerns raised by FAO members, demonstrating its legal qualification to operate. Over the following years, FAO continued to mobilize and remained active in filing complaints over ecological damage produced by mining operations. Yet this did not affect the viability of the project as residents of Cerro San Pedro remained the strongest supporters of the mining company. A local woman and employee of the mine encountered during a visit made to this municipality; when asked until when the mine would operate she responded: "hopefully for several more years" (Resident of Cerro San Pedro and mining employee, personal communication, February 10, 2014).

Prior consultation was neither offered by the government nor demanded by FAO. Opposition to San Xavier was not grounded in indigenous rights; it emerged in urban centers and was based on the destruction of historical monuments and potential environmental risks. More importantly, FAO was not representative of the residents of Cerro San Pedro who were in favor of the mining project. In 2015, after ten years of operations, San Xavier announced the abandonment of Cerro San Pedro arguing that the production of silver and gold had decreased along with mineral prices (Visión Industrial 2014). Amid accusations of environmental degradation by FAO, San Xavier committed to comply with environmental legislation in the closing of the mine, and to responsibly conclude labor contracts with local employees (La Jornada 2014).

The case of Cerro San Pedro shows the inability of environmental movements to gain support from local communities that are directly impacted by extractive projects. While mobilization resources were available for FAO, the absence of supportive political structure in Cerro San Pedro undermined the legitimacy of the anti-mining movement. Pro-mining families, on the other hand, did not negotiate with the company over the distribution of extractive resources and complied with the terms agreed between San Xavier and the Mexican government (Table 4.1).

Table 4.1 Type of Indigenous Group, Indigenous Mobilization Capacities and Outcomes

Case Study	*Type of Indigenous Group*	*Political Power*	*Prior Consultation*	*Outcome*
Challapata	Anti-extractivist (viable economy threatened by mining)	High mobilization capacity (representative Irrigators Association)	No	Suspension of mining project
Chetilla	Anti-extractivist (viable economy threatened by mining)	High mobilization capacity (representative community-based organizations)	No	Suspension of mining project
Capulálpam de Méndez	Anti-extractivist (viable economy threatened by mining).	High mobilization capacity (representative Usos y Costumbres municipal authorities)	No n	Suspension of mining project
Mallku Khota	Pro-extractivist (subsistence agro-mining)	High mobilization capacity (representative ayllu-centered political organization)	No	Cancellation of mining project
Chucuito	Pro-extractivist (viable economy not threatened by mining)	High mobilization capacity (representative municipal Aymara authorities)	No	Cancellation of mining project
Corocoro	Pro-extractivist (subsisting agro-mining economy)	Low mobilization capacity (unrepresentative ayllu-centered political organization)	No	Extraction
Cotabambas and Grau	Pro-extractivist (subsistence agro-mining economy)	Low mobilization capacity (unrepresentative municipal authorities)	No	Extraction
Cerro San Pedro	Pro-extractivist (viable economy not threatened by mining)	Low mobilization capacity (unrepresentative ecological organizations)	No	Extraction

Source: Author's elaboration.

Comparative analysis of cases

Chapter 2 indicated that national variables such as national political influence of indigenous movements (NIIM), the legal scope of the right to prior consultation (SPC) and the political ideology of the government (GI) do not account for variation in indigenous outcomes over the extractive industry. Chapter 1 indicated that the type of indigenous organization—mediated by NGO resources or created from bottom-up processes—is not the best predictor of indigenous outcomes over the extractive industry. The truth table (Table 4.2) shows all logically possible combinations of the aforementioned variables including indigenous political power (IPP) and prior consultation procedures (PCP), the two variables specified in this dissertation as conditions explaining indigenous outcomes over the extractive industry.

The cases presented in this chapter demonstrate that similar indigenous outcomes over the implementation of extractive projects are found across countries in spite of variation in the national variables indicated earlier. Likewise, the cases in this study exhibit wide variation in types of indigenous organizations. Hence, these variables do not appear to account for case results either. As has been demonstrated throughout this book, variation in IPP, combined with non-enforcement PCP, is what leads to different indigenous outcomes over extractive projects.

Table 4.2 Table B

Cases	*IPP*	*PC*	*NIIM*	*SPC*	*GI*	*TIO*	*SP*	*Outcome*
6	High	No	S	P	P	No	S	No extraction
7	High	No	W	M	R	No	S	No extraction
8	High	No	M	C	M	Yes	S	No extraction
9	Low	No	M	C	P	Yes	S	Extraction
10	Low	No	W	M	C	No	L	Extraction
11	Low	No	M	C	M	No	S	Extraction

IPP = Indigenous political power
High, Low
PCP = Enforcement of prior consultation procedure
Yes, No
NIIM = National Political Influence of Indigenous Movements
Strong (S), Moderate (M), Weak (W)
SPC = Scope of prior consultation
Progressive (P), Moderate (M), Conservative (C)
GI = Government ideology
Progressive (P), Moderate (M), Conservative (C)
TIO = Type of indigenous organization
NGO founded (N), Bottom-up organizing (B)
Yes, No
SP = Size of the population
Smaller than 30,000 (S), Larger than 30,000 (L)
Source: Author's elaboration.

An additional variable that varies widely across cases, yet does not lead to different levels of political power, is the size of the indigenous population (SP). The indigenous populations examined in this chapter range in size from 3,000 to 150,000 people; nevertheless, size was not determinant for the levels of political power found in each case.

Is political power the only thing that matters?

The cases presented in this chapter demonstrate that only politically powerful indigenous groups prohibited mining projects, whereas the weakest groups complied with extraction without negotiating compensation in exchange. A precondition of indigenous political power is having representative political organizations at the local level that can sustain several cycles of protest. In Challapata, the credibility of the Irrigators Association enabled them to successfully articulate a defensive discourse and mobilize support of broader indigenous groups finally achieving suspension of the mining project. In Chetilla, the effectiveness of the Community Assembly and the *Rondas Campesinas* in the areas of resource management and punishment of crime, enabled community leaders to successfully mobilize the population against the expansion of mining activities. In Capulálpam de Méndez, *Usos y Costumbres* municipal authorities reflect the legal choice of the population to elect their authorities through customary norms over the state election rules. The high levels of accountability between indigenous citizens and these authorities allowed the latter to mobilize support of the residents of Capulálpam de Méndez and suspend mining activities.

Unlike the cases of powerful indigenous communities discussed in the previous chapter, here indigenous groups saw mining projects as a threat to their local economies. Interestingly, yet unsurprisingly, the fact that prior consultation was not offered in these cases was not a detriment for indigenous banning of mineral extraction. Considering that one potential effect of prior consultation procedures is advancing division within indigenous communities, non-enforcement of this right might have enabled indigenous leaders to overcome dissention and maintain political unity. Thus, indigenous political power is a key element for preventing mining operations in indigenous territories. Still, spaces such as prior consultation where external actors could advance splits in the indigenous leadership must be precluded.

The second part of this chapter examined cases of pro-extractivist indigenous groups that complied with extraction but without negotiating significant economic benefits for their communities. NGO involvement was observed in all these cases; however, weak political organizations at the local level prevented the achievement of the movement's goals in each case. Anti-mining movements lacked representative political organizations at the local level capable of sustaining several cycles of protest or engaging in negotiations with the state or the extractivists. Moreover, the bulk of the population in Corocoro (Bolivia), Cotabambas and Grau (Peru), and Cerro San Pedro (Mexico) wanted mining projects to be implemented. The groups that wanted to negotiate the terms of extraction in the first two cases or to prohibit mining projects in the last case did not represent the interests of local communities.

The results obtained by these three groups are rather similar to those obtained by politically weak communities participating in prior consultation examined in Chapter 3. Political demobilization prevented all these communities from negotiating economic resources with the state. Yet prior consultation offered the consulted groups information about the projects that would be carried out in their lands. Governments generally announce the realization of prior consultation procedures in the websites of the state agencies in charge of undertaking consultations. These procedures usually attract NGOs attention who often participate in prior consultation meetings to guarantee that the information provided is reliable and that indigenous rights are respected. Without prior consultation, politically weak indigenous groups are more vulnerable to misinformation regarding extractive operations.

Conclusion

This chapter demonstrates that politically powerful anti-extractivist indigenous groups operating in the absence of prior consultation are generally able to prohibit extractive operations on their lands. Successful indigenous resistance in Challapata (Bolivia), Chetilla (Peru) and Capulálpam de Méndez (Mexico) did not demonstrate a willingness to negotiate extraction; their objective was to ban mining companies in order to secure their current economies. Previous chapters presented evidence of all the prior consultation procedures that have been conducted in Bolivia, Peru and Mexico over the extractive industry as of the writing of this book. In all these cases, governments obtained indigenous approval, with or without granting economic compensation for the consulted population. Moreover, indigenous division and intracommunity violence have followed indigenous participation in these procedures. Overall, evidence suggests that prior consultation if applied would have been a detriment for anti-extractivist goals.

On the other hand, the denial of prior consultation in the cases of politically weak indigenous organizations in Corocoro (Bolivia), Cotabambas and Grau (Peru), and Cerro San Pedro (Mexico) was prejudicial to the rights of these groups. Prior consultations may not have delivered negotiated economic compensation, given the organizational weakness of the local population (see Chapter 3). Such procedures, in turn, could have enabled a better informed community consent of the project.

References

Alanes, Victor, and German Condarco. 2005. *Challapata la Hermosa*. Oruro: Centro de Ecologia y Pueblos Andinos (CEPA).

ANAA. 2011. Asamblea Nacional de Afectados Ambientales. Available at: www.afectadosambientales.org/no-a-la-mineria-en-Capulálpam-de-Méndez-oaxaca/ (Accessed May 12 2015).

Aquino, Salvador. 2011. La lucha por el control del territorio en Capulálpam. Diferentes maneras acerca de la comprensión del subsuelo, el oro, la plata, la ley y el capital. Available at: www.encuentroredtoschiapas.jkopkutik.org/BIBLIOGRAFIA/MOVIMIENTOS_POLITICA_CULTURA_Y_PODER/La_lucha_por_el_control_territorio.pdf (Accessed January 4 2015).

Asociación para el Desarrollo Rural de Cajamarca. 2004. Diagnóstico Participativo del Páramo Jalca de Jamcate – Chetilla. Available at: www.paramo.org/files/recursos/Diagnostico_sitio_Jamcate___Cajamarca.pdf (Accessed July 28 2016).

Arellano-Yanguas, Javier. 2011. *¿Minería sin fronteras? Conflicto y desarrollo en regiones mineras del Perú*. Lima: IEP.

Bray, David, and Leticia Merino. 2004. *Las experiencias de las comunidades forestales en México: Veinticinco años de silvicultura y construcción de empresas forestales comunitarias*. México: National Institute of Ecology.

CEPA. 2011. Un No Contundente a la Minería. Available at: http://cepaoruro.org/index.php?option=com_content&view=article&id=721:un-no-contundente-a-la-mineria-en-challapata-derechos-de-los-pueblos-indigenas-25-08-11&catid=21:problemas-y-conflictos-socioambientales&Itemid=47 (Accessed December 1 2015).

Duran, Mario. 2017. Congreso Minero en Corocoro. Available at: https://corocoro-la-paz-bolivia.blogspot.mx/2017/10/congreso-minero-en-corocoro.html (Accessed March 3 2018).

Eabolivia.com. 2014. Empresa Minera Corocoro logra $us 11,2 MM de utilidad, November 5 2014. Available at: www.eabolivia.com/economia/20736-empresa-minera-corocoro-logra-us-112-mm-de-utilidad.html (Accessed February 3 2017).

Eisenstadt, Todd, and Karleen West. 2017. Public Opinion, Vulnerability, and Living with Extraction on Ecuador's Oil Frontier: Where the Debate Between Development and Environmentalism Gets Personal. *Comparative Politics* 49(2): 231–251.

Eju. 2009. Comibol retorna a Corocoro y la explotará a "cielo abierto, October 28 2009. Available at: http://eju.tv/2009/10/cobre-comibol-retorna-a-corocoro-y-la-explotar-a-cielo-abierto/ (Accessed June 2 2017).

Eju. 2012. Lidema: Explotación cuprífera deja sin agua a población de Corocoro, May 23. Available at: http://eju.tv/2012/05/lidema-explotacin-cuprfera-deja-sin-agua-a-poblacin-de-coro-coro/

El Comercio. 2016. "Prorrogan por décima vez intervención de FF.AA en Apurímac," September 7. Available at: http://elcomercio.pe/sociedad/Apurímac/prorrogan-decima-vez-intervencionffaacotabambasnoticia1929830?ref=flujo_tags_184863&ft=nota_1&e=imagen (Accessed July 3 2017).

El Diario. 2009. "Corocoro espera que se cumplan las promesas," January 14. Available at: www.eldiario.net/noticias/2009/2009_01/nt090114/5_20nal.php (Accessed June 4 2017).

El Economista. 2010. "Grupo suizo Xstrata invertirá USD 4.200 millones en proyecto minero en Perú," August 4. Available at: www.eleconomista.net/noticias/119263-

grupo-suizo-xstrata-invertira-usd-4200-millones-en-proyecto-minero-en-peru-html (Accessed September 24 2017).

Enlace, Mineria. 2014. Wild Acre Posterga Proyecto Peruano Colpayoc. Available at: http://enlacemineria.blogspot.com/2014/12/wild-acre-posterga-proyecto-peruano.htm (Accessed October 3 2017).

Environmental Justice Atlas. n.d. Database of Environmental Conflicts. Available at: https://ejatlas.org/conflict/Capulálpam-de-Méndez-contra-natividad-oaxaca (Accessed June 6 2018).

Gamez, Moisés. 2008. Internacionalización económica, historia y conflicto ambiental en la minería: el caso de Minera San Xavier. San Luis Potosí: Colegio de San Luis Potosí.

Gestión. 2012. Xstrata ha ejecutado más de US$ 50 millones del fondo social de Las Bambas, July 19. Available at: https://gestion.pe/economia/empresas/xstrata-ejecutado-us-50-millones-fondo-social-bambas-16005 (Accessed April 15 2017).

La Jornada. 2013. Capulálpam de Méndez contra la explotacion minera. Available at: www.jornada.unam.mx/2011/05/05/opinion/024a1pol (Accessed April 7 2017).

La Jornada. 2014. Deja Mineral San Xavier un daño irreversible en San Luis Potosi. Available at: www.jornada.unam.mx/2014/04/15/sociedad/033n1soc (Accessed May 23 2017).

La Patria. 2009. Campesinos anuncian bloqueos y marchas contra la hidrometalúrgica de Corocoro, November 1. Available at: https://lapatriaenlinea.com/?t=campesinos-anuncian-bloqueos-y-marchas-contra-la-hidrometalurgica-de-corocoro&nota=6782 (Accessed May 22 2016).

La Patria. 2009. FSTM Apoya Reapertura de Centros Mineros por Gobierno. Available at: http://lapatriaenlinea.com/?t=fstmb-apoya-a-reapertura-de-centros-mineros-por-gobierno&nota=7683 (Accessed July 13 2017).

La Patria. 2011. Corocoro recupera su condicion de capital cuprifera de Bolivia. Available at: http://lapatriaenlinea.com/?nota=65324 (Accessed October 16 2017).

La Rotativa. 2013. Chetilla celebró 13 años de la construcción de su hidroeléctrica, Available at: http://larotativa.pe/chetilla-celebro-13-anos-de-la-construccion-de-su-hidroelectrica/ (Accessed October 10 2017).

Lazcano, Miguel. 2012. El yacimiento descubierto por Kores vale $us 8.000 MM. La Razón, June 25. Available at: www.la-Razón.com/economia/yacimiento-descubierto-Kores-vale-MM_0_1638436198.html (Accessed November 10 2017).

Madrid, Emilio et al. 2012. Corocoro and Challapata: Defending Collective Rights and Mother Earth against Development Mining Fetishism. *Environmental Justice* 5(2): 65–69.

Madrid, Emilio. 2014. "Challapata: Resistencia communal a la desposesion de la mineria" In Thomas Perreault (Ed.) *Mineria, Agua y Justicia Social en los Andes*. La Paz: PIEB, 81–99.

Mineria de Bolivia. 2009. Gobierno firmó acuerdo con dos comunidades de Corocoro, November 28. Available at: http://boliviaminera.blogspot.mx/2009/11/gobierno-firmo-acuerdo-con-dos.html (Accessed July 17 2016).

Ministry of Health of Peru. 2005. *Análisis de la Situación de Perú en Apurímac*. Available at: www.bvsde.paho.org/documentosdigitales/bvsde/texcom/ASIS-regiones/Apurímac/Apurímac2005.pdf (Accessed August 7 2017).

Moreno, Gustavo. 2014. *Minería Conflicto Social y Dialogo*. Lima: Pro Dialogo.

Movement M4. 2012. Oaxaca: Autoridades zapotecas exigen cancelar concesion. Available at: http://movimientom4.org/2012/04/oaxaca-autoridades-zapotecas-exigen-cancelar-concesion-a-minera/ (Accessed May 2 2017).

Municipal council of Sustainable rural development. 2009. Plan de Desarrollo Municipal de Capulálpam de Méndez. Available at www.finanzasoaxaca.gob.mx/pdf/inversion_publica/pmds/08_10/247.pdf.National Census of Bolivia. 2012. Bolivia, características de población y vivienda. Available at: www.ine.gob.bo:8081/censo2012/PDF/resultadosCPV2012.pdf (Accessed April 09 2018).

National Institute of Statistics of Peru 2014. 6.3 Departamento Cajamarca: Población Total Proyectada y Ubicación. Available at: https://webcache.googleusercontent.com/search?q=cache:XfhQSHuw7ZAJ:https://www.inei.gob.pe/media/MenuRecursivo/publicaciones_digitales/Est/Lib1159/cuadros/cajamar/cajamar_6_3.xls+&cd=2&hl=es&ct=clnk&gl=mx (Accessed June 7 2018). National Institute of Ecology. 2007. La Comunidad de Capulálpam de Méndez. Available at: www2.inecc.gob.mx/publicaciones/libros/431/cap7.html (Accessed April 09 2018).

Observatory of Mining Conflicts in Latin America. n.d. Mining Conflicts in Latin America. Available at: www.conflictosmineros.net/ (Accessed May 09 2018).

Peña, Francisco, and Ednita Herrera. 2008. *Internacionalización económica, historia y conflicto ambiental en la minería: el caso de Minera San Xavier.* San Luis Potosí: Colegio de San Luis Potosí.

Pérez, Mario Alejandro, Julieth Vargas Morales and Zulma Crespo-Marín. 2018. Trends in Social Metabolism and Environmental Conflicts in Four Andean Countries from 1970 to 2013. *Sustainability Science* 13(3): 635–664.

Ramirez, Erika. 2013. Pueblo Mágico Amenazado por la Minería. Available at: www.contralinea.com.mx/archivo-revista/index.php/2013/06/18/pueblo-magico-amenazado-por-minera/ (Accessed September 09 2017).

Regional Government of Cajamarca.2013. Chetilla se desarrollará con turismo y agro. Available at http://www.regioncajamarca.gob.pe/noticias/chetilla-se-desarrollar-con-turismo-y-agro (Accessed June 7 2018).

Ribera, Octavio. 2013. *Estudio de Caso sobre Problemáticas Socio Ambientales en Bolivia.* La Paz: Lidema.

Segovia, Elías. 2013. "Visión regional de la conflictividad social asociada a actividades extractivas: El caso de Apurímac" In *Buscando salidas a la conflictividad social.* Lima: Desco. Available at: www.desco.org.pe/recursos/site/files/1021/international_alert.pdf (Accessed April 09 2018).

Servindi 2012. El idioma oficial en Apurímac y las Políticas Públicas. Available at: www.servindi.org/actualidad/23978 (Accessed April 19 2017).

Vargas, Miguel. 2010. *Lecciones Aprendidas sobre la Consulta Previa.* La Paz: CEJIS.

Visión Industrial. 2014. Minera San Xavier anuncia cierre definitivo en cerro San Pedro, SLP. Available at www.visionindustrial.com.mx/industria/noticias/minera-san-xavier-anuncia-cierre-definitivo-en-cerro-san-pedro-slp (Accessed Jun 6 2018).

Yashar, Deborah. 2005. *Contesting Citizenship in Latin America. The Rise of Indigenous Movements and the Postliberal Challenge.* New York: Cambridge University Press.

Chapter 5

Prior consultation and the expansion of extractivism in Latin America

Introduction

Today, the extraction of minerals and hydrocarbons is one of the main sources of political violence in Latin America. In the 1990s, the extractive industry sector was privatized to overcome the economic crises spurred by import substitution industrialization policies and the nationalization of the extractive industry made in former decades (Bebbington and Bury 2013). From the 2000s onward, indigenous peoples living nearby extraction sites have suffered the negative environmental and social impacts caused by the presence of foreign extractive companies (Slack 2009). Redistribution of extractive resources did not reach indigenous areas as rapidly as it reached Latin America's main urban centers (Arellano-Yanguas 2011).

Before prior consultation procedures were implemented, extractive projects were generally advanced without the consent of local communities. International pressure placed on extractive companies in the mid-1990s forced these companies to reach a deal with local people. Economic compensation to local communities was paid for the use of their lands for extractive purposes (Salas 2008; Arellano-Yanguas 2011). During this period, the asymmetry in power relationships between indigenous actors and multinational companies prompted accusations over low prices set by mining and hydrocarbon companies to be paid to disadvantaged indigenous communities (Salas 2008; Arellano-Yanguas 2011). Civil society organizations and international agencies encouraged states to play a more active role in the extractive industry with the understanding that state agencies were in the position to act on behalf of indigenous citizens (United Nations Declaration on the Rights of Indigenous Peoples 2007). Increasing conflicts and violence between indigenous populations and multinational companies over the control of valuable resources lying within community lands forced some governments to implement ILO Convention 169 along with prior consultation procedures with indigenous peoples.

Prior consultation was the formula developed by international human rights organizations to secure indigenous territories from unwanted impacts.

During the mid-2000s, after more than a decade of remaining ignored, some countries began to conduct prior consultation procedures. The previous chapters analyzed whether or not, and how, the implementation of the right to prior consultation in three Latin American countries during the past decade has contributed to the protection of indigenous territories from ecologically unsustainable industries.

The outcomes of prior consultation examined throughout the book suggest that ecological risks for indigenous territories are higher now that prior consultation procedures are undertaken. In turn, economic opportunities are available for some of the indigenous groups who approve extractive projects; however, internal division usually deepens after economic agreements take place. Finally, a possible solution for how prior consultation procedures could serve the best interest of indigenous peoples is offered.

The contradictions of prior consultation procedures

In recent years, Latin American governments began passing prior consultation legislation with the aim of pacifying conflicts surrounding indigenous territories. The extent to which indigenous voice was to be taken into account in policies impacting their lands, however, was ill-defined by ILO Convention 169. Thereby, states have been able to use their discretionary power to limit indigenous participation and soothe the effects of prior consultations.

The importance of the extractive industry in the region had already led some scholars to doubt the capacity of Latin American states to act autonomously in the realization of the right to prior consultation (Valdivia 2008; Gudynas 2009; Perreault 2013). During the 1990s, foreign investment in Latin American mining and hydrocarbon industries totaled 140 billion dollars (Bebbington and Bury 2013:44). Despite a fall in the prices of minerals and oil in the last years, a sizeable percentage of Latin American exports are still made up of these resources.

Giving veto power to indigenous communities over consulted extractive projects was seen by many state officials as detrimental to the state's capacity to manage mineral and hydrocarbon reserves for the public good (Ñiquen 2015). Most countries in Latin America legalized prior consultation procedures with indigenous communities as mandated by ILO Convention 169, but left final decisions regarding implementation of projects to the central government. In this regard, some scholars argued that prior consultations were used to validate extractive policies, as opposed to create a space for meaningful indigenous participation in state policies affecting their territories (Falleti and Riofrancos 2018; Flemmer and Schilling-Vacaflor 2015). This book provides evidence from three Latin American countries supporting these positions. Nonetheless, findings also show that some indigenous communities utilize prior consultation as a bargaining chip to obtain extractive resources.

To test the hypothesis that the economic significance of the extractive industry conditions prior consultation implementation in Latin America, this study examined Bolivia, Peru and Mexico. These three countries have sizeable indigenous populations in their territories, and at the same time, extractive industries are central to their economies. However, the selected countries vary with respect to the national influence of indigenous movements, the scope of the right to prior consultation, and government ideology, all of which are variables that the literature on social movements highlights as defining of political change and social transformation (Cohen and Arato 1992; Yashar 2005; Van Cott 2008; Lucero 2009). Despite these differences, Chapter 2 demonstrates that the results of prior consultation across countries were rather similar; in fact, in none of the cases examined in this book was a prior consultation held with the result that extractive industries were banned in the area in question after the consultation ended.

Indeed, all prior consultation procedures completed in Bolivia, Peru and Mexico have resulted in indigenous approval of extractive projects. Most of prior consultations in Peru and Mexico have been implemented in response to proposed hydrocarbon projects, whereas high levels of non-enforcement have been present in the mining industry of both countries. This study found that two factors related to the economic importance of the extractive industry explain the aforementioned prior consultation results. First, the majority of indigenous groups do not oppose extractive industries. For many such groups, as well as the state, the economic activity resulting from extractive projects represents a source of income. As such, conflict over mining and hydrocarbon projects is strategically used by indigenous leaders to negotiate economic gains for their communities (Arellano-Yanguas 2011; Arce 2014). This conflicts with the image of indigenous peoples in the environmental discourse of civil society organizations and international agencies, who often refer to indigenous populations as guardians of nature. As evidenced in Chapters 3 and 4, most indigenous groups today are currently unable to cover their basic needs through subsistence economies. For this reason, it is likely that most of these groups will choose profit over environmental protection when offered a stake in extractive projects.

The second factor conditioning prior consultation outcomes is the use of weak institutions by Latin American governments to avoid rejection from indigenous groups unwilling to accept extractive projects. Scholarly work shows that *de facto* discretionary power allows states to forgo enforcement or selectively enforce rights according to the interest they hold over the matters at stake (O'Donnell 1993; Levitsky and Murillo 2013; Amengual 2016). As evidenced here, many indigenous groups are pro-extractivist and are likely to comply with extraction after prior consultation is conducted. On the other hand, it is uncommon for anti-extractivist indigenous movements to participate in prior consultation procedures. This might be related to state non-enforcement of consultations in cases where indigenous approval of projects is not foreseeable. The fact that few or none of prior consultations have been applied in the mining industry of Peru and Mexico supports this argument. Whereas mining conflicts in Bolivia are not salient, Peru and Mexico are the two countries with more conflicts over mining projects (Observatory of Mining Conflicts in Latin America n.d.). One possible explanation for this is that the visible opposition that large-scale mining projects generate creates incentives for government to contravene ILO Convention 169 by skipping over consultation procedures in this industry.

Mining operations in Latin America have been primarily in hands of private companies since the 1990s. Foreign investment in this industry was followed by the introduction of new extractive techniques. Open-pit mining and cyanide "heap leaching," used in gold mining, spread across the region (Bebbington and Bury 2013:45). A characteristic of these new exploitation methods is that they do not require as much indigenous labor as do older mining techniques (Perreault 2014). Along with the lack of job opportunities for indigenous populations, more serious environmental impacts associated with open-pit mining prompted contentious stances by indigenous communities against modern mining operations (Slack 2009; Perreault 2014). Powerful anti-mining coalitions have emerged in various countries grounded in radical ecological mobilization. Social opposition to mining activities has frequently led to the suspension or cancellation of billion-dollar mining projects upon protestors' use of environmental discourses.

Although previous research shows that most indigenous movements actually pursue a fairer distribution of economic resources (Arellano-Yanguas 2011), Chapter 4 showed that in some cases, indigenous communities maintain anti-mining stances. This happens because these groups perceive that the damages that mining activities would cause to ongoing indigenous systems would be greater than potential benefits. Yet widespread environmental framing of mining conflicts makes it difficult to distinguish between anti-extractivist and pro-extractivists groups. Hence, Latin American governments' interests in avoiding delays in the allocation of mineral reserves might contribute to understand the absence of prior consultation in this sector.

Latin American states, however, have enforced prior consultations in the hydrocarbon industry and have been capable of reaching indigenous approval in each case. Traditionally, this industry has not engendered salient social opposition. The hydrocarbon industry is generally under the control of state-owned companies. The "resource nationalism" that emerged in the aftermath of the several waves of state nationalization of this industry in the 1930s, 1970s and 2000s in Latin America discouraged social mobilization over hydrocarbon extraction (Perreault 2013). It is for this reason that conflicts over hydrocarbon-related operations have mostly centered upon allocation of resources, while environmentally centered discourses have been less common. This partly explains why indigenous communities systematically approve hydrocarbon projects. In places such as the Amazon and El Chaco, indigenous compliance with oil and gas extraction observed in recent years starkly contrasts with the discourse used by indigenous movements when they mobilized over ILO Convention 169 in the early 2000s. In discourse, these earlier protestors demanded prior consultation to protect the environment and preserve ecologically harmonious indigenous livelihood. Once prior consultation procedures were offered, however, they did not result in indigenous rejection of extractive activities. Instead, it served as a bargaining chip with the potential to deliver significant economic resources for some indigenous communities.

Another similarity found in Bolivia, Peru and Mexico regarding prior consultation is that state agencies selected to conduct these procedures are those in charge of the extractive industry sector. Chapter 3 showed that in Peru, Perupetro's main function is to allocate hydrocarbon concessions to the most qualified oil companies. Simultaneously, this agency initiated consultations with indigenous populations about whether or not they want hydrocarbon projects to move forward. In Bolivia, the state oil company YPFB, in charge of hydrocarbon exploitation, is also in charge of consulting with indigenous groups. In Mexico, SENER is in charge of approving energy-based projects in the country while also conducting consultations with the indigenous. In each case, the playing field is stilted to the extractive industry rather than to the citizens whose approval is sought for extraction to proceed.

For governments, having this type of agencies conducting prior consultation might make sense in terms of functionality, as these agencies are familiar with extractive operations and with the places and populations living where these activities take place. However, considering that governments seek indigenous authorization for extractive projects, these agencies are likely to be biased in favor of extractive projects, and they can hardly be perceived as neutral by the consulted population. In other words, prior consultations should be moved from energy ministries to ministries or other agencies charged with defending the rights of citizens, specifically of indigenous peoples.

Finally, while this study demonstrated that governments are influenced by the economic interests created regarding extractive industries, findings also indicate that the state apparatus is not homogeneous. Anti-extractivist movements frequently gain support of some state agencies in spite of the pro-extractivist agenda held by the central/federal government. As illustrated by the cases presented in Chapter 4, state actors such as the governor of Oruro, the municipal mayor of Chetilla, local deputies in Oaxaca, and environmental state agencies such as Mexico's Profepa, supported anti-mining struggles in Bolivia, Peru and Mexico. In all these cases, the legal and political mobilization that generally accompanies social protests prompted the involvement of state officials contributing to validating indigenous anti-mining stances and the advancement of anti-mining goals. This demonstrates that although the economic importance of extractive industries conditions Latin American governments to privilege the implementation of extractive projects, there are parts of the state that can act independently (Bebbington and Bury 2013). Contradictions like these within the state apparatus can sometimes contribute to the realization of citizens' interests.

The opportunities created by prior consultation

Turning into an examination of the ways prior consultation can provide resources for indigenous peoples, previous chapters showed that some of the groups participating in prior consultation procedures have used them to negotiate economic resources with the state. This might encourage positions in favor of prior consultations as long as impoverished indigenous groups are finally able to access resources for their own administration. However, the results examined in this book call for caution. First, not all indigenous groups obtain the same economic results. This book's findings suggest that political power is a precondition for the indigenous to be capable of negotiating economic compensation with the state. Findings discussed in Chapter 3 demonstrated that highly mobilized, politically skilled indigenous peoples in Bolivia, Peru and Mexico were capable of persuading state officials to comply with their demands in the understanding that delays or blocking of extractive projects could be advanced otherwise. In turn, demobilized indigenous groups did not negotiate economic resources using prior consultation and complied with extraction upon the sole expectation of jobs and economic growth. The cases also showed that indigenous political power was linked to the existence of representative indigenous organizations at the local level that were capable of directing negotiations, as well as mobilizing their bases to demonstrate power.

Prior consultations in Bolivia, Peru and Mexico highlight a key fact long-studied by social advocates and legal agencies, which is that the legalization of rights does not automatically entitle the realization of those rights in practice (Rosenberg 1991; Epp 1998). Political scientists studying institutions in Latin America have pointed out that institutional innovation aimed at broadening citizen participation does not automatically lead to political change. However, it can offer bargaining tables to central political actors (Eisenstadt 2003). The ability to manipulate these negotiations to one's benefit depends on the specific characteristics of each negotiator. In this study, most powerful indigenous groups were found to be those who have long-standing experience in negotiating with the state or extractive companies. Frequently, these groups have a history of success in this type of negotiation and are knowledgeable in the use of environmental discourse and mobilization tactics to advance their demands.

The fact that only some groups can access extractive resources, evidenced in Chapter 3, shows that redistribution of these resources is still uneven across indigenous communities. Most disadvantaged indigenous communities, often found in nontraditional sites of extraction and lacking representative political organizations, have not been able to use prior consultation to their economic benefit (Flemmer and Schilling-Vacaflor 2015). Chapters 3 and 4 evidenced that politically weak groups that were consulted by the state obtained poor economic results that were not unlike the outcomes of communities that were not consulted. Thus, prior consultation procedures—as implemented today in Latin America—have not been able to overcome the power asymmetry existing also between indigenous peoples. In turn, by paying compensation only to politically powerful indigenous actors, governments reinforce the economic and political exclusion suffered by the most disempowered indigenous groups.

Nonetheless, the findings of this study do suggest that with prior consultation, indigenous groups are more likely to be properly informed about the extractive process. The case studies in Chapter 3 show that prior consultation generally activates the participation of Non-governmental organizations (NGOs) but also state agencies in charge of protecting citizens' rights. In Peru, officials from the Ombudsman Office and the Ministry of Culture play an important role in ensuring that Perupetro follows the legal standards enacted by ILO Convention 169, such as transparency and respect of indigenous political institutions. In addition, these procedures are public, and the agreements reached between indigenous representatives and state officials are registered in legal acts that are then placed on government websites. Through this process, the state is more likely to provide reliable information and remain accountable to the commitments made during prior consultation in comparison with private negotiations held between indigenous communities and extractive companies. More importantly, indigenous organizations now have access to legal documents binding state agencies to oversee extractive operations.

These two conditions—reliable information and legal documents containing state commitments *vis-à-vis* the consulted group—could eventually enable new forms of indigenous organization and socio-legal mobilization. In this spirit, past research has shown that the regular use of legal procedures can create knowledge and resources among citizens that can then be used to manipulate the law in their favor (Galanter 1974). This is exemplified by the case of indigenous Maya communities in Mexico, where formerly demobilized indigenous peoples have recently organized around the implementation of prior consultation over the use of transgenic soy. This example demonstrates that indigenous mobilization capacities can increase over time and these procedures could serve to strengthen indigenous organizations *vis-à-vis* future negotiation with the state. Hence, the analysis of indigenous outcomes in Bolivia, Peru and Mexico showed that prior consultation procedures do not necessarily define the distribution of extractive resources. What prior consultation does do, however, is creating a space for politically powerful pro-extractivist indigenous and state negotiators to reach economic agreements and settle disputes. Despite this, the relationship between key stakeholders and valuable resources continues to be influenced by the political power of relevant actors.

On the other hand, findings demonstrate that prior consultation is not useful for achieving anti-extractivist goals. The inherent negotiation condition in these procedures forces anti-extractivist groups to pursue social mobilization and confrontation strategies in the same way that similar movements did before prior consultation was implemented. In this regard, few things have changed for anti-extractivist movements. Moreover, some of these groups reject prior consultation as they see it as a threat to the unity of the opposition. As evidenced in Chapter 2, part of the strategy of anti-mining movements is not to participate in any form of negotiation with the state or extractive companies, including prior consultation. Community rejection to prior consultation could then be another reason why we do not see this type of group participating in these procedures.

Politically powerful indigenous groups are generally able to block extractive projects within their lands by using typical mobilization strategies such as protests, marches and blockades of roads and access to extraction sites. As Chapter 4 shows, reliance on functioning deliberation and decision-making mechanisms allows representative indigenous leaders to successfully lead several cycles of anti-extractivist mobilization in the absence of prior consultation procedures.

In coherence with that, new forms of collective action emerging among some indigenous communities consist in rejecting to participate in prior consultation procedures. Conversely, these communities claim that they are in a position to conduct their own consultations in order to decide whether they want a project executed on their lands (Gouritin and Torres 2018). These *auto-consultas* or self-consultations intended to overcome the shortcomings of prior consultations are rapidly spreading in countries such as Mexico and Guatemala. Indigenous self-consultations represent no more than the strict exercise of indigenous autonomy as long demanded to the government. Hopefully, *auto-consultas* will be an opportunity for indigenous peoples and their NGO supporters to realize that real self-determination and the protection of indigenous territories will not be achieved through a law, but through actual execution of self-government mechanisms.

Despite the shortcomings of prior consultation procedures in deterring potentially destructive industries, there is at least one way that the recognition of the right to prior consultation in domestic legislations can be useful to protect indigenous territories. Governments' ratification of ILO Convention 169 has created legal conditions for indigenous peoples to take cases of unconsulted projects to courts. State non-enforcement of prior consultation procedures can sometimes enable indigenous communities to seek judicial intervention. In various occasions, Supreme Courts in countries such as Mexico, Peru and Colombia have ordered the suspension of diverse types of projects arguing that governments had not conducted proper prior consultation with indigenous communities. Although governments in Latin America do not always comply with courts' rulings, sometimes Supreme Court decisions can impede the furthering of projects that could have negative impacts on indigenous territories.

Overall, the outcomes of prior consultation procedures suggest that social protest continues to influence the control of natural resources, even though prior consultation legislation is now in place. In the context of weak institutions, the use of strategic mobilization by indigenous political organizations in tandem with prior consultation demonstrates that the use of conflict is still effective in persuading the government of distributing extractive resources (Arce 2014). To a certain extent, prior consultation has reinforced the use of mobilization strategies by awarding sizable compensation to the groups capable of using these strategies. On the other hand, anti-extractivist groups continue to use social mobilization and protest to defend their lands from unwanted projects.

Prior consultation and the realization of indigenous demands

The aim of prior consultation was to provide institutional channels for the participation of marginalized indigenous groups in state policies targeting their territories (Falleti and Riofrancos 2018, Flemmer and Schilling-Vacaflor 2015). On the books, the inclusion of indigenous voices through prior consultation procedures would contribute to further indigenous movements' territorial demands. For sectors concerned with economic distribution, prior consultation could be useful to partially achieve this goal as it can enable politically skilled indigenous groups to obtain economic compensation in exchange for allowing the use of their lands for extraction. Evidence shows, however, that deep division and internal violence usually follow economic agreements reached in prior consultations.

Moreover, the evidence presented in Chapter 3 suggests that resources coming from extraction might not be completely beneficial to indigenous peoples. While Latin American governments have been incapable of delivering development in ways that are satisfactory to indigenous communities, indigenous administration of extractive funds does not appear to have resulted in a substantial improvement of indigenous living conditions either (Humphreys-Bebbington 2012). State agencies often lack the capacity to identify the most urgent social needs across indigenous communities, whereas indigenous organizations usually lack the capacities of addressing the complexities of structural economic and political inequalities faced by indigenous peoples in their everyday life. It is unlikely that cash resources negotiated in prior consultations are sufficient to have a long-term effect on the quality of indigenous living conditions. Likewise, misuse of prior consultation economic resources to some indigenous leaders' personal benefit prevents those resources to be used for indigenous communities' development (Vidaurre 2016). Direct economic compensation to indigenous peoples can provide precarious political stability for extractive projects. However, as people perceive that extractive resources do not create visible improvement in their living conditions, social conflicts eventually reappear (Arellano-Yanguas 2011). Still, the possibility that direct economic compensation paid to indigenous organizations can improve indigenous peoples' life remains to be explored.

Even when there is not sufficient evidence that access to economic resources in exchange for extraction entails sustainable development for indigenous peoples, findings indicate that the advancement of indigenous movements' demands regarding the safeguard of their territories and culture is not an effect of prior consultations as implemented today. Indigenous peoples' enjoyment of all human rights including the right to freely pursue their economic, social and cultural development is severely restricted by the absence of economic models that can be alternatives to industrialized resource extraction. Furthermore, the ecological risks associated with extractive projects could potentially reduce important sources of water and food upon which several indigenous groups still depend on to survive. If indigenous communities trading their lands for economic resources are not capable of attaining sustainable development, there may not be a territory to come back once extraction is over and the money from prior consultation negotiations runs out. For this reason, many indigenous rights organizations and their international allies do not perceive that prior consultation is a mechanism to foster the realization of indigenous rights. In the eyes of many human rights organizations and environmental activists, governments use prior consultation to co-opt indigenous leaders and buy their support for extraction.

In addition, this book argues that the preservation of indigenous territories free from extractive companies—long advocated by a sector of the international NGO community—results from viable indigenous economies and representative political organizations, not from prior consultation procedures. In sum, the results of indigenous struggles in Bolivia, Peru and Mexico demonstrate that as long as indigenous communities remain in extreme poverty conditions, their voice will continue to go unheard and their demands for a development model that is respectful of their territories and tradition will remain unmet.

Policy implications for the protection of nature

Extractive conflicts in Latin America are among the most violent in the region as they tend to radicalize causing numerous deaths and injuries. The participation of indigenous peoples in this type of conflict is significant and is usually associated with the environmental defense of indigenous ancestral territories. Even while resource-based violence is on the rise and more people get killed every year (The Guardian 2017), a slowdown in extractivism does not seem to be the trend in the region. In 2015, Bolivia's president Evo Morales lifted prohibitions to explore hydrocarbons in 7 of 22 national parks and ecological reserves in the country. Furthermore, Morales highlighted the support of the Guaraní indigenous people saying that he was pleased to find out that indigenous groups are not manipulated by international NGOs (El Universo 2015). Likewise, Rafael Zoeger, former president of the state agency Perupetro in Peru, announced that hydrocarbon exploration in ecological reserves can be done responsibly and that extant legislation forbidding extraction in these areas needed to be modified (Servindi 2016). More recently in Mexico, the government passed the Biodiversity General Law, which, among other things, enables extractive operations such as mining and fracking in ecologically protected areas (Lira 2018).

The implementation of the right to prior consultation which was intended to include indigenous peoples in policy making processes regarding their natural environments has failed to deter industrialized extractivism. Nonetheless, the study of prior consultation outcomes in Latin America has important implications for how indigenous peoples worldwide can be better positioned *vis-à-vis* the extractive industry. In recent years, much attention has been given to the scope of prior consultation. Indigenous rights activists and lawyers have pushed for more substantial recognition of indigenous voices in state policies. For many, this will only result by giving veto power to consulted indigenous groups. Today, free, prior and informed consent (FPIC) by indigenous peoples, instead of mere consultations, is demanded by human rights and environmental organizations but also by some international agencies (FAO 2014). Legal activists tend to focus on the procedural aspects of prior consultation and whether governments follow ILO 169 standards in order to obtain indigenous FPIC. All these issues are important for guaranteeing indigenous rights; moreover, it is likely that granting indigenous communities veto power over the implementation of extractive operations in their lands could enhance their leverage in prior consultation.

However, findings presented through this book do not indicate that changes in prior consultation legislation will bring about different results in terms of indigenous prohibition of extraction. One of the main arguments this book makes is that the importance of the extractive industry conditions not only the way Latin American states address indigenous prior consultation rights but also how indigenous groups engage with extractive projects. As shown by this study, one of the main drivers of indigenous struggles is economic. Pro-extractivist groups mobilize to profit from extraction, and anti-extractivist groups mobilize to protect ongoing economic systems that are based on the preservation of their natural resources. Both groups use environmental causes to frame their grievances, but in the cases examined in this book environmental protection is the driver of conflicts only when environmental resources represent safeguards to indigenous peoples for avoiding poverty. Therefore, any form of implementation of prior consultation procedures, even one that grants veto power to indigenous groups, will be embedded in these conditions. The case of Bolivia, where the most progressive legislation of prior consultation exists, illustrates this argument.

The findings of this study also suggest that because prior consultation is negotiation, state agencies in charge of overseeing indigenous rights could see more benefits by focusing on strengthening indigenous political organizations. In turn, environmentalists could obtain better results by strengthening indigenous economic models in order to create conditions for anti-extractivist attitudes to increase among indigenous communities. As shown by case studies presented in Chapter 4, working economies are often linked with representative political authorities that have credibility among the population. Capulalpam de Mendez in Mexico, Chetilla in Peru and Challapata in Bolivia are examples of powerful indigenous organizations capable of mobilizing their communities to defend their economic systems from potentially destructive mining projects. As demonstrated in Elinor Ostrom's research, self-governing communities develop long-range, robust and cooperative arrangements to ensure that local resources are not degraded by the actions of external appropriators (Pacheco-Vega 2014). Only by securing indigenous peoples an adequate environment in which they can freely develop alternative economic models, can we expect an increment in the number of successful environmental defenders.

Another important policy implication of this study is that enforcement of prior consultation could diminish unnecessary state repression by offering negotiation spaces to pro-extractivist indigenous groups and state actors. Prior consultation procedures the way they are implemented today allow some indigenous groups to reach economic deals without having to engage in violent confrontations with state forces. A better way of presenting prior consultation than as a right to include indigenous voice in policy making could be as a right to negotiate the economic terms of extraction. Under this logic, negotiation procedures should be available for all groups living close to extraction sites; however, the decision to engage in consultation should belong to indigenous communities and should be made upon the awareness that extraction will follow. This would eliminate the uncertainty regarding the utility of prior consultation and would possibly contribute to new forms of indigenous organizing. As explicit negotiations, prior consultation procedures could be more beneficial for indigenous participants. In addition, other mechanisms—different from prior consultation—should be available for anti-extractivist groups to channel their demands. Otherwise, violence will continue to increase as well as the number of indigenous activist who are killed for defending their territories.

Finally, evidence on indigenous struggles over extractive projects suggests that environmental protection should be addressed differently in the future. Linking ecological causes with indigenous rights was an effective strategy to achieve legal transformations in the 2000s. In the present day, however, it may be more useful to clearly distinguish between the necessity of having adequate mechanisms for protecting the environment and the urgency of improving indigenous peoples living conditions. Although these two issues are often related, it is critical to find neutral political actors that can supervise the impacts of the extractive industry sector. While some indigenous groups have demonstrated to be the most radical ecologists to defend their territories, the fact that most indigenous communities live in extreme poverty and are many times stakeholders in extractive activities prevents most of these groups to be neutral when overwatching the impacts of resource extraction. Perhaps a better solution to address environmental protection of ecologically fragile areas is to search inside the state apparatus for neutral agencies that can veto ecologically unsustainable projects. Another alternative could be that these functions are given to an international agency as it has been proposed by some countries in several United Nations assemblies. The potential undermining of national sovereignty is always an argument made against international intervention in states' affairs, but negotiations over this matter could deliver proposals that be acceptable for governments in the near future.

References

Arce, Moises. 2014. *Resource Extraction and Protest in Peru*. Pittsburg, PA: University of Pittsburg Press.

Amengual, Matthew. 2016. *Politicized Enforcement in Argentina: Labor and Environmental Regulation*. New York: Cambridge University Press.

Arellano-Yanguas, Javier. 2011. *¿Minería sin fronteras? Conflicto y desarrollo en regiones mineras del Perú*. Lima: IEP.

Bebbington, Antohony, and Jeffrey Bury. 2013. *Subterranean Struggles. New Dynamics of Mining, Oil and Gas in Latin America*. Austin: University of Texas Press. DOI: 10.7560/748620.

Cohen, Jean L., and Arato, Arato. (1992). *Civil Society and Political Theory*. Cambridge, Mass: MIT Press.

Eisenstadt, Todd. 2003 Thinking Outside the (Ballot) Box: Informal Electoral Institutions and Mexico's Political Opening. *Latin American Politics and Society* 45: 25–54.

El Universo. 2015. Bolivia buscará hidrocarburos con mucha fuerza en siete parques naturales, July 21. Available at: www.eluniverso.com/vida-estilo/2015/07/21/nota/5031097/bolivia-buscara-hidrocarburos-mucha-fuerza-siete-parques (Accessed May 13 2017).

Epp, Charles. 1998. *The Rights Revolution: lawyers, activists and supreme courts in comparative perspective*. Chicago: Chicago University Press.

Falleti, Tulia, and Thea Riofrancos. 2018. "Endogenous Participation: Strengthening Prior Consultation in Extractive Economies." *World Politics* 70(1): 86–121.

Flemmer, Riccarda, and Almut Schilling-Vacaflor. 2015. Unfulfilled promises of the consultation approach: the limitations to effective indigenous participation in Bolivia's and Peru's extractive industries. Paper presented at the *Alacip Conference*. Lima, July 22–24.

FAO. 2014. "Respecting Free, Prior and Informed Consent. Practical Guidance for Governments, Companies, NGOs, Indigenous Peoples and Local Communities in Relation to Land Acquisition." Governance of Tenure Technical Guide No. 3. Rome. *Food and Agriculture Organization.*

Galanter, Marc. 1974. Why the "Haves" Come Out Ahead: Speculations on the Limits of Legal Change. *Law & Society Review* 9(1): 95–160. Litigation and Dispute Processing: Part One (Autumn, 1974).

Gouritin, Armelle, and Marcela Torres. 2018. "Indigenous Peoples' Right to Consultation and Their Emerging Claim for Sel-Consultation." Paper prepared for *Lasa Conference.* Barcelona, May 27–30.

Gudynas, Eduardo. 2009. Diez tesis urgentes sobre el nuevo extrativismo. Contextos y demandas bajo el progresismo sudamericano actual. *CAAP/CLAES* 187–225.

Humphreys-Bebbington, Denisse. 2012. "Las tensiones Estado-Indigenas debido a la expansion de la industria hidrocarburifere en el Chaco boloviano." In Leonith Hinojosa (Ed.) *Gas y Desarrollo. Dinamicas Territoriales Rurales en Tarija-Bolivia.* La Paz: Fundacion Tierra, 131–150.

Levitsky, Steven, and Maria Victoria Murillo. 2013. "Building Institutions on Weak Foundations: Lessons from Latin America" *Journal of Democracy* 24(2) (April 2013).

Lira, Ivette. 2018. Ley de la Biodiversidad es un regalo para la minería y el fracking y un atentado a la ecología, alertan. Available at: www.sinembargo.mx/05-02-2018/3380865 (Accessed May 18 2018).

Lucero, Jose Antonio. 2009. "Decades Lost and Won: Indigenous Movements and Multicultural Neoliberalism in the Andes." In John Burdick, Phillips Oxhorn and Roberts Kenneth (Eds.) *Beyond Neoliberalism in Latin America: Societies and Politics at the Crossroads.* New York: Palgrave Macmillan, 63–81.

Ñiquen, Alberto. 2015. "Paulo Vilca: No sólo algunos empresarios se oponen a los derechos de los indígenas, también funcionarios públicos." *Rights and Resources,* August 3. Available at: https://rightsandresources.org/es/blog/espanol-la-mula-paulo-vilca-no-solo-algunos-empresarios-se-oponen-a-los-derechos-de-los-indigenas-tambien-funcionarios-publicos/#.Wsu4NC7waM8 (Accessed February 27 2016).

O'Donnell, G. 1993. "On the State, Democratization and some Conceptual Problems: A Latin American View with Glances at some Postcommunist Countries." *World Development* 21(8): 1355–1369.

Observatory of Mining Conflicts. n.d. Mining Conflicts in Latin America. Available at: www.conflictosmineros.net/ (Accessed January 8 2018).

Pacheco-Vega, Raul. 2014. Ostrom y la gobernanza del agua en México. *Revista Mexicana de Sociología* 15(1) January–March. DOI: 10.22201/iis.01882503p.2014.0.46485.

Perreault, Tom. 2013. "Nature and Nation: The Territorial Logics of Hydrocarbon Governance in Bolivia." In Anthony Bebbington and Jeffrey Bury (Eds.) *Subterranean Struggles: New Geographies of Extractive Industries in Latin America.* Austin: University of Texas Press, 67–90.

Perreault, Tom. et al. (Ed). 2014. *Minería, agua y justicia social en los andes: experiencias comparativas de Perú y Bolivia.* La Paz: Justicia Hídrica, Centro de Ecología y Pueblos Andinos; Fundación PIEB.

Rosenberg, Gerard. 1991. The hollow hope. Can courts bring about social change? Chicago: Chicago University Press.

Salas, Guillermo. 2008. *Dinámica social y minería. Familias pastoras de puna y la presencia del proyecto Antamina (1997–2002).* Lima: IEP.

Servindi. 2016. Proponen explorar y explotar en áreas protegidas August 11. Available at: www.servindi.org/11/08/2016/plantean-explotacion-y-exploracion-en-areas-protegidas (Accessed March 9 2017).

Slack, Keith. 2009. "Digging Out from Neoliberalism: Responses to Environmental (Mis) governance of the Mining Sector in Latin America." In John Burdick, Phillips Oxhorn and Roberts Kenneth (Eds.) *Beyond Neoliberalism in Latin America: Societies and Politics at the Crossroads.* New York: Palgrave Macmillan, 117–134.

The Guardian. 2017. Environmental Defenders Being Killed in Record Numbers Globally, New Research Reveals. Available at: www.theguardian.com/environment/2017/jul/13/environmental-defenders-being-killed-in-record-numbers-globally-new-research-reveals (Accessed February 28 2017).

Valdivia, Gabriela. 2008. Governing Relations between People and Things: Citizenship, Territory, and the Political Economy of Petroleum in Ecuador. *Political Geography* 27: 456–477.

Van Cott, Donna Lee. 2008. *Radical Democracy in the Andes.* New York: Cambridge University Press.

Vidaurre, Laura. 2016. Guaranís denuncian la desaparición de 6.5 millones de dólares. *El Periódico,* April 19. Available at: http://elperiodico-digital.com/2016/04/19/Guaraníes-denuncian-la-desaparicion-de-65-millones-de-dolares-de-la-apg/ (Accessed January 27 2018).

Yashar, Deborah. 2005. *Contesting Citizenship in Latin America. The Rise of Indigenous Movements and the Postliberal Challenge.* New York: Cambridge University Press.

Chapter 6

Conclusions

Latin America's extractive industry through the lens of green criminology

Green criminology scholars have offered extensive evidence on the environmental harm that industrialized exploitation of natural resources causes to nearby communities and their ecosystems (Stretesky and Lynch 2011; Long et al. 2012; Pearse et al. 2013; Ruggiero and South 2013; White 2013). In attempting to explain why conflicts over the control of natural resources occur, Kuijpers (2012: 14) argues that many of these conflicts are driven by economic variables. In this vein, others have identified similar motivations for environmental crime, asserting that it results from the selfish desire for capital accumulation (Pečar 1988: 116 cited in Brisman et al. 2015). In Latin America, exploitation of mineral and hydrocarbon reserves remains one of the most lucrative businesses for multinational corporations. Companies' need for profit leads them to direct significant efforts to controlling lands potentially containing minerals, oil and gas. In turn, governments' need for the revenues generated by the exports of these resources prompts state actors to "assist" corporations by facilitating their access to the valuable resources (Zilney et al. 2006; Ruggiero and South 2013; White 2013).

An extensive body of literature demonstrates that the close relationship between state actors and multinational corporations is one important cause of global environmental degradation (Paulson et al. 2015: 268). Neoliberal discourses that have dominated politics for the last 30 years in most parts of the world call for a minimalist state whereby government power in regulating environmental risk is eroded (Flournoy 2011: 299). According to the neoliberal model, private investors are the main drivers of national economies and are thus responsible for economic growth. Neoliberal governments create lax licensing procedures and corporate benefits to attract foreign investment. In Latin America, flexible regulations and non-enforcement of legislation that could be inconvenient to mining and hydrocarbon companies leave indigenous communities living in resources-rich lands highly vulnerable to the negative impacts of extraction. Furthermore, neoliberal policies are usually accompanied by support of state forces in the event of conflicts that could delay corporations' economic operations (Hristov 2009). This reality is premised, again, on the notion that private economic activities benefit the national interest and, as such, governments must guarantee conditions for economic development by whatever means necessary. As a result, dozens of activists and protestors lose their lives every year, victims of the intersection of state repression and corporate—and government—interests. The implicit alliance between governments and multinational corporations in the expansion of extractive projects at the expense of local communities and their natural environments has led some criminologists to catalogue both types of actors as "partners in crime" (Ebus and Kuijpers 2015: 144).

Heavy dependence on the export of commodities deepens the influence that the extractive industry has on Latin American law enforcers, moving beyond simply influencing government ideology. During the left-turn that defined regional politics of the 2000s, progressive presidents came to power upon anti-neoliberal discourses. New governments promised to address the unequal distribution of resources and ecological degradation caused by extractive economic models. In countries such as Ecuador and Bolivia, leftist governments displayed innovative legislation in order to protect Mother Nature. Nonetheless, dependence on commodity export revenues to implement redistributive policies pushed new presidents to continue and even advance extractivist projects, this time with greater state participation (Gray 2010; Hinojosa 2012).[1]

In Latin America, indigenous populations are at the center of resource-based disputes. Large-scale resource extraction often leads to the displacement of local communities already living in these areas or negative environmental impacts that, in turn, adversely affect the survival of such groups (Brisman et al. 2015:18). Today, governments are committed to the development of megaprojects in indigenous lands without guaranteeing that indigenous peoples' minimum needs for subsistence are met. In addition to ongoing political and economic exclusion, these groups risk the loss of the lands that have allowed them to preserve their culture to the present day. Ultimately, resource-based disputes between indigenous peoples, multinational companies and governments clearly illustrate how Latin America's structural inequality has been deepened by neoliberal policies.

Beyond extensive damages to the environment, health and culture, resource frontiers are places wherein gross violations of human rights are on the rise. In Latin America, human rights defenders and environmental activists are in constant danger, and among them, indigenous members are in a particularly vulnerable situation (Gouritin 2018). Over the last decade, hundreds of indigenous activists have been murdered for defending their lands from invaders attempting to profit from their natural resources. A Global Witness report on Honduras, for instance, indicates that land activists are more likely to be killed in this country than anywhere else in the world (Global

Witness 2017). This report was prepared after Honduran indigenous activist Bertha Cáceres was killed in 2016, just one year after being awarded the Goldman prize, the world's most prestigious recognition for environmental grassroots work. Likewise, in 2017, after receiving dozens of death threats around his defense of forests from logging projects within indigenous community lands, Mexican environmentalist Isidro Baldenegro was killed. Like Cáceres, Baldenegro had been awarded with the Goldman prize in 2005 (Mundo 2017). More recently, in 2018, Mexican activist Guadalupe Campanur Tapia, famous for defending community lands in the indigenous municipality of Cherán, was found dead in the state of Michoacan.

These are only three examples from the long list of indigenous people murdered over the past few years in Latin America. Most of these killing go unpunished—the result of a lack of identification of the individuals responsible of the murders, as well as what appears to be a lack of prosecutorial will (The Guardian 2017). Making matters worse, recent reports indicate that a significant amount of human rights violations in these cases are perpetrated by state officials (2016 report prepared by the Mexican Center of Environmental Law or CEMDA, cited by Gouritin 2018:4).

In a context of persistent and deep economic inequality and generalized violence, it should come as no surprise that the implementation of the right to prior consultation has failed to protect indigenous territories in the ways envisioned by its most forthright advocates. This book has shown how governments from different ideological backgrounds in Bolivia, Peru and Mexico make use of diverse political strategies to misuse the right to prior consultation for the advancement of billionaire extractive projects. The outcomes of prior consultation legislation examined in previous chapters shed light on the ways states manipulate policy to sidestep indigenous rights. Findings also show how in many parts of the region the extractive industry shapes indigenous movements' goals by transforming legitimate environmental concerns into demands for economic compensation. The global management of natural resources by governments and multinational companies creates high economic expectations among the most disempowered indigenous communities. This helps to explain why indigenous communities accept extraction when consulted by the government. Moreover, the evidence presented herein suggests that prior consultation procedures as implemented today contribute to the commodification of indigenous territories. This has the potential of accelerating the disappearance of numerous indigenous cultures across Latin America.

Pro-extractivist and anti-extractivist indigenous peoples

This book highlights some of the key strategies utilized by Latin American governments under the auspices of prior consultation procedures in order to circumvent obstacles to extractive projects. At the same time, research on indigenous municipalities in three different countries with sizable indigenous populations and prominent mining or hydrocarbon industries sought to demonstrate the complexity of indigenous struggles over the extractive industry. The conflicting relationship between indigenous communities and mining and hydrocarbon industries, when examined more closely, is in all cases a dispute over the uneven distribution of wealth. Environmental values, as understood by first-world environmentalists, are often used as discursive strategies to overcome economic exclusion and historical dispossession. Indigenous protestors strategically link indigenous rights to ecological livelihoods, and they often claim that minerals and hydrocarbons must remain unexploited, given that extractive industries will harm their environment.

Yet previous research on extractive conflicts in Peru demonstrates that there are two types of social movements in relation to the extractive industry. The first type is made up of indigenous groups seeking to economically benefit from extractive projects, whereas the second type seeks to prohibit extractive activities (Arellano-Yanguas 2011; Arce 2014). This book's findings corroborate the existence of these two diametrically opposed types of movements, expanding previous findings in Peru to Bolivia and Mexico. Case studies presented in Chapter 4 demonstrate that in some cases, indigenous struggles are borne out of radical opposition to extractive projects as they threaten native economies that rely on the preservation of natural resources. Prior consultation outcomes presented in Chapters 2 and 3, however, suggest that most of the time, indigenous communities are willing to work with the extractive industry. The latter applies as long as indigenous groups can have access to the economic benefits produced by mining or hydrocarbon operations. The most remarkable example of this is the case of politically salient indigenous Guaraní communities in the El Chaco desert of Bolivia. These groups historically mobilized around environmental causes to claim the ownership of great expanses of lands enriched with sizable gas reserves. Once the government granted them with the right to prior consultation in 2005, the Guaraní used it to obtain million-dollar compensation for allowing extraction within their lands. It is important to mention that the Guaraní in Bolivia's Chaco are not doing anything new by negotiating resources through prior consultation, nor are Amazonian tribes living near oil block 192 in Peru. Economic negotiation was always present among Guaraní and Amazonian groups living nearby extraction sites. However, with prior consultation, these groups have a new tool to demand economic distribution of extractive profits for their communities.

As indicated earlier, however, both pro- and anti-extractivist groups frame their disputes using similar environmental discourses, making it difficult to distinguish between the two. Building upon past research, this book offered a comprehensive conceptualization of pro-extractivist and anti-extractivist indigenous groups. Whereas the bulk of literature on indigenous movements focuses on the repertoires of social action used by indigenous actors and their transnational allies (Keck and Sikkink 1998; Devlin and Yap 2008; Urkidi and Walter 2011), this study brings attention to the economic conditions present in various indigenous locations to assist in explaining the divergent motivations underlying indigenous actions on extraction. Chapter 1 suggests it is likely that indigenous groups living upon subsistence activities and isolated from broader economic markets, or in areas where the extractive industry has operated for long period, will be pro-extractivist. In turn, indigenous peoples with ongoing viable economies in place that are threatened by the extractive industry will generally be anti-extractivists.

By analyzing indigenous economic conditions at each research site, this study also confirms the notion that anti-extractivist indigenous groups carry out protests to protect their means of existence (Guha and Martinez-Alier 1997). Previous studies have relied on the existence of strong agricultural models generally associated with indigenous peoples to explain anti-extractivist mobilization (Arce 2014; Arellano-Yanguas 2011). The analytical framework introduced in Chapter 1, however, pays special attention to the viability of economic activities more than the activity itself. In this sense, new models emerging among indigenous communities, such as ecotourism, were found as another source of opposition to the extractive industry.

As indicated by Broad and Cavanagh (2017), over the last two decades, political ecologists have offered extensive evidence demonstrating that it is the poorest people who are the most concerned about the environment as these groups depend on intact ecosystems for their subsistence. Latin America's indigenous people are among the poorest populations in the subcontinent, and many of indigenous tribes still depend on their surrounding natural resources to survive. Violent conflicts between indigenous communities rising to defend their territories have often followed state-corporation attempts to implement extraction in their lands. Systematic indigenous approval of extractive projects resulting from prior consultation procedures, however, would suggest that most of these groups are, in fact, willing to give up their territories—and intact ecosystems—in exchange for economic compensation.

This book used a green criminology perspective to broaden the understanding of prior consultation outcomes in Latin America. By acknowledging that an economic and political alliance between states and multinational companies exists to further profitable extractive projects, the book shows how selective enforcement or non-enforcement of prior consultation procedures enables state actors to circumvent indigenous groups that are more likely to reject extractive projects. On the other hand, government abandonment of indigenous people, in addition to the fact that processes of dispossession initiated several centuries ago have left many of these groups with unproductive lands, prompts many of them to accept the extractive industry in the hopes of escaping extreme poverty.

This book's findings also expand upon political ecology approaches to resource-based conflicts. Previous chapters provide evidence indicating that indigenous groups genuinely opposing extractive activities generally have viable economic systems that rely on the preservation of their natural environment. Typically, this type of indigenous group is connected to broader economic markets often found in urban centers and capital cities, and indigenous members do not have to migrate to other cities in search of jobs. Viable economic systems are usually linked to representative political organizations at the local level. As shown in Chapters 3 and 4, these organizations have credibility *vis-à-vis* community members because of their effective management of natural resource for the benefit of the community. These findings resonate with past research demonstrating that when communities are empowered through the community control of resources, collective action can lead to positive environmental outcomes (Broad and Cavanagh 2017). In the cases examined in this book, effective control and administration of resources in Challapata (Bolivia), Chetilla (Peru) and Capulalpam de Mendez (Mexico) enabled indigenous organizations to overcome division, mobilize the population and ban industrialized mining operations.

In the case of pro-extractivist indigenous communities, representation by political organizations can also exist and is required for negotiating economic compensation with the state. The source of their power, however, does not come from successful administration of natural resources as this type of group generally inhabits unproductive areas with insufficient economies. Connections with Non-governmental organizations (NGOs) and other types of external support can help to create and strengthen political organization under these circumstances. The next section addresses these apparent connections.

The alliances between indigenous peoples and environmental organizations

Previous chapters find that representative political organizations at the local level are in many cases a precondition for sufficient indigenous political power to deter or to profit from extractivism. Findings from Chapters 3 and 4 confirmed that representative political organizations able to mobilize their communities are necessary for demonstrating power and gaining leverage in negotiation, as well as for opposition movements to counteract state repression. These findings also indicate that while connections to NGO actors can strengthen indigenous organization, these are not necessary for the success of anti-extractivist opposition. It does not appear that NGOs or other types of organizations detached from indigenous societies can fulfill the functions of political representation and mobilization of indigenous citizens. Although external actors can and often do contribute to articulating grievances into powerful discourse, gathering support of diverse actors, providing resources for mobilization and reaching broader audiences, case analysis demonstrated that indigenous mobilization can succeed without NGO involvement, such as in the cases of the Quechua community of Chetilla (Peru), the Yaqui tribes in Sonora (Mexico) and the Zapoteca people in Capulálpam de Méndez (Mexico). In turn, findings indicate that pro-extractivist and anti-extractivist protestors alike can fail to achieve their goals despite NGO support such as in the cases of the Mosetén in La Paz (Bolivia), Cotabambas and Grau in Apurimac (Peru), and Cerro San Pedro in San Luis Potosí (Mexico). Likewise, the fact that anti-extractivist communities who prohibited extraction did not receive NGO founding for self-organization confirms that protestors are usually able to find mobilization resources with or without alliances with external actors (McAdam and Boudet 2010). These findings are in line with Elinor Ostrom's influential studies concluding that self-governing communities are sufficiently capable of defending their territories from foreigners seeking to jeopardize their local control of natural resources (Pacheco-Vega 2014).

Moreover, this book demonstrates that NGO participation does not always overlaps with anti-extractivist indigenous attitudes. Findings revealed that it is precisely those indigenous organizations that emerged in the 1980s with NGO support who end up demonstrating pro-extractivist attitudes, given that they complied with extraction once offered the chance to profit from it. This is confirmed by the cases of the Guaraní groups in El Chaco and indigenous organizations in Amazonia, both of which systematically approved hydrocarbon projects in Bolivia and Peru. Arguably, such an apparent contradiction relates to the fact that international NGOs are concerned with ecological conservation above all else. NGO actors might have succeeded in empowering indigenous leaders politically but have not been capable of addressing the economic needs of the majority of community members (Pratt 2007). Conversely, in places where ongoing economic models offer alternatives to indigenous communities, *Rondas Campesinas* and *Usos y Costumbres*, bottom-up political organizations, have been able to sustain opposition until companies have withdrawn operations.

Indigenous economic viability is one crucial way of ensuring conditions for the emergence of anti-extractivist stances among indigenous communities. Environmentalists should direct their efforts toward securing the conditions for the development and sustainment of alternative economies if they want to be able to compete with rapid cash disbursements associated with the extractive industry. Ultimately, the evidence presented in this book indicates that raising the quality of life of indigenous peoples would be more useful for ecological defense than advocating for the implementation of prior consultation.

Economic agreements and indigenous division

Another important issue this book stressed, and that should be considered by actors advocating for prior consultation in countries where these procedures remain unimplemented, is indigenous political division. While it is intuitive that not all indigenous communities are united in their beliefs, the allocation of economic resources that sometimes accompanies prior consultation may make these procedures more divisive than uniting in many communities. The cases presented throughout the book show that those groups whose political organizations are politically skilled are generally capable of negotiating a significant amount of money in exchange for permitting extractive operations. Nonetheless, the cases presented in Chapter 3 evidence that aside from consultation outcomes, some of the indigenous communities who negotiated with the state also suffered increased political division in the aftermath of prior consultation. Disagreements between factions over the approval of extraction or the amount of the compensation accepted by indigenous leaders can generate high levels of internal violence. This is the case of the Yaqui people in Mexico, where division over the approval of the construction of a gas pipeline in community lands exacerbated past conflicts among Yaqui members leading to one person dead and several others injured.

From a legal standpoint, state intervention through prior consultation should serve to guarantee indigenous rights to territories, natural resources and culture (Inter-American Commission of Human Rights 2009). In the past, multinational corporations negotiated directly with indigenous communities when attempting to access their territories. Many abuses against the most vulnerable indigenous groups were committed in the aim of obtaining community lands for extractive purposes. Now through prior consultation, state actors have come to occupy the place of mining and hydrocarbon companies in negotiations with indigenous leaders. Still, the outcomes of prior consultation procedures are not promising.

The emergence of indigenous movements at the beginning of the 2000s was understood by many as a radical critic to hegemonic neoliberal ideologies that base development on unlimited exploitation of natural resources (Escobar 2018). The fact that indigenous communities are approving extractive projects in exchange for profits, however, reinforces widespread visions that assign monetary values to nature. Indigenous movements could stop representing legitimate interlocutors contesting economic models based on the expansion of economic growth. With this, proponents of alternative development models that conceptualize nature as a subject of rights instead of a source of profit (Gudynas 2015) could lose one of their most important voices.

Environmental activists and legal advocates worldwide would benefit from knowledge of the Latin American experience. International agencies and NGOs should take precautions when pressuring governments to apply prior consultation procedures in countries where extractive industries are prominent. As evidenced in this book, state actors are generally capable of finding ways to use prior consultation to their—and corporations'—advantage. Furthermore, other governments beyond Latin America could use these procedures to give legal validity to ecologically unsustainable extractive projects.

Is Latin America's dependence on the extractive industry insurmountable?

As of today, economic models based on the exports of commodities are predominant in Latin America. To paraphrase Argentinean scholar Maristella Svampa (2013), the region has moved from the Washington consensus, which resulted in governments' commitment to adopt neoliberal policies, to the Commodities consensus. This new "consensus" suggests an implicit and generalized commitment to the exportation of raw and semi-industrialized materials, which further dispossesses indigenous communities of their lands and natural resources, and produces new forms of dependence and domination (Svampa 2013: 32).

One distinctive characteristic of countries' dependence on commodity exports is that long-term viability and prosperity of the national economy are generally sacrificed to the immediate benefits believed to flow from commodity booms (Carrington et al. 2015:256). At the local level, two of the most negative impacts that undiversified economies have relate to severe impacts on the environment, as well as people's health (Brisman et al. 2015:15). As argued earlier in this book, extractive operations are often carried out in areas inhabited by indigenous peoples. Economic incentives created by the expectation to get jobs at extractive companies encourage community members to abandon their land-based work in favor of working as low-skilled employees. Yet the profits generated by these activities only give environmental degradation an appearance of acceptability in these communities. What is more, on many occasions, indigenous workers end up in unsafe and highly contaminated locations in spite of perils to their health and personal security.

The prior consultation outcomes examined in Bolivia, Peru and Mexico seem to reinforce the argument of the "resource curse," whereby a strong dependence on export revenues from extractive industries increases inequality and violence. This book has presented evidence indicating that in spite of government ideology, national influence of indigenous movements and the scope of the right to prior consultation given in domestic legislation, states and multinational companies continue expanding resource frontiers. Despite these findings, recent evidence also indicates that some governments do not necessarily comply with the Commodity consensus. In 2017, El Salvador became the first Latin American country to ban any kind of gold mining in the national territory. In 2010, Costa Rica placed a ban on open-pit mining techniques. More recently in 2018, Ecuadorian President Lenin Moreno carried out a national referendum in which the government asked the population, among other things, if mining operations should be forbidden within protected natural areas. The population voted "yes" to placing bans on mineral exploitation, demonstrating a rejection of the aggressive extractive policies put in place by former administrations.

Certainly, El Salvador and Costa Rica have the advantage of not being economies dependent on extractive industries. Interestingly, both countries do not have sizable indigenous populations either. In Ecuador, on the other hand, where the extractive industry is prominent and the indigenous population is numerous, to what extent the referendum results will be fully implemented by President Moreno remains to be seen. Having made this point, such cases should be explored further as they might be indications that the era of unquestioned extractivism is coming to an end (Broad and Cavanagh 2017). These cases bring some hope into Latin America—the fact that some governments are seriously addressing the environmental harm that extractive industries cause is worth consideration. The general picture, however, indicates that most governments lack sufficient incentives to give priority to the protection of the environment. Under the current global scenario where underdeveloped countries are the main providers of natural resources for industrialized countries, the alliance between state actors and multinational companies is likely to endure.

Limitations and topics for future research

It is worth highlighting several important limitations of this book. First, the chapters do not offer empirical evidence on the participation of anti-extractivist indigenous groups in prior consultation procedures because they did not find any such cases; only cases of pro-extractivist groups, presented in Chapter 3, were found. The inability to find cases of anti-extractivist groups participating in prior consultation procedures is likely the product of states' unwillingness to consult on mining projects for which indigenous opposition is generally greater, at least during the timeframe within which fieldwork was carried out. Likewise, this also relates to the fact that many indigenous groups opposing to the extractive industry—aware of the negotiation condition inherent in prior consultation—refuse to be consulted. Yet the inability to test this combination limits the scopes of this study to the extent that it cannot be known if prior consultation could transform anti-extractivist indigenous attitudes into pro-extractivist stances. In addition, it cannot be known for sure if anti-extractivist groups who decided to participate in prior consultation would be able to maintain opposition till the end of the procedure. Nonetheless, previous research has documented the enhancement of indigenous divisions as a result of prior consultations (Bascopé 2010; Rodríguez-Garavito et al. 2010). Moreover, these findings were corroborated by the cases of the Aymara and the Mosetén in Bolivia, the Achuar, Quechua and Kiwchua in Peru, and the Yaqui in Mexico, all cases of indigenous groups participating in prior consultation and experiencing subsequent splits in their political organizations. Together, this evidence suggests that prior consultation procedures have the ability to break indigenous leadership and further extractive projects.

Another limitation of this study is that because prior consultation procedures are relatively recent in the region, it is still not possible to know for sure what the effects of these procedures will be among politically weak indigenous organizations. Whereas this study has predicted the emergence of stronger forms of indigenous organizing around prior consultation procedures, no empirical evidence was found to support this claim. Likewise, it is still too early to know if the implementation of prior consultation procedures can impact the ways the extractive process is conducted within areas inhabited by indigenous peoples. While this study measured the outcomes of indigenous groups over the extractive industry, outcomes related to how prior consultation impacts extractive companies should be considered. Future research should address this limitation by studying the behavior of extractive companies after commitments to oversee extractive operations were made by the state in prior consultations.

An additional limitation of this study is related to the possibility of corroborating the finding that direct economic compensation paid by the state to indigenous organizations is not actually beneficial to indigenous peoples. It remains to be explored if prior consultation funding serves to improve living standards in indigenous communities as opposed to the state administration of those resources. Chapter 4 demonstrates that in Peru, state agencies have been incapable of using extractive funds to deliver development in ways that are satisfactory to indigenous communities. Likewise, administration of those funds by indigenous organizations in Guaraní territories in Bolivia does not appear to have resulted in a substantial improvement of indigenous living conditions either (Humphreys-Bebbington 2012). Future research should pay greater attention to the effects of indigenous administration of extractive resources on indigenous peoples' living conditions. It is worth examining whether or not the indigenous management of economic funds derived from extractive operations is more effective in "delivering well-being" to indigenous communities than the state administration of extractive funds. Advantages and shortcoming in each type of administration could shed light on more effective distribution and administration of extractive resources.

Future research should more deeply explore the impacts that indigenous self-consultations, or *auto-consultas*, have on the defense of indigenous territories. This book has examined their value in deterring potentially destructive mining projects. Yet a systematic examination of the conditions under which these self-consultations produce better results for anti-extractivist movements could shed light on new strategies that environmental activists could pursue in the years to come.

Finally, by applying the green criminology perspective to indigenous struggles over mining and hydrocarbon projects in Latin America, this book attempts to demonstrate that the key impact of prior consultations has been to replace concerns over environmental harm to indigenous territories with economic negotiation. Under this prior consultation framework, conflicts between anti-extractivist indigenous peoples, state actors and multinational companies are likely to increase. On the other hand, prior consultations with pro-extractivist groups could contribute to expand resource frontiers deeper into new territories.

Note

1 In most countries, especially in the hydrocarbon industry, extraction remains in the hands of state-owned companies. However, in terms of the environment, this has not necessarily implied an improvement.

References

Arce, Moises. 2014. *Resource Extraction and Protest in Peru*. Pittsburg: University of Pittsburg Press.

Arellano-Yanguas, Javier. 2011. *¿Minería sin fronteras? Conflicto y desarrollo en regiones mineras del Perú*. Lima: IEP.

Bascopé, Ivan. 2010. *Lecciones aprendidas sobre la Consulta Previa*. La Paz: CEJIS.

Brisman, Avi, Nigel South, and Rob White. 2015. "Toward a Criminology of Environmental-Conflict Relationship" In Avi Brisman, Nigel South and Rob White (eds) *Environmental Crime and Social Conflict. Contemporary and Emerging Issues*. England: Ashgate Publishing Limited, 1–38.

Broad, Robin, and John Cavanagh. 2017. Historic Wins for Democracy and Rights in El Salvador. *Ethics & International Affairs*, June 19. Carnegie Council. Available at: www.ethicsandinternationalaffairs.org/2017/historic-wins-democracy-rights-el-salvador/ (Accessed February 23 2018).

Carrington, Kerry, Russel Hogg, and Alison McIntosh. 2015. The Hidden Injuries of Mining: Frontier Cultural Conflict. In Avi Brisman, Nigel South and Rob White (eds.) *Environmental Crime and Social Conflict: Contemporary and Emerging Issues*. Ashgate Publishing Limited, 241–264.

Devlin, John, and Nonita Yap. 2008. Contentious Politics in Environmental Assessment: Blocked Projects and Winning Coalitions. *Impact Assessment and Project Appraisal* 26(1): 17–27. DOI: 10.3152/146155108X279939.

Ebus, Bram, and Karly Kuijpers. 2015. The State-Corporate Tandem Cycling Towards Collision: State-Corporate Harm and the Resource Frontiers of Brazil and Colombia. In Avi Brisman, Nigel South and Rob White (eds.) *Environmental Crime and Social Conflict. Contemporary and Emerging Issues*. Aldershot, 125–152.

Escobar, Arturo. 2018. Farewell to Development. In Great Transition Initiative. Available at www.greattransition.org/publication/farewell-to-development (Accessed April 09 2018).

Flournoy, Alyson. 2011. Three Meta-Lessons Government and Industry Should Learn From the BP Deepwater Horizon Disaster and Why They Will Not. *Environmental Affairs* 38: 281–303.

Global Witness. 2017. Honduras: The Deadliest Country in the World for Environmental Activism. Available at: www.globalwitness.org/en/campaigns/environmental-activists/honduras-deadliest-country-world-environmental-activism/ (Accessed June 7 2018).

Gouritin, Armelle. 2018. *Extractivism and Renewable Energies: Human Rights Violations in the Context of Socio-Environmental Conflicts. Illustration Using Wind Farms in San Dionisio del Mar, Oaxaca*. European Union: Heinrich Böll Foundation. Available at: https://eu.boell.org/sites/default/files/extractivism_and_renewable_energies_hr_violations_in_the_context_of_socio_environmental_conflicts.pdf (Accessed June 7 2018).

Gray, George. 2010. "The Challenge of Progressive Change under Evo Morales. In Kurt Weyland (Ed.) *Leftist Governments in Latin America: Successes and Shortcomings*. New York: Cambridge University Press, 140–179.

Gudynas, Eduardo. 2015. *Derechos de la Naturaleza*. Buenos Aires: Tinta Limón.

Guha, Ramachandra, and Juan Martínez Alier. 1997. *Varieties of Environmentalism. Essays North and South*. London: Earthscan.

Hinojosa, Leonith (Ed.). 2012. Gas y desarrollo. *Dinámicas territoriales rurales en Tarija, Bolivia*. La Paz, Bolivia: Fundación Tierra–CERDET.

Hristov, Jasmin. 2009. *Blood and Capital: The Paramilitarization of Colombia*. Ohio: Ohio University Press.

Humphreys-Bebbington, Denisse. 2012. Las tensiones Estado-Indigenas debido a la expansion de la industria hidrocarburifere en el Chaco boloviano. Inter-American Commission of Human Rights. 2009. Derechos de los pueblos indígenas y tribales sobre sus territorios ancestrales y recursos naturales. Available at: http://cidh.org/countryrep/TierrasIndigenas2009/Cap.VIII.htm (Accessed July 24 2017).

Keck, Margaret, and Kathryn Sikkink. 1998. *Activists beyond Borders: Advocacy Networks in International Politics*. Ithaca, NY: Cornell University Press.

Long, Michael, Paul Stretesky, Michael Lynch et al. 2012. Crime in the Coal Industry: Implications for Green Criminology and Treadmill of Production. *Organization & Environment* 25(3): 328–346.

McAdam, Doug, and Hillary Boudet. 2010. Site Fights: Explaining Opposition to Pipeline Projects in the Developing World. *Sociological Forum* 25(3): 401–427.

Mundo. 2017. Matan en México a Isidro Baldenegro, el conocido activista ambiental ganador del prestigioso premio Goldman. Available at: www.bbc.com/mundo/noticias-america-latina-38672959 (Accessed January 29 2018).

Pacheco-Vega, Raul. 2014. Ostrom y la gobernanza del agua en México. *Revista Mexicana de Sociología* 15(1) January-March. DOI: 10.22201/iis.01882503p.2014.0.46485.

Paulson, Nels, Kim Zagosrszy, and D. Chris Ferguson. 2015. "On Harm and Mediated Space: the BP Oil Spill in the Age of Globalization" In Avi Brisman, Nigel Souht and Rob White (Eds.) *Environmental Crime and Social Conflict Contemporary and Emerging Issues*.

Pearse, Guy, David McKnight, and Bob Burton. 2013. *Big Coal: Australia's Dirtiest Secret*. Sydney: New South.

Pečar, J. 1988. 'Kriminološko' javno mnenje. *Zbornik znanstvenih razprav* 48: 105–125.

Pratt, Brian. 2007. Advocacy in the Amazon and the Camisea gas project: Implications for non-government public action. *Development in Practice* 17(6): 775–783. DOI: 10.1080/09614520701628246.

Rodríguez-Garavito, César, Meghan Morris, Natalia Orduz, and Paula Buriticá. 2010. *La consulta previa a pueblos indígenas: los estándares del derecho internacional*. Bogotá: Universidad de los Andes.

Ruggiero and South. 2013. Toxic State–Corporate Crimes, Neo-Liberalism and Green Criminology: The Hazards and Legacies of the Oil, Chemical and Mineral Industries. *International Journal for Crime, Justice and Social Democracy* 2(2): 12–26.
Stretesky, Paul, and Michael Lynch. 2011. Coal Strip Mining, Mountaintop Removal, and the Distribution of Environmental Violations across the United States, 2002–2008. *Landscape Research* 36(2): 209–230.
Svampa, Maristella. 2013. «Consenso de los Commodities» y lenguajes de valoración en América Latina. Available at: www.unesco.org.uy/shs/red-bioetica/fileadmin/shs/redbioetica/Consenso_de_Commodities.pdf (Accessed April 10 2018).
The Guardian. 2017. Environmental Defenders Being Killed in Record Numbers Globally, New Research Reveals. Available at: www.theguardian.com/environment/2017/jul/13/environmental-defenders-being-killed-in-record-numbers-globally-new-research-reveals (Accessed February 28 2017).
Urkidi, Leire, and Mariana Walter. 2011. Dimensions of Environmental Justice in Anti-Gold Mining Movements in Latin America. *Geoforum* 42: 683–695. Barcelona: Institut de Ciència i Tecnologia Ambientals.
White, R. 2013. Resource Extraction Leaves Something Behind: Environmental Justice and Mining. *International Journal for Crime, Justice and Social Democracy* 2(1): 50–64. DOI: 10.5204/ijcjsd.v2i1.90 (Accessed December 20 2017).
Zilney, Lisa Anne, Danielle McGurrin, and Sammy Zahran. 2006. Environmental Justice and the Role of Criminology: An Analytical Review of 33 Years of Environmental Justice Research. *Criminal Justice Review* 31: 47–62.

Index

Note: Page numbers in bold and italics indicate tables and figures, respectively